STRONGHOLD

STRONGHOLD

A HISTORY OF
MILITARY ARCHITECTURE

Martin H. Brice

Schocken Books · New York

1 Frontispiece *This view of Harlech was taken from the south. Between the prominent house in the foreground, and the first low mantlet wall of the castle, is a deep dry ditch, crossed near the round house on the right (the east) by a bridge, itself protected by a barbican. There was no need for a ditch on the west (the left) because of the precipice. This latter is screened by flanking walls to cover the steep and narrow pathway connecting the castle with the quay below. This area is known as the Outer Ward, the Middle Ward being that within the low mantlet wall.*

The dominant feature of Harlech is the massive curtain wall, 24 metres high and enclosing the Inner Ward. Proceeding clockwise from the south-east, the three great corner towers are Garden (Mortimer) Tower, Weathercock (Bronwen) Tower and Chapel (Armourer's) Tower, their names reflecting some bygone use or resident. The Prison (Debtor's) Tower is out of sight behind the twin-towered and bastioned gatehouse. Besides being defensive in nature, this provided accommodation for the garrison, more dignified apartments being located in a range of buildings along the other sides of the Inner Ward. The windows of the Great Hall can be seen in the west curtain wall. Note the remains of the machicolation which once fringed all the walls, towers and turrets.

First American edition published by Schocken Books 1985
10 9 8 7 6 5 4 3 2 1   85 86 87 88

Designed by Gillian Gibbins
Manufactured in Great Britain
ISBN 0–8052–3938–3

Library of Congress Cataloging in Publication Data
Brice, Martin Hubert, 1935–
    Stronghold: a history of military architecture.
    Bibliography: p.
    Includes index.
    1. Fortification—History.   2. Military architecture—History.   I. Title.
UG401.B85 1984   355.7'09   84–10903

Contents

2 *Fort Laramie in 1849, in what was to become the American State of Wyoming.*

In common with all peoples confronted with different cultures the Indian tribes find themselves drawn towards the trading opportunities offered by the fort, even though it also acts as a cavalry base and staging post for military and commercial operations which will eventually destroy their way of life. Meanwhile, the pioneers, fearing the primitive peoples outside, have surrounded themselves with blank-faced walls, their corners protected with square blockhouses. It is easy to see how, in spite of being located in wide open spaces, such enclosed communities in any age could become obsessed with petty intrigue, jealousy and gossip.

Note the two timbers supporting a weak section of wall. It is usually assumed that bygone artisans built to last, but even the most massive castles were always in a continual state of maintenance, dilapidation, repair, neglect and reconstruction.

Acknowledgements

For providing material and information, making research facilities available, assisting with typing and the production of illustrations, checking and commenting on the typescript, and generally helping with advice and encouragement, I am particularly grateful to the following individuals and organisations:

Aldershot Military Historical Trust, David Allen, Alton Area Library, Alton History & Archaeology Society, Timothy Auger, Basingstoke Reference Library, Sylvia Brice, Rose Coombs, Tony Cross, Devizes Museum, Ermine Street Guard, Fort Widley, Jenny Fox, Roger Fox, Gordon Frater, Ivor Guy, Charles W. Hawkins, Gordon W. James, David Jones, Laura Kemal, James S. Lucas, John Maulkin, Dennis Mayne, Tony Merriman, Newbury Building Society, New Zealand House Library, Harry Pond, Royal United Services Institute (London), Nigel Saul, Southsea Castle, Sussex Combined Forces Museum (Eastbourne), Jack Sweet, Tilbury Fort, Winchester Central Reference Library, Winchester Lending Library, Wish Tower (Eastbourne), Miss Yamashita, York Story Exhibition.

My thanks are also due to the Trustees of the Imperial War Museum for permission to reproduce the extract from the archives of the Department of Sound Records quoted on pp. 152–3.

And for permission to reproduce the photographs grateful acknowledgement is due to the following institutions and individuals:

Courtesy of the Aldershot Military Historical Trust: 79. The Collection of Air Commodore H.F.V. Battle (by courtesy of Nicholas Battle): 19; 36; 65; 73; 74. China Travel Centre: 62 and front cover. Rose Coombs: 90 and front cover. Crown Copyright (by courtesy of the Department of the Environment): 26. By courtesy of the Danish Tourist Board: 3; 27. By courtesy of the French Tourist Office: 41. By courtesy of the German National Tourist Office: 51; 102; 103. By courtesy of the Greek Tourist Authority: 20. By courtesy of the Indian Railways Board: 66. By courtesy of the Japan National Tourist Office: 63. Aerofilms: 31. Mansell Collection: 2; 39; 68; 69; 70. By courtesy of the High Commissioner for New Zealand: 64. Pacific School of Religion: 17. Popperfoto: 52. Jack Sweet: 97. United States National Archives: 80; 98; 99; 100 and back cover.

The map of the Maginot Line on p.164 is based on the one reproduced in *Architecture of Aggression* by Keith Mallory and Arvid Ottar, published by Architectural Press Ltd.

Other illustrations are from the collections of B.T. Batsford and Martin H. Brice.

Every care has been taken to discover the owners of copyrighted material, but if necessary acknowledgements have been omitted or any illustrations included without due permission, we trust the copyright holders will accept our apologies.

Author's note

Dimensions are given in metric form as this is now the standard measurement of archaeology. An exception has been made in the case of weapon calibres and in certain other measurements for which there is no precise equivalent.

Place-names display a certain inconsistency, both in their spelling and in their description. For example, 'Gallia', 'Gaul', 'France' and 'North-West Europe' may all be used in quite close proximity when referring to medieval places. I make no apology for this. In each case, I prefer to use the historically contemporary name for the area, but I believe it is important for the reader to know exactly where the place was, even if that means giving it a modern political name or other geographical description in common use today.

No attempt has been made to convert by-gone currencies into present-day values or terminology.

In the diagrams and maps, 'North' is always at the top, unless otherwise stated. The scale given is necessarily an approximation.

CHAPTER ONE

Stronghold

> Withdrawn and ruinous it broods in umbra: the immemorial
> masonry: the towers, the tracts. Is all corroding? No.
> Through an avenue of spires a zephyr floats; a bird whistles;
> a freshet bears away from a choked river. Deep in a fist of
> stone a doll's hand wriggles, warm rebellious on the frozen
> palm. A shadow shifts its length. A spider stirs . . . . *And
> darkness winds between the characters.*
> (Mervyn Peake, *Gormenghast*;
> Eyre & Spottiswoode, London 1977)

Masada, Mai Dun, Maginot and Monte Cassino, Tintagel, Taku, Gormenghast and Laramie, Douaumont and Eben-Emael, Colditz, Corregidor and Camelot, Krak des Chevaliers, Chateau Gaillard and Joyous Gard, The Wall, The Kremlin, The Pentagon, The Tower; their names reverberate across the centuries, their histories and legends echo through the mind, blurring fact and fiction until it is almost impossible to tell which castles were real and which were imaginary.

The very word 'castle' conjures up a whole range of images from the sugary Walt Disney picture of a pinnacled fairytale palace, to the dark and sinister lair of Count Dracula. The legends abound; treachery, loyalty, gallant knights and horrible ghosts. Everybody has heard about cascades of boiling oil, torture chambers and dungeons. There are stories of sorcerers, ogres and damsels in distress. Some castles, garrisoned by a handful of half-starving men, held out almost indefinitely; others, defended by regiments, fell at the blast of a single trumpet.

In such stories castles are rarely regarded as the refuge of the common people; usually they are portrayed as the private domain or secret lair of some powerful being; an evil dragon or wicked baron, an all-wise judge or a god-like king who, in a time of *his* own choosing, will emerge with magical or military armament of invincible force, to destroy his enemies, punish the disaffected, succour the afflicted and reward the faithful. And until that time comes, the hidden denizen sleeps or rests or makes his plans within the innermost sanctum of his mighty stronghold. Not far away is his treasure, that which he delights in, that which is closest to his heart. Around him is his army, a hierarchy of spectral or uniformed retainers, their wants supplied by weaponmakers and cooks, whose products fill countless storerooms in the bowels of the fortress. Such bounty must be protected against the greed of envious outsiders. Until the master of the stronghold is ready to emerge, his strength must be husbanded, defended by wall and portcullis, drawbridge and moat, sentried battlements and long-ranged patrol, armed soldiers and demonic arts.

That is the traditional image of the stronghold of legend. It is also as near a portrait of the stronghold of fact, as makes no difference.

Forts and castles may sometimes be used as refuges for the common people, but that is not their primary function. In most ages the common people have been left to fend for themselves. Admittedly some rulers have provided their subjects with purpose-built towers or shelters

3 *These terraced houses are married quarters built for the families of 600 of the seamen serving in the Royal Danish Navy during the reign of King Christian IV (1588–1648). His aim was to build up a powerful fleet and army to dominate the Baltic and its shores. Like many other Protestant monarchs of the period he derived the necessary finance from the acquisition of ecclesiastical property.*

These houses at Nyboder in Copenhagen are early examples of the concern of state and civic authorities for the welfare of the people in their charge. Those which were still standing in 1866–93 were rebuilt and modernised. One is now a museum, while the others still make good homes, as can be seen from this photograph.

4 *There has always been some interaction between military and civilian architecture. In earlier times it was mainly in the realm of grand architecture. Medieval masons could be employed on cathedrals and castles; nineteenth-century bricklayers built railways and forts. During the twentieth century the widespread introduction of married quarters has resulted in a complete overlap of building for both municipal and military authorities. This modern block of flats has been erected for British army families at Aldershot, but in some places soldiers', sailors' and airmen's families are accommodated in housing built for civilian tenants and leased from local government councils.*

5 *The business end of the portcullis in the fortified gateway leading to the Inner Ward at the Tower of London. Originally known as the Garden Tower (because it adjoined the Constable's garden), it was often used to confine notable prisoners, including the boy-King Edward V and his brother, the Duke of York. They died there in mysterious circumstances and since then the place has become known as the Bloody Tower.*

into which they can flee in time of strife, waiting passively until the trouble has swept over or around them. But in contrast, forts and castles, whether baronial or military, whether prehistoric, medieval or modern, are intended as bases of active operation. And as such they all have certain features in common.

They must have somewhere for the master of the stronghold to live and plan his schemes and keep safe what is most valuable to him. There must be some place which will serve as a judicial chamber for the trial and punishment of the transgressor. There must be somewhere for his bodyguard to live and train, somewhere for their armament and provisions to be prepared and stored. And finally all this material, all these people must be kept safe until the lord of the fortress decides that the time has come for his army to be unleashed upon his foes. And so the stronghold must be provided with outworks and observation towers, a labyrinthine entrance and a network of spies, an armament of bows and arrows, cannon and missiles. And it is these external defence works which most impress the

outsider; massive ramparts or impregnable walls perched upon lofty eminences and mounting towards the sky.

From this stronghold infantry were able to patrol a distance of up to six to seven kilometres away, while cavalry swept the countryside over a radius of 16 kilometres. Castles were also sited for tactical purposes, as well as being used as a base of operations. The longbow had a range of 200 metres; the crossbow could project its heavier armour-piercing bolt over 350 metres, a skilled

6 *The ruined curtain wall to the bottom left of this photograph of Rochester Castle was built by Bishop Gundulf in 1087–9. As the river then came right up to the cliff supporting the foundations it was probably the sector least likely to be attacked. Accordingly, some time after 1220 (in the reign of Henry III), a large hall was built against the upper level of this wall, thus making it even thicker. The row of joist-holes for its floor can be seen above the pointed arches of the undercroft which supported the hall. The north-west bastion dates from 1378–83.*

man being able to pick off a target 50 metres beyond that. That meant that archers firing from the position shown in figure 6 could hit men trying to cross the old bridge over the Medway, its line indicated by the lower approach road between the new bridge and the square dark building on the far side of the river, and by the cars parked just in front of the modern staircase in the north-west bastion of Rochester Castle. Catapult artillery, too, would have a similar range from its location either on the walls or in the bailey.

A final function of castles was to act as watch-towers. It might be thought that they would not be very good for this because the number of trees in those days would have effectively cloaked movement along the forest trails. However, observant visitors to existing castles may notice that there are often open spaces just where a road emerges from woodland to cross a stream, or where a short stretch of distant river is just visible between high cliffs. The sentry would know the exact places which an enemy would have to pass and he would be waiting for that flash of sun on armour or spear, the faint clatter of hooves on loose stones. Obviously only the longest-sighted, sharpest-eared would be chosen for lookout duty in time of danger – a task for otherwise untrained boys. And no-one could fail to notice the extra columns of smoke beyond the far hills, fires of encampment or pillage, which marked the pro-gress of a hostile army.

One of William the Conqueror's earliest acts after his victory at Hastings in 1066 was to order the erection of a timber headquarters for the administration and military control of London. The site chosen was just within the old Roman Wall, the highest navigable point for seagoing ships in the River Thames.

In 1078 he ordered the construction of a stone tower to replace the wooden building, while the whole area making up the enceinte (or precinct) of the stronghold was to be enclosed by a stone wall instead of the existing earth rampart. Both were completed about 1097. The central building acquired the name 'The White Tower' after 1240, when Henry III had it whitewashed inside and out.

By then a number of other alterations had been carried out, but it was Henry III who began to reconstruct the fortress into a concentric castle, each inner wall being able to direct fire over the heads of defenders on the lower outer walls. This work was continued during the reign of his son, Edward I. Subsequent monarchs made appro-priate alterations to maintain the Tower's effec-tiveness as a royal military stronghold.

The main residential and defensive building in a Norman stronghold was originally the 'tower' or 'great tower'; hence this fortress is 'The Tower of London' and not 'London Castle'. Later the term 'donjon' was employed for the tower, but that became transferred to a cell (or 'dungeon') in the tower where prisoners were kept. In medieval times such an airless, lightless hole was called an 'oubliette', from the French word *oublier*, 'to forget' – you put the prisoners there and forgot about them. Meanwhile the great tower or donjon had become known as a 'keep'. To avoid close repetition, all three words – 'tower', 'don-jon', and 'keep' – are employed in this book when referring to Norman and medieval castles with-out strict regard to contemporary usage.

Castles have a long history. Donnington Castle was built in 1386 and was still a stronghold during the English Civil War when it was thrice besieged; on each occasion being held for King Charles I by Colonel John Boys. His 200 infantry, 25 cavalrymen and four cannon faced as many as 4,000 soldiers from 31 July to 22 October 1644. During the Second Battle of Newbury on 27 October 1644 Donnington Castle was a vital strongpoint on the Royalist battle line. It not only covered their subsequent withdrawal, but also served as the safe repository for the Crown Jewels and the Great Seal of England. Such a treasure could not be allowed to fall into the hands of the Parliamentarians, and once again Sir John Boys refused to surrender, even though comparatively isolated and assaulted by the army of Sir William Waller from 28 October to 10 November 1644. The siege was then raised and the treasure restored to the king.

For a while Donnington Castle served as a base for a Royalist force striking at Parliamentarian lines of communication. Its final ordeal began on

7 *The Tower of London is one of the world's most famous military structures and treasure-houses, being the home of the Crown Jewels of England. It has also been an arsenal and a zoo. In this photograph, five periods of military architecture can be seen. On the right is one of the surviving sections of London's Roman Wall. About 35 metres beyond the people in the background, behind the invisible – and now dry – moat, is the low mantlet wall marking the perimeter of Edward I's fortress. Set some 30 metres behind that is the Curtain wall, enclosing the Inner Ward. This was laid out in the reign of Henry III; the Bowyer Tower (evidently associated with the storage of bows and arrows) and the Brick Tower (far left) are but two of the thirteen towers providing flanking fire along the Curtain Wall.*

Rising above them are the Waterloo Barracks, built in 1845, to accommodate the soldiers making up the garrison of The Tower. The 7th Regiment of Foot (also known as the Royal Fusiliers or City of London Regiment) was raised in 1685 and today forms part of the Royal Regiment of Fusiliers. The Regiment is

quite separate from the Yeomen Warders of the Tower (commonly called Beefeaters), who are uniformed civilians, not soldiers. Such a division of responsibilities must have been usual in most strongholds in most periods, enabling household routine, neighbourhood administration, the defence of the walls, and the despatch of patrols and striking forces, to be carried out quite separately from – but in full co-operation with – each other.

Note how the Victorian architect has given the Waterloo Barracks a harmonising mock-medieval appearance. The same was true of Tower Bridge opened in 1894. Its top can just be glimpsed to the left of the roofed turrets of the White Tower, which rises more than 27 metres above the Inner Ward.

8 *The great gatehouse-keep of Donnington Castle in Berkshire was built by Sir Richard de Abberbury in 1386. Richard II granted permission for the residence to be fortified because of the uncertainty of that troubled period. Standing 20 metres high, its walls are of flint, with five courses of stone. It was besieged three times during the English Civil War, with much of the siege activity involving artillery bombardments and infantry assaults on outlying trench systems, but there were attempts to storm the castle by means of scaling-ladders. The lesser walls and towers suffered severely and have largely disappeared, but the great gatehouse-keep has survived 21 months of artillery bombardment and 600 years of weathering – a fitting emblem for the local building society.*

14 November 1645. By now the king's cause was hopeless, but Colonel Boys still held out, until Charles I himself sent word that 'Hee shoulde gette the beste conditions that he could for himselfe and his.' The Parliamentarians under Colonel John Dalbier were magnanimous in victory and when Sir John Boys surrendered on 30 March 1646 they allowed him and his men to march out with colours flying and drums beating.

But it was not only castles that required solid defences to keep corporeal enemies at bay – some ecclesiastical properties required them also. The Benedictine Abbey of Mont St Michel, in the bay between the Brittany and Cherbourg Peninsulas, was founded in 966. Because of its own wealth and because of the trading prosperity of the lay community which grew up around it, it was a tempting target, especially for cross-Channel raiders from England. These pirates may well have been attacked themselves by French corsairs at some previous date; unable to avenge themselves upon the perpetrators of the crime, they might well pillage and destroy some other French town which had nothing to do with the feud. It was a form of privateering engaged in by seamen from both sides of the Channel, encouraged – or punished – by their respective mon-

archs, according to the dictates of their foreign policies when not actually at war. It meant that during the Middle Ages – and later – all Channel ports of any significance had to be defended against assault, while simultaneously serving as bases for amphibious operations and as markets for the disposal of loot.

The Abbey still stands, a testimony to the skill of its builders – as with many of the strongholds of earlier times. Long after the master of the stronghold, his loyal followers, his humble subjects, his hated foes, have all returned to dust; long after their ideals and fears and their civilisation itself have faded into half-forgotten myth; long after the internal structures of habitation and manufacture, of administration and entertainment, have all disintegrated and crumbled – the walls and ramparts remain, to impress and bewonder the observer, an outsider in time and place.

Thus it is with the prehistoric hillforts of Britain.

9 *Cadbury Castle, north of Yeovil in Somerset, has been inhabited intermittently since the days of Early Neolithic hunter-gatherers about 3600 BC. Its most distinctive feature is the multivallate Iron Age hillfort which crowns its summit, but its fame rests on its reputation as the site of Camelot. The legends of King Arthur may well be derived from the very earliest prehistoric folk-memories, but there was a definite though shadowy Romano-British leader who continued the struggle of Ambrosius Aurelianus against the Anglo-Saxon invaders about AD 500 – a campaign which reached its climax at the Battle of Mons Badonicus. Recent archaeological excavation at Cadbury Castle has revealed the refurbishing of its defences in the period following the collapse of the Roman Empire, together with the remains of a feasting hall similar to those described in the earliest Arthurian chronicles. It does seem as though Cadbury's claim to be the ancient Camelot is the strongest to date. The place is notoriously difficult to capture on film in its entirety. This photograph was taken from the A303 road to the West Country and shows the wooded ramparts of Cadbury Castle between the two mounds of Pen Hill (on the left) and Warren Hill (on the right).*

CHAPTER TWO

Green ramparts

Caesar learned from these people, that he was not far from
Cassivellaunus' town, which was screened by woods and
marshes, and big enough for a great number of men and
cattle. For what the Britons call a town, is some place in
tangled woodland, fortified with rampart and ditch, and in
which they are accustomed to congregate to evade enemy
assault.
(*De Bello Gallico* V, xxi)

Digging a trench and heaping the soil on the inner perimeter of the excavation is the easiest permanent method of marking a boundary. It can be improved by reinforcing the earth with sticks or stones, and by planting a quickset thorn hedge along the top of the bank. Such an enclosure would be of particular service to semi-nomadic peoples, either pastoralists shifting their herds every season, or primitive farmers forced to move every other year when the ground was exhausted, but eventually returning when it had recovered. No matter how long they had been away, they would not have to do much to refurbish the site. Dead bushes would be rolled into the ditch, where their thorns would provide further protection against marauding beasts. Until new planting had reached maturity, the gaps would be filled with woven hurdles.

Such thorn enclosures, known as *bomas* or *zarebas* were – are still – used by African tribes like the Masai to protect their cattle against animal and human predators. And as a military obstacle, even when subjected to high explosive bombardment during the First World War, the spiky vegetation proved as formidable as barbed wire; it was only vulnerable to fire.

Thus, right at the beginning of this narrative of the development of fortification, we have two of

several themes which run right through history.

The first is that primitive, antique, obsolete, obsolescent, modern and prototype weapons and structures can exist and be employed at the same time – and not only in different parts of the world, but in the same areas and in the same societies. Just because something new has been invented, does not mean that everything of earlier design is immediately abandoned. The old continues in use until a dominant leader imposes change, or until it demands too much effort to keep it in good repair, or until it is destroyed by enemy action. Even in the last circumstance, it may be rebuilt to the old design, the vanquished people attributing their defeat to moral or spiritual decline rather than inefficient weaponry.

The second continuous theme is that the same piece of architecture can be employed for a multitude of purposes with hardly any change in its basic structure. For example, a twentieth-century stadium can have been built for the performance of a variety of sporting activities in honour of some international ideal. And yet, in addition, it can, at various times, accommodate religious services, political rallies, musical festivals, commercial markets, emergency housing, reserve foodstocks, contraband under customs bond, prisoners of war, soldiers under training,

10 *This massive barrier of dead thorn bushes has been erected by Hampshire conservationists to temporarily restrict access to parts of Old Winchester Hill nature reserve presently undergoing reinstatement. Such a natural barricade is cheaper and less offensive than barbed wire. Though of peaceful intent in this instance it would be a formidable obstacle in wartime to anybody trying to get through without using incendiary or mechanical means of removal. Interestingly, some parts of the reserve, which adjoins an Iron Age hillfort, are permanently closed to the public because of the unexploded bombs there, relics of the Second World War when it was used as a mortar training range – a military association which bridges two thousand years.*

anti-aircraft equipment, and even be ploughed up altogether for growing crops. It is therefore unwise to be dogmatic about what some prehistoric earthwork was used for over the whole of its 2,000-year existence. Even places of apparently obvious religious or ceremonial significance may have been tended and guarded by warrior-priests in the same way as the Knights Templar and other orders protected the Holy Places of Jerusalem during the Middle Ages. Conversely, a conquering rival may very well deliberately use a captured stronghold as a cattle enclosure to defile and desecrate its sacred precincts.

It does seem, however, that the earthworks known as causewayed camps were not built with defence in mind. They are marked by a series of concentric ditches, one to two metres deep, bridged by numerous causeways affording easy access from every direction to the central, circular, banked enclosure. The most famous is on Windmill Hill near Avebury in Wiltshire. Covering 8.5 hectares, it was laid out over an even earlier site about 3250 BC, but it is not the oldest causewayed camp so far discovered. That honour goes to Briar Hill, which is near Northampton and dates from 4400 BC.

There is evidence that the Neolithic peoples built some causewayed camps with a palisade on top of a continuous bank within the interrupted ditch. However, the first certain hillforts with rampart and ditch of military function were the creation of the Bronze Age.

As its name implies the period from 2000 to 500 BC in Britain was characterised by the increasing employment of weapons and ornaments cast first in copper, and subsequently in an alloy of copper and tin. Suitable ores for the extraction of these elements are not very common. The use of such metal objects, especially in juxtaposition with artefacts of gold, therefore implies that their ownership was generally restricted to a powerful aristocracy. They controlled the sources of their metallurgical wealth and hence dominated the agrarian economy of their times.

We cannot tell how many kings or chieftains or high priests carved out realms for themselves, but it certainly seems that political power in southern Britain was focused on the religious and funerary monuments of Salisbury Plain. Stone circles, henges, and groups of round barrows occur elsewhere, but are smaller in scale, indicating local worship and governance. Some areas of Britain are devoid of such structures, although Beaker and Bronze Age relics have been found there. It can thus be argued from such archaeological evidence that the pervading atmosphere of the Bronze Age was one of stable empire, which – whether benevolent or authoritarian – enabled isolated communities and lonely travellers to farm and mine and trade in peace, and to pay their dues of corn and metal and service without interruption. There was no fear of attack by foreign invader or aggressive outlaw, and so social energies could be devoted towards the raising of spiritual edifices, rather than the construction of military defenceworks.

It was the arrival of the Hallstatt culture (named after the Austrian region where it originated) with its knowledge of ironworking about 500 BC, which ended that prehistoric idyll. Iron ore has to be smelted at a higher temperature than the bronze metals, and this could only be attained in a primitive, bellows-operated, open-hearth or kiln-like blast-furnace. Even then, all that could be produced was a slaggy, spongy 'bloom' of ore, charcoal and impure metal. The foreign matter had to be hammered out, while still hot. The smith then forged the residual wrought-iron into currency bars or swords or whatever utensil was required. This was a complicated procedure, but once it had been mastered, iron offered far greater possibilities. For a start, there are widespread deposits in Britain of suitable ore from which iron can be obtained. Any local chief who could secure the services of a smith could now make his own money and his own weapons. The British Isles became a land of perpetual civil war, a patchwork of little kingdoms, each with its own hilltop capital set behind rampart and ditch. And when, at the end of the pre-Christian era, there were threats of invasion from the continent of Europe, the hillforts were rebuilt with extra defenceworks of increased complexity.

That has been the accepted view of prehistorians for most of the twentieth century. However, from 1969 onwards, Carbon-14 dating techniques have suggested that Scottish and Welsh 'Iron Age' hillforts believed to be no older than 200 BC may in fact have been built about 700 BC. And an example in England is Hambledon Hill in Dorset. What seems to have originally been a funerary causewayed camp in the Neolithic period was, in about 1500 BC, turned into a defended site a thousand years before the construction of the great hillfort which is its most prominent feature today. On the other hand, excavation has indicated that Cadbury Castle in Somerset, though inhabited in the Neolithic and late Bronze Ages, had no defensive structures before 550 BC.

Perhaps the Bronze Age in Britain was not the golden time of peace and plenty as it has so often been suggested. Perhaps it was as faction-ridden as later societies, its hillforts completely obliterated by subsequent rebuildings. That was the case with most other metalworking cultures in the rest of Europe, the Mediterranean and the Middle East. For example, what is called a *castro* or bastioned citadel was a feature of the structures built by the Chalcolithic peoples in central Portugal about 3200–2900 BC, one of which is the hilltop site of Vila Nova de Sao Pedro in Ribatejo province. A wall of limestone blocks with a rubble core surrounds an area about 25 metres in diameter. Excavation has revealed that the wall (which is about 6.5 metres thick) has been laid on

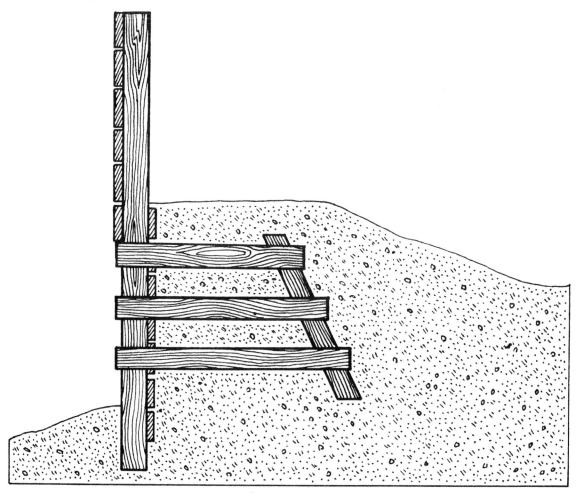

10 m

A

top of a properly levelled expanse of pounded limestone mortar, itself covering an earlier settlement. In the foundations could be traced the outlines of nine or ten semi-circular bastions, so positioned that archers could provide flanking fire cross the front of the wall. There are also hints of two – perhaps three – bastioned walls at 20 metres' distance from the central citadel. It therefore seems likely that this was the stronghold of some chieftain of the early Copper Age.

And so, such Bronze Age defenceworks as do exist today in Britain no doubt reflect the gradual break-up of that hegemony as the weather turned colder and wetter, harvests became uncertain, local communities began to hoard grain, and the central government found it increasingly difficult to insist on the payment of tribute. At first only noticeable on the periphery of empire, such defiance would eventually spread, the disintegration of centralised influence being accelerated by the introduction of the ironfounding techniques described earlier. Whether that metallurgical skill was brought by mass invasion from the Continent, by a conquering aristocracy, or by the natural spread of ideas, is immaterial. The end result of all those factors was the same. From 500 BC onwards, the hillfort became a permanent feature of the British landscape. Favoured sites, which had been occupied intermittently from the Neolithic period, now became fortified settlements, habitations which were both refuge and stronghold. Whatever their size, wherever their

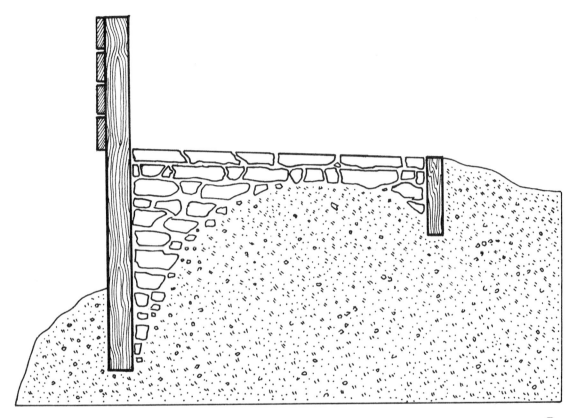

B

location, their defences were basically similar, simple and effective.

And that also applies to hillforts in northern France. It is not entirely clear whether the similarity of prehistoric sites on both sides of the Channel reflects an identical solution to the same socio-military problem, or whether one influenced the other. Challenge and response in adjacent cultures can be so quick that they often appear to be simultaneous when inventive minds on both sides are considering the matter; that one happens to be the first to be credited with its origination is often due to accidental delay affecting his rival's work.

When it came to building hillforts, whether in Britain, France or elsewhere in Europe, the

11 *Conjectured sections through two types of rampart at Cadbury Castle.*
A. A wooden wall and framework with earth infill.
B. A wooden palisade with stone facing and rampart walk.

procedure was the same. First of all, a site was selected, probably one which was already of some significance to the people in the area (Old Winchester Hill in Hampshire and Maiden Castle in Dorset, for example). It was sometimes on an isolated hilltop (Hod Hill in Dorset) and sometimes on the projecting spur of a ridge (Ham Hill in Somerset). Occasionally political consider-

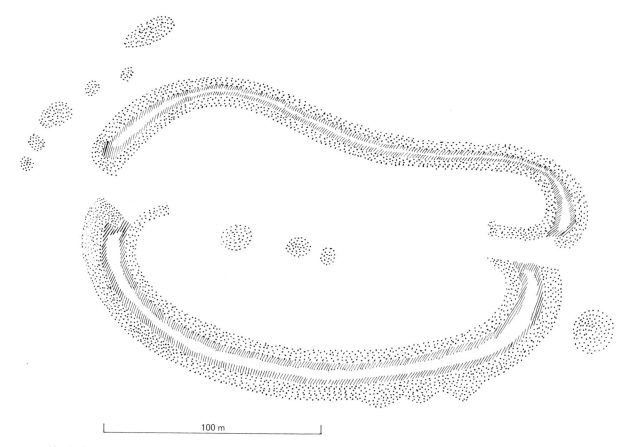

100 m

12 A plan of the hillfort at Old Winchester Hill in Hampshire. Built about 500 BC, the highest inner rampart still rises some seven metres above its fronting ditch. The whole site covers about 5.7 hectares and was formerly known as Windover Hill. Long barrows and round barrows indicate that the site was significant to earlier cultures. Indeed, the southern outer rampart has been built over three Bronze Age round barrows, incorporating them into the structure like bastions. There are suggestions of a porter's lodge inside each entrance.

ations dictated the fortification of some locality in a lowland region of forest and marsh, as reported by Julius Caesar. But even there, advantage was taken of rising ground to lift the settlement above the water level. This was the case at Wheathampstead in Hertfordshire, the capital of the Catuvellauni.

If the area were completely waterlogged, the only local material was wood and that had to be used. The Hallstatt D settlement of 600 BC at Biskupiec among the marshes of the Masurian Lakes in north-east Poland was surrounded by a timber wall of box-like construction, reminiscent of a very compact, rectangular trestle railway bridge. The huts were linked by a series of duckboards and wooden causeways, the foundations being either vertical piles or simple but enormous log jams like beaver lodges. Such a community would have been extremely vulnerable to incendiarism, which was also true of the Glastonbury and Meare Lake villages in Somerset. Indeed, it is unlikely that these latter sites were originally of military significance at all.

For many years it was believed that Iron Age houses were built on stilts in the Somerset swamps as protection against attack. It is now considered that the villages were there before the water, farmsteads established on the rich land of the Somerset Levels during the drier period of the late Neolithic and early Bronze Ages. When the

13 *The reverse side of the rampart at Hod Hill. A modern fence follows the ancient line of the palisade and rampart walk.*

weather became very much wetter about 500 BC, and Sedgemoor again flooded, the villagers were forced to build levees around their homes to keep the water out, then raise their houses on piles, and finally abandon the site altogether. The same would be true of the Fens, and Scottish and Irish valley bottoms, where similar sites or crannogs have been discovered. However, although these crannogs and lake villages may not have been of military intent *originally*, their very location must have made them difficult to approach, so that they became defensible places of refuge in time of danger. There are accounts of crannogs being so used in Ireland as late as the sixteenth century AD.

Returning to the construction of hillforts proper, once the location had been decided upon, a trench was dug all the way round the intended site, the earth being thrown up on the inner rim of the excavation. They left a fairly level space (or berm) between the edge of the ditch and the growing heap of rubble. If the region were rocky,

the loose stones and boulders were manhandled into position. When an appropriate height had been reached, the rampart was consolidated, its top levelled off and the rear of the bank sloped downwards towards the centre of the enclosure. Meanwhile, the outer face of the rampart was being made vertical. Finally it was revetted with wattle hurdles or stonework, depending upon the right sort of wood or rock being available. The rampart was then surmounted by a continuous palisade, probably backed by a duckboard or pounded-stone walkway.

A somewhat different system was employed at Murcens in Lot-et-Garonne in south-west France. Horizontal timbers were laid in parallel rows about 60 cm apart, being joined by transverse beams. The gaps between were filled with earth. Stones were used to face the front and to provide a layer on top of the earth, on which more timbers could be laid and secured until the whole structure had a layered appearance; a *mille-feuille* of stone (fireproof) and wood (providing resilience against battering-rams). The Murcens *oppidum* still shows indications of this timber/ stone layering.

Huenberg hillfort overlooking the Danube south of Binzwagen, was built about 600–550 BC. It had clay-brick walls and bastions on stone foundations along its north-west perimeter. It is so similar to Mediterranean walled cities that it has been suggested that the local chieftain must somehow have obtained the services of an architect from the south to design his fortress. (It may be argued that the terms 'architect' and 'designer' are inappropriate words to use of unlettered workers before the introduction of writing, mathematics, paper and surveying instruments. The fact remains that all these works were laid out under the direction of master-builders who may have had to keep the whole plan in their head and do all their calculations by a mixture of inspired guesswork and mental arithmetic; that they never committed any of that to paper does not make them any less worthy of the title 'architect' or 'designer'.)

Excavations at Cadbury Castle have indicated that the wooden stockade at the top of the rampart was an integral component of the earth bank when it was built about 500 BC. Postholes were dug, big enough to take vertical timbers about 15 cm in thickness. The posts (about 1.2 metres apart) were joined by rows of horizontal planks and braced by an arrangement of angled and horizontal timbers to the rear. The whole structure ('h-shaped' in section) was filled in with earth and rubble.

Inevitably the timbers rotted and the rampart eventually had to be rebuilt. The ditch was deepened to quarry slabs of solid rock which were used to pave the sloping rampart walkway behind the wooden palisade. This fence was only along the top of the rampart, the lower part being faced with lias slabs kept in position by the upright posts supporting the palisade. To an outsider Cadbury's ramparts must have had all the appearance of a stone wall rather than an earthen bank, an impression shared by most hillforts when newly completed.

We thus have an early example of yet another of the themes which run all through the history of military architecture: that magnificent edifices are symbols of pride as much as protective structures, intended to overawe the lord's own subjects as well as deter the enemy. In the case of Cadbury Castle, the new rampart was too much of a showpiece; the lias slabs began to split into smaller and smaller splinters; those which remained had not been keyed into the core, so they started to slip out; and when the upright timber posts rotted, the whole lot began to crumble away.

And this, too, is a theme which recurs again and again. The most impressive and prestigious of fortresses are not necessarily the strongest, disintegrating or revealing some weakness in their defences just when their protection is most needed. Even strongholds impregnable on their foundation day need constant repair and modernisation to maintain their integrity. But daily observation does not reveal anything really wrong with such enormous structures until it is too mammoth a task to undertake without considerable debate regarding its true necessity. The temptation, then, is to put it off until other lesser – but seemingly more urgent and more easily attainable – projects have been dealt with; and by then it is too late.

One of the simplest hillfort maintenance tasks to organise (using slaves or promising inducements to freemen) and undertake, was the occasional cleaning out of the ditch and straightening its sides. The soil and debris thus removed were thrown out on the outside perimeter, coincidentally resulting in the additional obstacle of a counterscarp bank. The ground beyond would be cleared of vegetation, thus forming a sloping glacis on which any attacker was exposed to killing missiles during the whole of his approach to the earthwork.

Understandably, hillfort builders took advantage of any natural cliff or precipitous slope when laying out their fortress. It not only enhanced the defences, but saved labour, for the amount of work involved was colossal. Modern attempts to reproduce the situation, by volunteers excavating a short section of ditch and then calculating how many prehistoric people were involved and how long it took them to complete the entire project, are interesting but unrealistic. After all, the speed at which a modern infantryman digs a foxhole when being mortared is quite different from the rate at which he turns over the soil when out in his garden to escape a family argument. And so no modern experiment can recreate the real or imagined pressures which motivated those Iron Age artisans.

It may not simply have been fear of foreign invasion or rival brigandage. Always in the background of Celtic society there must have been the shadowy influence of the Druids, religious commissars contributing the fear of eternal damnation as extra incentive for completing the work on time. Perhaps summary punishments such as flogging or death were inflicted upon those slaves who did not fulfil their work norm. Or perhaps such pain was dealt out to their families, held hostage by some cruel overlord. Or perhaps they were all free men and women – and children – toiling unstintingly for the preservation of their beloved homeland and leader. Or perhaps the hillfort-builders were a special breed of men, experts in their professions, selling their services to the highest bidder, taking their families with them and living in temporary accommodation, moving from one project to another as nomadic architects and artisans, like the canal and railway builders of the nineteenth century AD. But perhaps even gangs of forced labour, working at their lord's command, tackled their jobs with enthusiasm, their seasonal servitude something of a holiday from routine life and responsibility, with free food and drink provided every night, plus extra beer – and women – for the team which shifted the most dirt during its period of duty.

All these factors – or at least the promise or threat of them – have influenced people in working hard, in devoting themselves to the cause, in sacrificing themselves for the common good, in modern times. There is no reason to suppose that the people of prehistoric times, of the Iron Age, of the medieval period, or of any other era in any other society, were any less susceptible to similar mental and physical persuasions.

However, building Iron Age hillforts was not just a case of digging fast and furiously. Skilled carpentry was required and – by implication – some form of long-term forestry management. One of the easiest modern calculations to make from archaeological evidence is the volume of material to be shifted or delivered for any particular project. For example, the timber facing and palisade of the earliest rampart at Cadbury Castle (with a circumference of 1100 metres) would have involved at least 21 kilometres of planking, quite apart from the 900 vertical posts and all the supporting structures, and the gates. It was not just enough to select suitable trees, fell and cut them up into planks. There were also hurdles for stock-control and wattle-and-daub housing, as well as reinforcing earth ramparts, while primitive ironworking demanded charcoal – and lots of it.

All this points towards the coppicing of certain areas of woodland, which in turn enabled those bigger trees left standing to grow straight and tall, suitable for planks and posts which might have to be renewed every 20 years or so. Whether the sanctity of such woodland was preserved by religious taboo (recalled today in such folklore ceremonies as Oak-Apple Day and the wassailing of fruit trees) or whether it was maintained through fear of physical retribution by the king and his retainers, we cannot tell. But however the prohibition on indiscriminate felling was enforced, somebody in authority had to think ahead, probably ahead of his or her own lifetime. Someone in authority believed that whatever the future held, there would always be a place for hillforts. And they did, after all, remain in service for almost a thousand years.

Of course, during that time span, some were abandoned, new ones were built, and old ones were improved. Indeed, from 500 BC onwards, it seems that a number of chiefs had achieved kingly dominion over the whole of Britain. There were some small enclosures around remote villages or farmsteads, but these were more to keep stock in and wild animals out, rather than military architecture. Apart from these examples, most of the lesser hillforts were abandoned about this period, power becoming concentrated in a few massive and complex structures, whose size reflected the growing importance of their overlords.

The commonest method of modernisation was to dig extra ditches and ramparts beyond the existing ones, turning univallate hillforts into bivallate and multivallate hillforts. However, it should not be assumed that *all* univallate hillforts predate *all* multivallate hillforts. That is not the case, as has been indicated by Carbon-14 dated samples from a number of earthworks. Nevertheless, the multivallate design did help to counter the new weapon, the sling.

From about 250 BC onwards there was a series of further influences from across the Channel, probably in the nature of warrior-adventurers with lower-class servants, rather than a mass-migration of peoples. The first to arrive were representatives of the La Tene culture, named after their place of origination in Switzerland. They introduced the chariot to British warfare and were followed by Belgic and Gallic immigrants under pressure from Germanic tribes and – after 58 BC – from Roman legions. Which of these groups introduced the sling, which of them really set the fashion for constructing multivallate hillforts, is yet another question. Certainly the Veneti of Britanny were expert slingers, but they were amongst the last to arrive, after their maritime power had been smashed by Julius Caesar in 56 BC. Even so, they may well have introduced the weapon earlier through their links with the south-west peninsula of Britain. Indeed, the men of Portland were proficient with the sling-shot, retaining that skill for so many centuries that Thomas Hardy later referred to their abode as 'The Isle of Slingers'.

One can picture a canny warrior-trader from the Dorset coast demonstrating the advantages of the new weapon. First he might hurl a throwing-spear, the standard anti-personnel missile of the day. It would strike the ground about 30 paces distant. And then he would whirl the sling about his head, release the shot – and a condemned prisoner tied to a post a hundred paces away sagged lifeless with shattered skull. Perhaps the watching chieftain would leap to his feet with excitement; perhaps he witnessed the display unemotionally. Either way, he was impressed. He was being offered a weapon which outranged the defences of his rivals' strongholds. After that it was easy for the warrior-salesman to insist that only his people could train the slingers properly, and to persuade the chief that it was no good using just any old round stone from a river bed. Nor would shot of baked clay do. Only the pebbles of Chesil Beach had the right shape and weight for use as sling-shot; and every slinger would need hundreds, perhaps thousands, of stones at his position as ready-to-use ammunition. It was only later that the chief realised that the same demonstration had been performed at every hillfort in the land, and that he too must now extend his own defences to take account of the range of the new weapon.

Of course, such a scene is mere fancy, but there is no illusion about the reconstruction of so many British hillforts in the last three centuries of the pre-Christian era. However, before describing these alterations in detail, there is one other matter of Iron Age weaponry to be considered, and that is the almost total absence of reference to the bow as an anti-personnel weapon. It has been suggested that arrows were difficult to mass produce and were liable to warp in the damp Iron Age climate. But, even so, it is surprising that there has not been more evidence for war-bows in hillforts. After all, they should have been easier to handle and aim, more accurate than a sling for the same amount of training and practice. Bows were certainly used in hunting – and perhaps that is why they were hardly used in war. Like a modern shotgun (banned from the trenches of the First World War, where it would have made a most effective weapon), the bow was for killing animals, not warriors. References to the bow in ancient warfare tend to speak of it in rather contemptuous tones: Paris the womaniser, wounding the hero Achilles in the heel; the arrow loosed 'at a venture' which smote King Saul between the joints of his armour; the Parthian shots of desert horsemen, who would not stand still and fight like men; even the Battle of

Hastings might have ended differently if King Harold had not been hit in the eye by the legendary arrow.

But if the bow was unfair, how was it that the sling, a similar equaliser in the hands of the ignoble, became acceptable? Perhaps the answer to that lies in the story of David and Goliath. It was a shepherd's weapon, used by children to protect their flocks. Perhaps in time of assault it was the custom for those same boys and girls to defend the ramparts with their slings, laying aside their childish weapons for adult spear and sword when they became men and women (there are references to Celtic women fighting alongside their menfolk). It could well be considered acceptable if the sling were only used in the hands of youngsters. If a warrior stopped a child's slingstone . . . why, even dead, he would still be an object of derision to his fellows; he should have known better than to get so close.

Again, this is mere hypothesis, but it should be remembered, throughout the story of military architecture, that there are all sorts of seemingly ridiculous reasons why things were done in a certain way. The object of warfare in any age is the exercise of power. In practical terms, that involves the capture of real estate (with or without your enemy still in living occupation), or the capture of your enemy's body or mind (even if this only involves converting him to the idea that you ought to be left alone). Warfare therefore does not necessarily mean death and destruction, and it is possible for it to be conducted according to such rules as will permit the opposing wielder of power to submit to your authority without loss of face and without his personal loss of life. Each age has its conventions, its secret weapons and its ultimate deterrents, which hold the ring while the warriors put their cause to the test of battle,

14 *This view from the inner rampart at Danebury hillfort shows how someone at the far base of the outer rampart was nevertheless visible to the defenders.*

regulated by such chivalric ideals as seem proper to them. This is reflected in military architecture as much as in any other martial activity.

And so, for whatever reason it was introduced, however it came to be employed, and whoever wielded it, the sling was responsible for altering the early hillforts and changing the landscape of Britain.

It was not simply a matter of digging extra ditches and heaping the material up on the inner rim to form yet another rampart. At Cadbury Castle (as at Maiden Castle, Danebury and most reconstructed hillforts) this was done in such a way that the whole of the climb formed an obstacle-strewn killing-ground. Imagine what an attacker had to overcome to attain his objective.

He might be one of a hundred warriors charging up the hill, their cohesion and impetus broken up by stumbling over boulders and tree-trunks deliberately placed there. Our hero found himself climbing a bare slope six metres across, just before he dropped into a ditch four metres deep. Here he was safe – if he pressed himself against the rock wall opposite, and tried to ignore the sling-shot which ricocheted and bounced around him. To get out and resume the attack, he had to scramble up a six-metre rock face like the roof of a house, which gradually sloped to a gentle incline. It was no place to linger and get his breath back, not with a hail of sling-shot smashing about him. He raced up the ten-metre slope and tumbled into a shallow vee-shaped ditch, too wide to afford shelter. He could not retaliate. To do that, he had to stand up straight, draw his spear-arm back, or whirl his sling about his head, and aim at a target which appeared momentarily at a gap in the wooden palisade far above him. And all the time, sling-shots were striking his comrades, stunning, blinding, numbing wrists. Some had broken their legs and stabbed themselves on their own spears when they dived into the ditch; they, too, were hit again and again. The attacker could not stay here. Driven on by fear and honour, he scaled a near-vertical ten-metre slope, falling forward another three metres into a precipitous trench with sharp stakes (probably poisoned) and dead thorn bushes at the bottom. By now, he was alone. But all he had to do was

climb the last 15 metres of the slope – he might be able to grasp hold of the downward-pointing splintery stakes and thorny branches sticking out from clefts in the rock. He could clamber over the stockade, past the thrusting spears of the defenders inside; and then at last, our warrior-hero could bring his own spear and sword into action and capture the stronghold – all on his own.

No, it did not seem very likely. No, the best chance of capturing a hillfort was by attacking the gates. The causeway might lead uphill, but at least it should be a steady gradient.

But even here the defenders had their little surprises. There were no aerial reconnaissance photographs to show which of several entrances through the outlying earthworks was the true one. Today, they are simply grassy mounds, but when occupied they would have been vertical stone or wood-revetted walls, three or four or more metres high, enclosing narrow alleyways, which twisted and turned and were obstructed by tree-trunks with their branches lopped off and sharpened to form *chevaux de frise*. Some corridors ended in blank walls or led the invaders down into the ditches. Even if the attackers managed to scramble up and seize one of these flanking walls, they were no nearer entering the hillfort. That particular rampart could be an island; the defenders could scurry back across a little footbridge to the safety of the inner palisade, tossing the plank into the ditch below. The assailants were now marooned and exposed to the fire of every slinger in that sector. Of course, by sheer force of numbers, the invaders might break down, or storm and open the gate. But that was only the outer gate. The whole operation had to be repeated before the inner gate could be breached; and, in between, there was a deep ditch, at the bottom of which lay the wreckage of the bridge which normally crossed it in time of peace.

No, attacking the gate could result in just as many casualties as storming the ramparts. Nor was it any good thinking of running round the hillfort and attacking from the other side to catch the defenders off-guard. All they had to do was hurry from one inner rampart to the other, while you had to go all the way round at the base of the hill. You could split your force into two and try a co-ordinated diversionary and main assault. But again, the defenders could do the same, and there would be no advantage. To achieve overwhelming superiority, it would be necessary to obtain the co-operation of another tribe – and they were not to be trusted. They would not understand the blowing of horns and the banging of drums which was your signal for the co-ordinated attack to begin. In any case, the defenders could imitate those sounds on their own instruments, effectively jamming and confusing your communications network. It might be possible to set fire to the dead thorn bushes in the ditch and hope it would spread to the wooden palisade, the gates and the hurdles revetting the rampart face. But that would only stand any chance if it had been a dry season, and the Iron Age in Britain was noted for its rainfall. In any case, every hillfort had its own well or means of collecting water from the roofs of its buildings and then storing it; it was not only for drinking and watering stock; it was also for putting out fires.

Though weapons and methods of construction may have changed, and even though strongholds may have become continental in size, these problems of carrying a fortress by storm have not altered since the days of hillforts. If properly situated and designed, the defenders can always bring their firepower to bear on any approaching force. They can rush from one side to the other to concentrate against attacks from different directions more quickly than the enemy can move all the way round the outer perimeter out of range of the defenders' weaponry. Only if the assailant has overwhelming superiority of numbers can he carry out a co-ordinated assault, but that involves problems of control; if the attacks are unsynchronised, they may well be beaten off piecemeal.

The same rules apply to sieges of hillforts as to later fortresses. If properly provisioned, the keeper of the stronghold is sitting on a great store of food and ammunition, while the besiegers have to bring everything they need with them. Alternatively, they will have to spend much of their energy scouring the countryside looking for food and antagonising those local people who for some reason or other have not sought refuge inside the fortress. If the invaders are not careful they may find themselves having to fight a guerrilla war as well as carry out a siege. And at any time they may have to deal with a field army coming to help the people inside.

For food reserves many hillforts were big enough to contain a herd of grazing or fodder-consuming cattle. At the same time, excavation has revealed large numbers of storage pits, each about one to two metres deep and two to three metres across. It has been estimated that there are as many as 5,000 at Danebury dug out of the solid rock, although they were not in use all at the same time. They were lined with wickerwork, filled with wheat or barley from the surrounding fields, covered with a lid and kept airtight with a clay seal. In that manner, about 2,900 litres of corn (either threshed grain or in the ear) could be kept in good condition for many months before being taken out for grinding. (The British besieged at Lucknow during the nineteenth century AD also relied on grain stored in pits for some of their provisions.) When empty, the pits could be re-used once, perhaps twice, but in spite of subsequent purification by having fires lit in them (usually of contaminated storage baskets) each pit only had a maximum life of a couple of years, before being affected by mould. The holes were then used as rubbish dumps and new storage pits dug. If, in the course of their excavation, the pit-diggers broke through into an old one, the gap in the side of the new pit was built up with rock to preserve its integrity.

The existence of these storage pits indicates the presence of something more than gifted leadership, inspiring heroic defence or the hurried construction of massive earthworks. Whether the pits contained sacks and baskets of grain, or whether the corn was stored loose, someone had to decide when the pit was to be opened. Certainly bulk storage suggests that the corn was doled out at specific times, perhaps unfairly with warriors getting priority, but definitely according to some form of rationing. Whether the hillforts were governed by democratic or dictatorial principles the person responsible for issuing corn must have done so with some sort of royal or druidical authority; storage pits imply a primitive

15 *The entrance to Danebury hillfort in Hampshire as it is today.*

bureaucracy.

The inhabitants of the hillfort were thus provisioned against lengthy siege and were well-nigh impregnable against direct assault. In fact, there does not seem to be any archaeological evidence for frontal attacks on hillforts during the Iron Age. An exception may be Battlesbury Camp in Wiltshire, which has what appears to be a war cemetery outside the north-west entrance. This does not necessarily mean that the place was stormed, but that the warriors were buried near where they had fallen outside the ramparts. (However, the presence of the skeletons of a woman and a child does raise other, unanswerable questions.)

Nor may the destruction of gates by fire be positive evidence of incendiary assault. In most

hillforts the entrances were flanked by guard-rooms or huts surmounted by observation towers. Carelessness with a fire kindled for warmth on a bitterly cold night could eventually engulf the gates and part of the rampart palisade.

All Celtic tradition and the reports of literate visitors indicate that the warriors emerged from the strongholds to do battle. Naked except for gold ornaments, their bodies stained with woad and carrying a long rectangular shield, they shouted insults at the enemy's champions. Individually or in small groups, they fought with spear and sword against similar numbers of opponents. The victors spoiled the dead and took possession of the territory in dispute. The losers fled back to their hillfort to recover, before resuming the conflict or before acknowledging their new overlord. The hillforts themselves remained unassailed, inviolate, although there was always the danger that someone, tiring of the

16 *Old Winchester Hill (in the centre of this photograph) may not be located on the very highest peak flanking the Meon Valley in Hampshire, but it is certainly the most dominating site. Wherever you are in the valley bottom you cannot escape being aware of it – a sentiment probably much stronger when the hillfort was occupied, even making allowances for denser woodland. Whether a lookout up on the hill could see what a rebellious peasant or foreign warrior was doing and wanted to keep secret, is immaterial; the latter would undoubtedly feel that the hill itself had eyes and was watching every move. (Modern soldiers experienced exactly the same uncanny sensation at the foot of Monte Cassino in Italy in 1944.)*

siege, might assassinate the chief in his lair, or betray the secret of the gate to an enemy. The fear was a very real one; treachery and the punishments meted out to traitors form yet another feature of Celtic traditional storytelling – and also run right through the history of castles and fortresses.

So, to ensure that only the proper people entered the hillfort, gatehouses were constructed at the entrance, as indicated by excavation at Cadbury Castle. Such guardians also guaranteed that only the proper people *left* the hillfort. Excavations of hillforts have revealed a large number of rectangular and circular wooden or wattle-and-daub houses of varying sizes, to provide dwellings, stores and workshops, and archaeologists often comment on the high standard of metalwork or pottery they find. The hillforts of Britain were thus self-contained units, with their own industries, and it is not likely that any chief would allow *his* skilful blacksmith to desert and serve a hated rival. Ramparts and walls, palisades and ditches, keep the law-abiding citizenry in their place, just as surely as they keep out the foreign aggressor.

Prehistoric hillforts were true strongholds, where the lord dwelt, enjoying the accumulated and increasing wealth of his people, safe from attack, and a base for launching his warriors upon his enemies. All this suggests that the hillforts of Britain fulfilled a rather different function from those in Gaul. There were fewer *oppida* (or towns), but many more *vici* (or undefended villages) in Gaul than in Britain. This may simply mean that British archaeologists have not found many *vici* – or it may imply that the Gallic hillforts were refuges to which the populace could flee in time of trouble.

Anyway, whatever was happening over on the Continent, the life of the hillforts of Britain went on as it had done for centuries. There were squabbles between petty chiefs and battles between rival kingdoms. There were alarms and rumours of invasion from across the Channel. Celtic sentiment could swing from despair to overweening self-confidence. In times of fear and crisis, ditches and ramparts were refurbished, stocks of sling-stones built up, new chariots constructed and decorated with the heads of defeated foes. With such an access of strength came the renewed conviction that the combination of hillfort-stronghold and warrior-hero would defeat any invader – even the Romans, of whom much had been heard in the last century of the pre-Christian era.

And then in 55 BC, the Romans set foot on British shores. They came bearing – no doubt without realising it – the accumulated military lore of a variety of cultures reaching back over 2,000 years and stretching from Gaul to Africa, Persia and the borders of India. The Romans had their own ideas about military architecture; and they had their own ideas on how to deal with other people's.

CHAPTER THREE

The fertile crescent

And it came to pass, when the people heard the sound of the
trumpet, and the people shouted with a great shout, that the
wall fell down flat, so that the people went up into the city,
every man straight before him, and they took the city. And
they utterly destroyed all that was in the city, both man and
woman, young and old, and ox, and sheep, and ass, with the
edge of the sword. And they burnt the city with fire, and all
that was therein: only the silver, and the gold, and the vessels
of brass and of iron, they put into the treasury of the house
of the Lord.
(Joshua, 6: 20–1, 24)

Ignoring such mythical battles as the Titans'
assault on the stronghold of the gods on Mount
Olympus (which may be the exaggerated folk-
memory account of an actual Old Stone Age
event), the earliest references to sieges and fortresses occur in the Bible, Homer's Iliad, and in
similar records of the peoples of the Mediterranean and Middle East. However, Troy, Jericho,
Jerusalem, Mycenae and Carchemish are only a
few well-known names out of many. Like the
hillforts of Britain, the strongholds of the Biblical
and Classical world were self-contained settlements, surrounded by walls and towers. They
were constructed with whatever local material
and expertise were available, and influenced by
response to changing weaponry. They were often
erected upon the ruins of previous settlements,
each civilisation excavating enough of its prede-
cessor to lay its own foundations.

Such an architectural palimpsest may be as
many as nineteen layers deep, as archaeologists
found at Jericho on the west bank of the River
Jordan. There the earliest settlement was of the
Neolithic period, about 7000 BC. It covered four
hectares and predated the invention of pottery,

its 3,000 citizens fashioning dishes and bowls out
of limestone. And yet they enclosed their town
with a free-standing stone wall 2 metres thick, 7
metres high and 800 metres in circumference, plus
a tower 7.5 metres in breadth. The whole was
surrounded by a ditch 8.2 metres wide and 2.7
metres deep. The existence of this ditch suggests a
military purpose for such construction, which the
walls and tower alone would not necessarily
signify. For although the early strongholds of the
Mediterranean and Middle East were usually
fortified cities, not all cities were fortified in
military style.

The Sumerian cities of Mesopotamia, like Ur
and Lagash, whose foundations date back to
3500 BC, were impressive structures, rising high
above the irrigated flood-plain of the Rivers
Tigris and Euphrates. But the mighty ziggurats or
step-pyramids which dominated their silhouette
were not of military intent. They were lofty
temple-palaces, sacred high places, raising
priests, priestesses and god-kings nearer the
divinities in the sky. Admittedly there were walls,
similarly of sun-baked brick, but these served to
insulate the religious from the profane, and to

separate the urban from the rural.

There was certainly warfare, but this was an affair of heroes in war-carts and of phalanxes of infantry, manoeuvring, fighting and dying in the empty spaces between the rival city-states. Sieges and assaults on the towns themselves did not figure in those early campaigns. This was partly because the walls had to be built very broad at the bottom to support the weight of all the layers of bricks above. That meant that they could not be undermined, while the lack of suitable timber in Mesopotamia precluded the construction of siege-towers and even of scaling ladders tall enough to reach the top of the wall, and simultaneously strong enough to bear the weight of several armed men all at one time.

Besides, the object of Sumero-Akkadian warfare was to kill the god-king and his warriors, thus proving your superiority so that you gained monopolistic control of the canals and crops of the valley, and seized the material riches and wealth-producing population within the opposing city. The destruction of the means of producing that fertile and industrial bounty was not part of that warfare. Copper spearheads were designed to kill people and leave property intact.

Admittedly, Sargon of Akkad (2371–2316 BC) 'turned Kazalla into dust and heaps of ruins; he destroyed even the resting-places of the birds'. But Sargon was exceptional. He was recorded as making a particular point of wrecking the walls of cities he captured. And it was no good trying to defend a town against him. His warriors either rushed the gates or built a sloping rampart of earth as high as the wall and swarmed over that way.

But Sargon was a barbarian from outside Sumeria itself, the sort of person the Median Wall was built to keep out. Erected, some say, about 3500 BC, it covered some 70 kilometres from the Tigris to the Euphrates. It is not clear whether it was a definite military obstacle, or merely a frontier demarcation. Some authorities declare that the Median Wall dates from 800 BC, although this might indicate later construction along the old foundations. Certainly, enough of it existed in the time of Alexander the Great (336–323 BC), for it to be regarded as the boundary between the provinces of Mesopotamia (to the north-west) and Babylonia (to the south-east). But, however it was constructed and whatever its intent, it did not keep out invaders.

Nevertheless, a thousand years of invasion and war passed without the destruction of the Mesopotamian irrigation canal system. Dynasties came and went. Occasionally a city was sacked. Sometimes new capitals replaced others, but more often the old ones (first Ur and then Babylon) flourished under the new regimes. It does seem as though there was some sort of military taboo against the total destruction of property for the sake of it. Once the warrior-priests had put their cause to the test of battle, even the human beings they conquered were not slaughtered but enslaved. No doubt some people pined for the old days; others must have merely accepted one remote foreign aristocracy for another.

The earliest Egyptian civilisation presents a somewhat similar picture, regarding the necessity for military architecture. Founded by the legendary King Menes about 3100 BC, the city of Memphis (a corruption of Men-nefer) was given that name signifying 'The White Walls'. But although it was surrounded by whitewashed ramparts, that does not necessarily mean that the city was intended to withstand assault or siege. Such a wall hindered unauthorised admission, thus preserving the god-king's spiritual and physical security. It also protected the State's (i.e., the royal and temple) reserves of food from starving rioters in time of famine.

However, the god-kings of ancient Egypt put their trust in two other forms of defence against rebellion at home and enemies abroad. The first was the cohesive nature of Egyptian society, religion and government, enabling massive engineering effort to be directed into the construction of spiritual monuments, funerary art and dogmatic bureaucracy, which in turn reinforced the god-king's unifying hold over the country.

The second factor in Egypt's security was distance. A foreign army coveting corn in Egypt had to cross the Mediterranean to the north or – if coming from the south – march or boat down a long, winding, cataract-obstructed river valley.

Enemies to east and west would have to traverse barren desert before they began to pose any sort of threat to the god-kings at Memphis. Admittedly, small raiding parties of maritime or desert nomads might get through, but it was hardly likely that great armies could survive the watery or sandy wilderness. And by the time the logistics capable of sustaining such masses of men had been devised and the resources accumulated, the Egyptian Pharaohs had raised their own standing army, meeting the foe as far from the cities and fields of Egypt as possible.

Neither policy – of unification at home and isolation from enemies abroad – worked perfectly all the time (no policy could over two thousand years), but both policies were effective enough for the Egyptians to return to them again and again. To help keep the foreign foe at bay so that Thebes and their homeland cities need not be fortified except for show, the god-kings of the Middle Kingdom (2052–1786 BC) built military strongholds on the borders of their empire. Like existing fortified cities in the Middle East they had square or semi-circular bastions projecting from the walls to provide flanking fire, but they were quite different in concept. They were not refuges for peasants nor centres for trade and industry. Their sole purpose was the provision of accommodation and supplies for frontier troops. They were so located that any attempt to bypass them would involve a lengthy trek through the wilderness. Nor could they be ignored; the soldiers inside would then come out to harass the rear of the invader's column, driving it into the Pharaoh's oncoming field army. In any case, the invader might not want to ignore the frontier fortress, but might prefer to put the question of the ownership of disputed territory to the gods of war.

But the ancient Egyptians did not simply rely on the whims of Anhur and Sekmet, the god and goddess of war. Buhen below the Second Cataract and built during the XII Dynasty (1991–1786 BC) was provided with battlements and balconies to protect the archers on the walls and enable them to fire vertically down upon the heads of soldiers trying to cross the dry ditch and assault the walls. At the same time the Egyptian army was trained in siege techniques, which mainly involved digging tunnels to undermine the walls, while above ground there were wheeled scaling-ladders and battering rams, all under covering fire from archers.

By the time of the New Kingdom, which began in 1567 BC, the Egyptians had adopted two new weapons systems from their temporary conquerors, the Hyksos. The first was the double-convex composite bow of wood, horn and sinew, so bound or glued together that at rest it seemed to be bent the wrong way round. When strung and pulled, it had a maximum range of 400 paces. The other development was the single-axle chariot with spoked wheels, which provided mobility for archers and spearmen. This resulted in a more economical deployment of soldiers in peacetime. New fortresses built on the boundaries of the re-expanded empire did not need to be as large as their precursors, because they each housed a smaller number of troops. The *migdol* (which was the name later given to this type of fort) was a base for soldiers patrolling the frontier zone or standing guard over an oasis or road junction, its archers' arrows dominating the route into Egypt. Any sign of disaffection, or invasion, and a charioteer would be despatched at full speed to alert the Pharaoh's field army. Repair and replacement of horses were provided by chariot workshops and staging posts along the road.

When the Egyptians themselves came up against a fortified city they usually attempted an immediate assault, hacking at the gates with axes and storming the walls by means of scaling-ladders. While so doing, they slung their rectangular shields over their backs which acted as protection while leaving their hands free. That was how the Canaanite city of Megiddo was captured in 1468 BC.

If the initial assault was not successful, the Egyptian general (Pharaoh himself was not always present in the field) called it off before there were too many casualties. He then settled down for a long siege, wearing the defenders out with limited attacks, until they either surrendered, were so weakened that they could not man the walls, or succumbed to some ruse which induced them to open the gates. That was what happened at Jaffa in Palestine. Thot (Thutmose III's general) pretended to abandon the siege, sending 200 baskets or sacks of tribute as offerings to the victorious citizens. Once inside, a soldier emerged from each container. They formed up and captured the gates, so that the Egyptian army outside could come in.

Kadesh in Syria, however, was protected by the confluence of the Orontes and a tributary, plus an artificial canal joining the two rivers. That city was only taken by Thutmose III after a protracted siege. Indeed, it was such a formidable place that when Ramses II defeated the Hittites under Mutallu in 1288 BC, he made no attempt to pursue the retreating enemy into Kadesh, but himself withdrew to regroup his own army and consolidate his existing hold on southern Palestine.

The Hittites were a race of warrior-priests whose capital had been founded about 1800 BC at Hattusas (present-day Boghaskoy) some 150 kilometres east of modern Ankara. It had a stone wall, pierced by nine gates, the inward-curving jambs being composed of single pieces of solid rock. The Battle of Kadesh marked the beginning of a period of eclipse for both the Hittites and the Egyptians, their contracting empires matched by the growing strength and rivalries of formerly subject States in Palestine and upper Mesopotamia.

Eventually the Egyptians were once again confined within the Nile valley, but the Hittites disappeared altogether, their traditions carried on by mercenary advisers who made their military expertise available to the rulers of the new states. The most famous was Uriah the Hittite, whose wife Bathsheba was coveted by King David of the Israelites. Although of warrior tradition, Uriah seems to have been more of a staff officer than a front-line soldier, relaying messages from General Joab to headquarters at Jerusalem. Joab was then (about 1000 BC) besieging Rabboth-Ammon (the citadel overlooking present-day Amman in Jordan). The Ammonites made a sortie and withdrew under covering fire from their archers on the ramparts above. In hot pursuit, the Israelites got too close to the wall and Uriah – placed in that situation by David's secret

instructions – was killed.

Officially, what the assault party had done was expressly against King David's standing orders, which referred to the fate of a certain Abimelech. He had been one of the Judges of Israel in an earlier century. Conducting a campaign against rebel strongholds in central Palestine, his preferred plan of action was to storm a fortified city and drive the inhabitants into a single tower. He then piled brushwood around the base of the structure and set fire to it. The defenders either burned to death as the flames spread through the wooden doors, floors and partitions, or were suffocated by the smoke. It had worked well enough at Shechem: 'all the men of the tower of Shechem died also, about a thousand men and women'. But at Thebez, Abimelech was overconfident. Going personally to set light to the pyre, he was struck on the head by the upper part of a millstone thrown down by a woman on top of the tower. His skull was fractured, but he was determined that no female should have the credit for killing him. He therefore commanded his armour-bearer to finish him off with his sword – which he did. 'And when the men of Israel saw that Abimelech was dead, they departed every man unto his place', presumably without waiting for the destruction or surrender of the tower of Thebez.

From such accounts and from archaeological evidence we can thus recreate an impression of military architecture and its employment in Palestine and Syria from 1200 to 800 BC. The region was divided into a continuing shifting patchwork of rival religions, cultures and kingdoms, each with a fortified city as its capital. The object of warfare was the possession of empty territory for an expanding population. Campaigns were therefore waged to capture the enemy's strongholds and destroy *his* population. So each city was equipped with at least one tower of refuge into which – at the last – all the survivors could flee, hoping that some divine or human intervention would drive off the enemy before he achieved his aim of total kill. The siege of Thebez shows that such intervention could occur enabling the defenders to emerge and repossess their homeland – and then go on to steal somebody else's!

Each city acted as a refuge for the peasants in the surrounding area. In return, the villagers had to pay taxes to the rulers of the city, presumably when they passed through the gates to trade in more peaceful days. It soon came about that the definition of a city was that it was walled whereas a village was not. And so, the temples, houses, workshops and market-places of the townsfolk were surrounded by a stone or brick wall 2.5–6 metres thick and as high as the foundations would allow; 10–12 metres in the case of Mizpah or Tell-en-Nasbeh, built about 900 BC. From the period of King Solomon (974–37 BC) onwards, skill in stonemasonry had advanced so much that stones up to two metres in dimension could be so hewn that they fitted together perfectly and indissolubly without mortar. However, the wall of Mizpah was laid in clay mortar, while that of Lachish was of sunbaked brick. The outside of the wall could be covered with lime plaster to a height of 5.5 metres, making it more weather-proof and more difficult to scale, besides being more neat and impressive. By now, the old unbroken, smooth-lined wall had been replaced by one which not only went up and down following the rise and dip of the terrain, but which also went in and out (alternating re-entrant and salient). The walls were crenellated with alternate high and low sections (or battlements). At intervals, a rectangular tower jutted out as much as two metres beyond the line of the wall, its base often further protected by a circular bastion. This not only enabled the defenders to fire at anybody assaulting the wall or adjacent towers, it also made the towers themselves more difficult to damage because there was no corner from which stones could be easily dislodged. That is, if anybody had been able to cross the glacis fronting the wall. This was a great sloping apron of beaten earth eight metres across and absolutely devoid of cover. The glacis itself was only accessible after crossing a ditch and climbing a retaining-wall or stone shield up to 20 metres in height. To make things even more difficult for the attacker, the whole complex could be encircled by yet another wall, as at Lachish near Gaza in Judah. When that was done, the gatehouse defences became even more important, for they provided the only practical means of reinforcing the defenders on the outer wall or of withdrawing them if that became necessary. The gates were composed of solid wooden boards strengthened with metal and secured with wooden beams and bronze (later iron) bolts. An invader would have to smash his way through two or three such gates, either set at angles to each other or with narrow alleyways in between – or both. Certainly the walls on either side and the ceiling above would be hollow, narrow holes or slits enabling the defenders to maintain a deadly rain upon the attackers in the semi-darkness between the gates.

Most cities had a much simpler entrance. That at Mizpah was formed by overlapping the walls by nine metres. It is particularly interesting archaeologically, as the foundations of the guardrooms can be seen, while the outer court of the gates has stone benches for the transaction of legal and other business. It was inevitable that walls and their gateways eventually came to be regarded as regulators of trade as much as branches of military defence.

Of course, none of this construction was of any use if the defenders died of thirst, which could happen within a few days in a Mediterranean climate. The inhabitants of Megiddo – on the west bank of the Jordan – took special care to ensure that that did not happen when they constructed their city defences about 1100 BC. The only reliable large-capacity well was located more than 40 metres outside the line of the city walls, a mere inconvenience in peacetime but a fatal circumstance under siege. The Megiddans therefore tunnelled down 18 metres to construct a stairway leading through the rock to tap the spring at its source.

But Megiddo was not simply a refuge for frightened people; it was also the King of Israel's northern base of operations as shown by another development there. This was the construction of stables for horses which had been introduced in the reign of Solomon to draw war-chariots, instead of mules. (Some authorities say that these buildings date from the slightly later Omri-Ahab period of 885–853 BC.) The stables comprised five sheds with two rows of eleven stalls in each. The roof was supported by stone pillars, which also

17 *An artist's reconstruction of the walls of the Biblical city of Mizpah, based on the results of an excavation conducted by the Pacific School of Religion, under Professor William F. Bade.*

served as hitching-posts. In front of the compound was a courtyard with a large cistern for watering the horses.

One of the subject races who found new freedom when the Hittite Empire broke up was a nation living in northern Iraq and worshipping a fearsome God of War, Blood Sacrifice and Fertility named Asshur. From him they derived their own title, the Asshurians. (Coming down to us as the 'Assyrians', they have ever since been confused in the Western mind with the 'Syrians', who took *their* name from a different geographical region.)

Hesitantly at first, but with growing confidence, the Assyrians (employing cavalry for the first time) embarked upon the conquest of the entire Middle East. By 745 BC they had occupied the whole of the Fertile Crescent from the Persian Gulf to the coast of Syria, with other client States sending tribute to their capital at Nineveh. But even this was not enough. Assyrian domination had to be 100 per cent. They waged total war; they

insisted upon unconditional surrender. Enemies who rejected that demand were slaughtered and their city pulled down around their ears. Survivors were blinded with spears, impaled upon stakes, or buried alive in the flaming debris. And that included non-combatants, men, women and children. In fact, the fear of terrible death might induce them to rebel against their warriors and open the gates to the Assyrians. When that happened, the city's leaders were skinned alive and the rest of the people shipped off to some remote province of the empire, another conquered race being settled in their former abode.

Sometimes, however, such terror-tactics had exactly the opposite effect, uniting everybody within the city in determination to resist; they were all going to die anyway, so it might as well be heroically. Sometimes they resisted long enough for plague or other affliction to smite the Assyrians, or for their army to have to be withdrawn to meet some other crisis elsewhere in the empire.

But the Assyrians did not usually give up. To deal with such recalcitrance, they developed a highly efficient siege-train. Assault troops swam across moats and rivers using inflated goatskins; boats ferried larger items of equipment across and pontoon bridges were assembled. There were scaling-ladders nine metres in length, while tunnellers undermined the walls using long crowbars to prise apart individual blocks of stone. The same principle was employed in the most novel device, a development of the battering-ram. Its tip in the form of an axe, the baulk of timber was pounded away at the gate or wall until a crevice or indentation had been made and into which the point could be forced. It was then levered from side to side until bricks and stones or chunks of wood came loose and the hole grew and grew until the wall collapsed or the gate was smashed in. Being very heavy, the ram was suspended from a gallows, so that the engineers could swing it to and fro and from left to right. This structure was protected by a domed tower about five to six metres high, carried on a six-wheeled armoured frame about 4.5 metres long and pushed into position by the men inside. A lighter four-wheeled version came into service under Tiglath-pileser III (744–727 BC).

All this activity was conducted under cover of fire from slingers (also introduced by Tiglath-pileser III) and archers. The latter shot arrows of a new design, their iron heads barbed to make them very difficult to pull out, thus inflicting fearsome wounds. The bowmen were usually ensconced behind large portable shields or were carried in wheeled towers to overlook the walls. Besides being individual marksmen, the archers and slingers were trained to fire in volleys, thus enhancing the devastating effect of their missiles.

The Assyrians were often able to storm a city at the first assault. Their insistence upon contributions of manpower from conquered states meant that for the first time, the besiegers – having sufficient discipline, organisation and troop reserves – could mount simultaneous attacks, always outnumbering the defenders at any one point on the perimeter.

And if all else failed, the Assyrians settled down for a lengthy siege. They were not warrior-heroes, easily bored with inactivity and always ready to go off in search of fresh adventure; Assyria was a nation-in-arms; their whole society was a full-time professional army. So, they obeyed orders, dug in, mounted limited attacks, and waited for the people inside to starve to death

or be bled to death by steady attrition – or surrender and be massacred. Sargon II (the Biblical Shalmaneser) besieged Samaria for three years, until the city capitulated in 722 BC and ten of the Tribes of Israel disappeared for ever.

Being an expanding empire, the Assyrians do not seem to have introduced anything new in military architecture themselves. When Sennacherib rebuilt Nineveh, he simply made its fortifications more grandiose than anything before. Its walls were of brick 15 metres thick and 50 metres high, with many shallowly projecting buttresses. The wall was surrounded by a moat fed by the River Tigris and the total perimeter was said to be 80 kilometres in extent.

The bricks employed in this work – and indeed in most of the projects mentioned in this chapter – were about 10 centimetres square and 30 centimetres in length. They were of two sorts: baked (i.e. dried in kilns) and unbaked (i.e. dried in the sun). The former were red and very hard; the latter softer and of a whitish appearance. They were bonded together with clay or lime mortar or bitumen (which oozed from the oil-bearing rocks of the region).

The question is, how could such massive works have been accomplished in the days before cranes and mechanised earthmoving equipment? The answer undoubtedly lies in three parallels from the twentieth century AD.

The first is of thousands of Chinese peasants, men and women (some cradling babies) scooping up earth with simple shovels, dumping it in baskets, emptying the baskets in the appointed place, and tamping down the level surface with their feet – to create airfields for B-29 Super-fortresses to bomb Japan.

And when it comes to attaining height, many Western servicemen abroad remember seeing barracks and other tall buildings being erected by local labour. At Aden in the 1950s the Arab contractors assembled a lofty scaffolding of small pieces of timber, all lashed together. It looked most ramshackle, but there are no reports that such constructions ever collapsed. The concrete came out of the mixer into a series of large shallow bowls, each one being passed from hand to hand, all the way up the staging, until tipped

18 *This reconstruction of medieval builders at work can be seen in The York Story Exhibition in that city's Church of St Mary. Note the pulley, ladder and staging and how the scaffolding is lashed together. It may look crude, but it enabled towers and spires over 100 metres high to be erected. In fact it was how all building above the ground floor was done from prehistoric times until the recent invention of metal scaffolding and clips. Records of such fatal accidents as did occur suggest that these were due more to momentary carelessness (such as stepping backwards without thinking) rather than frequent collapses of scaffolding.*

into the appropriate shuttering. The empty pans were then passed back down a different route to the mixer in a continuous cycle. Every so often, the foreman blew his whistle and the gangs changed places in such a way that nobody was engaged on heavy or awkward work all the time.

However, it is unlikely that the Assyrian overseers would have been so considerate. It may

well be that the experiences of British soldiers of 1942–5, building the Burma-Siam Railway, were more typical of prisoners-of-war throughout history, rather than those servicemen captured in Europe with rights guaranteed by the Geneva Convention.

Similarly, the Assyrians required thousands of slaves to knead and mould the clay, fire the kilns and build their walls, which in turn involved further punitive expeditions against vassal states which had not fulfilled their quotas of forced labour. And that in turn prompted a lot of people to give serious thought to improving their own defences.

Such work was necessarily hasty, improvisation not invention being the order of the day. It was mainly devoted to three expedients: rebuilding and strengthening dilapidated walls; mass producing plenty of hand weapons and missiles; and building up stocks of food and water for all the inhabitants.

Anticipating a fresh offensive by the new Great King of Assyria, Sennacherib (704–681 BC), King

Hezekiah's tunnellers excavated an underground channel, bringing a stream of water into the city of Jerusalem. Also, in Judah, the citizens of Lachish crowned their walls with a wooden balcony from which the archers could fire vertically downwards upon the assaulting troops (what was called in the Middle Ages AD a brattice).

But these cities were not meant to be strongholds, defensible bases of operations, from which, at the appointed time, an all-conquering army would sally forth. No matter how complex their fortifications, they were simply refuges, places where frightened people could hide more-or-less passively, until the Assyrian storm had swept past them, or – more likely – had carried them away.

But at Jerusalem in 701 BC, for once the Assyrians under Sennacherib had too much to do. While his main army besieged and captured Lachish, Sennacherib despatched another force to Jerusalem, demanding Hezekiah's surrender. The embassy was rejected, but before Jerusalem could be assaulted, an epidemic virtually wiped

19 *A prospect of the ruins of Babylon, showing how the buildings and walls were constructed of brick. The tourist is an RAF officer in mufti, representative of another empire which ruled Mesopotamia between the two world wars.*

out the Assyrian host. Sennacherib had no alternative but to raise the siege and withdraw the survivors, taking with them the plundered population of Lachish.

Few cities were as fortunate as Jerusalem. Sennacherib's successor Esarhaddon (681–669 BC) had his eyes on grander plunder, the Kingdom of Egypt, no less. The 'White Walls' of Memphis succumbed to battering-ram, undermining engineers and stormtroops after just half-a-day's operations. Thebes (screened by water defences) fell in the next reign, that of Ashurbanipal (668–633 BC).

But no empire lives for ever. A great coalition of vassal states outfought the Assyrian field army and in 612 BC took Nineveh itself after a three-month siege. The walls, for all their splendour, were unsound. Undermined by the flooding of the Tigris, they began to disintegrate. Sardanapal, the last of the Great Kings of Assyria, set fire to his palace and threw himself into the flames.

For a time, the Chaldeans were masters of Babylonia. Under Nebuchadnezzar II, they tried to combine world empire with harsh autocracy; the sack of Jerusalem in 586 BC and the Jewish exile in Babylon are well-known examples of his policy. No doubt many of the Jews were employed in Nebuchadnezzar's rebuilding of Babylon. Its surrounding wall was 18 kilometres in circumference, with a reinforcing tower-buttress every 20 metres. The inner surface of the wall was composed of six metres of unbaked brick; then came 9.2 metres of rubble, retained by a fronting wall of baked brick 7.6 metres thick. The surrounding moat was fed by the Euphrates, which flowed right through the centre of the city. However, Nebuchadnezzar had learned the lesson of Nineveh. So that the foundations of his city walls should not be washed away, the urban side of the moat was lined with three metres of brick. The wall's greatest weakness was its number of gates, eight in total and of splendid magnificence. The Euphrates itself made two gaps in the wall, but the stream was so deep that it could not be employed as a means of entrance by soldiers, while there were probably devices to prevent unauthorised boats passing through. It was all very impressive, but the city of Babylon was still taken by the Medes and Persians under Cyrus. From 539 to 538 BC he pretended to besiege the city, throwing up fieldworks apparently to prevent contact between Babylon and any outside allies. However, they were in fact screens to cover the construction of canals. At the right time, the Euphrates was diverted into them, its level dropping so dramatically that a large force of Medes and Persians was able to enter the city along both sides of the river-bed.

And so Babylon fell to Cyrus and his successors. They permitted a much greater degree of local self-government than under the Assyrians and Chaldeans. Nevertheless, although enlightened rulers, they were just as obsessed with the dream of world domination – which brought them into conflict with the Greeks.

CHAPTER FOUR

The Greeks

It is men who make the city, and not walls or ships with no
men inside them.
(Nicias of Athens, reported by Thucydides)

The Hellenes were not all one race, but were a synthesis of differing peoples and cultures, who had invaded the southern Balkan Peninsula and the Aegean Islands over a period of two thousand years. The topography of the country was hardly conducive to unity, and the area remained one of separate city-states. Each had its own mountain stronghold or *acropolis*, its natural defences improved with stone ramparts. That these were of military purpose is suggested by the Heroic legends and indicated by archaeological excavation.

The palace-city of Mycenae (between Corinth and Argos) was founded about 3000 BC, attaining its full splendour about 1350 BC. Crowning a precipitous cliff, the citadel comprised houses of stone and wood for nobles, priests, warriors, poets and artisans. The royal palace (a complex of state chambers, public rooms and storehouses), sacred enclosure and tombs (so full of precious funerary objects that early archaeologists called one 'The Treasury of King Atreus'), were located on the highest point. On terraces around the acropolis were gardens, vineyards and orchards. The whole self-contained community was surrounded by a wall of massive blocks, known to later Greeks as 'cyclopean stones' – it being assumed that the architect had been Cyclops the Giant. The ceremonial entrance to Mycenae was via the famous Lion Gate, three metres high and three metres wide.

Perhaps by their very size, such impressive structures acted as deterrents to direct assault. Or

perhaps at some early stage in development each State's acropolis was declared a sacred area, a refuge for women and children, respected by all combatants. Whatever the reason, most battles were decided in single or group combat by strutting, boastful – and sulking – heroes. That was how the legendary Troy was besieged for ten years. It was hardly a direct assault on the walls. Even the final destruction of the city (that event being dated to 1184 BC) was achieved by infiltrating a commando party by means of the Wooden Horse – a trick of epic memory, but not a frontal assault.

So, as the city-states developed and were able to field larger armies, they still fought as infantry in the debated land at the edge of the *poleis'* sphere of influence. (The aggressor could always provoke a battle by threatening to burn his opponent's crops.) Once the cause of dispute had been put to the test of battle, the vanquished acknowledged the victor's triumph by sending heralds to ask for an armistice to bury the dead.

There were city walls, but they were as simply functional as the situation would allow; they were not built as symbols of military grandeur. When they had the opportunity the Greeks preferred to devote most of their architectural effort to temples and the arts. Even militaristic Sparta lacked buildings of spectacular belligerence. Their contribution to military architecture was the barrack block, where all male Spartans between the ages of seven and thirty lived under martial discipline. According to tradition, Lycur-

gus (the founder of Sparta about 776 BC) had forbidden the construction of defensive walls, thus forcing the citizens to trust in their own valour for their protection. (And harking back to the days of the Minoan civilisation of 2000–1400 BC, it is interesting to note that the city of Knossos had no defensive walls at all, relying entirely on maritime power to keep foes at a distance.)

The situation became somewhat different during both the Persian invasions of 490–479 BC, and the Peloponnesian War (431–404 BC) between

20 *A general view of the stronghold of Mycenae in Greece.*

Athens and Sparta. These had much of the nature of civil wars, vendettas or blood feuds, in which old scores were paid off without regard to any code of behaviour. In such an atmosphere, cities became refuges rather than strongholds, their walls rebuilt or strengthened.

The Peloponnesian Greeks fortified the Isthmus of Corinth against the invasion of Xerxes and his Persian host in 480 BC, but this was probably more in the nature of fieldworks rather than military architecture. That same year the Delphic Oracle advised that 'When all was lost, a wooden wall should still shelter the Athenians.' Those non-combatants who put their trust in land fortifications hurriedly erected timber barricades; they died behind them, in the flames of their city. Those Athenians like Themistocles, who believed the Oracle was referring to wooden war galleys, took the fleet to sea and defeated the Persians at Salamis. It would not be the last time in history that a nation's warships have been eulogised as its 'wooden walls'.

With the Persian threat annihilated, Themistocles set about the reconstruction of Athens in 478 BC, encircling the city with walls 12 kilometres in circumference and 3.5–4.5 metres thick. Themistocles intended that they should be 36 metres high, so loftily unassailable that they could be manned by senior citizens and children, while all the warriors served in the fleet. In fact, after a period of continuous labour by all sections of the community cutting, trimming, shifting and laying blocks of stone, the height was restricted to 18 metres – which proved more than adequate. At the same time, walls of similar dimensions were erected to protect the naval dockyard at Piraeus. To ensure safe passage between Athens and the port upon which her prosperity depended, two more walls were built from Athens to the sea at Piraeus and Phaleron. The work was undertaken from 457 to 456 BC, but the area enclosed was too large to be defended. Accordingly, the Phaleric Wall was abandoned, its materials probably being used in the construction of a wall running parallel with the more northerly wall between Athens and Piraeus. Being a mere 170 metres apart, each sector of the seven-kilometre Long Walls could be defended by the same body of men, rushing from one rampart to the other. These walls served Athens well, for the city – even when ravaged by plague – could not be taken by storm, and its leaders were free to pursue a policy of maritime warfare. Athens was thus a stronghold from which her fleet – refitted – could be launched again and again against her enemies.

The object of the Peloponnesian War between the Greek city states was the political and commercial domination of Greece and the Greek colonies in the Mediterranean. All rivals were to be eliminated, all the men and most of the non-combatants being killed and the survivors enslaved. In such circumstances, when cities were attacked, they were defended by men, women and slaves with a desperation only matched by the vengeful slaughter when the invaders broke in and fought their way house by house under a hail of missiles and building materials. Such was the engagement in the streets of Plataea north of Athens in 431 BC, when the occupying Thebans were forced to surrender and were all killed.

And yet direct assault on a city was rarely immediately successful; the number of attacking warriors was usually not enough to outnumber even a small garrison at any one point. So primitive siege techniques had to be employed, techniques which improved under the impetus of war. The second siege of Plataea from 429 to 427 BC gives some idea of what was involved. First, the Spartans cut down all the fruit trees in the area and surrounded Plataea with a palisade. Then they built a long sloping ramp of earth and timber against the walls of Plataea, to enable scaling-ladders to reach the parapet. As fast as they did so, the Plataeans (who totalled 480 men and 110 women) kept raising the height of their own walls with layers of bricks and wooden balconies covered with hides as protection against flaming arrows. At the same time, they tunnelled out under their own foundations to undermine the Spartan mound so that it kept subsiding. The Plataeans also constructed a crescent-shaped switch-line, its two horns against the original walls and enclosing the danger-area. If the Spartans did break through, they would have to repeat the whole operation to pierce the switch-line.

The most perilous time came after three months, when the enemy heaped up bundles of brushwood impregnated with sulphur and pitch. The resulting blaze would have engulfed the whole city, if it had not been extinguished by an opportune thunderstorm.

This form of attack was not repeated, perhaps because of some ancient treaty which would have meant that Sparta would have to relinquish her prize if the city were taken by force. The Spartans and Thebans then determined to starve the garrison into voluntary capitulation. They therefore built a roofed and watch-towered double wall 4.5 metres wide all the way round the city. With ditches on either side and continuously patrolled, it effectively cut off all escape from Plataea and prevented the arrival of the oft-promised relief column from Athens – not that one was ever despatched. The Plataeans held out for two years, and then under cover of a nocturnal winter storm, they sallied out, placed ladders between two watch-towers on the investing wall, and killed the sentries. One of the party dislodged a tile, but the Spartan guard turned out carrying torches, and so were easy targets in the darkness. Some 200 Plataeans got away, but famine soon compelled the remainder of the garrison to surrender. They were tried 'for making war on Sparta', found guilty and executed.

The siege of Plataea was typical in that most Greek cities were blockaded in some way. The Greek city-state economy depended upon imports of food, either from the surrounding countryside or from over the sea. The slightest interruption of that trade – and the citizens faced starvation. For them it was a matter of holding out until a friendly fleet or army arrived and drove the besiegers away.

The siege of Plataea also illustrates the difference between fortifications and fieldworks. The former are of a permanent architectural nature; the latter, no matter how well designed and stoutly constructed, are of temporary purpose only. Other ancient fieldworks were employed at the siege of Syracuse in Sicily, a colony of Corinthian foundation. Blockaded by an Athenian fleet from 415 BC, its landward walls were paralleled by an Athenian double-wall similar to that constructed by the Spartans at Plataea. However, the Syracusans pushed out their own fieldworks across the line of the intended investment. The first two Syracusan counter-walls were taken and dismantled by the Athenians, but the third was successfully completed and held against the Athenians, thus ensuring that supplies, reinforcements and intelligence could always get through to Syracuse. The subsequent defeat of her fleet and the failure of the Sicilian Expedition was the beginning of the end for the Athenian Empire. In 404 BC Athens itself was besieged and forced to surrender by Lysander of Sparta without being stormed.

Among the terms of the peace treaty was the dismantling of the Long Walls, which was done to the sound of Spartan music and dancing. The Long Walls were later rebuilt and some other cities (such as Corinth) copied this form of parallel fortification, but they were never as impressive nor as effective, being too large in extent to defend against the new equipment and skilled engineers now being employed by the dictators and emperors of the Mediterranean and Middle East with the resources of half the known world at their disposal.

Among the devices used by the Syracusans in the defence of their city was an incendiary substance said to be of pitch, sulphur, tow, frankincense and pine-sawdust. It is not clear whether this was thrown out in burning lumps or whether it was used in flaming arrows to set siege equipment on fire. There are also rumours about this time concerning the use of some sort of tube projecting flame, the earliest reference to 'Greek Fire'. Mention of this mysterious substance will be made from time to time, and it seems evident that its principal constituent was naphtha or some other flammable chemical derived from petroleum which occurs naturally in the Middle East.

Other equipment was employed by Dionysius of Syracuse (405–367 BC) when he pushed mobile battering-rams and siege-towers along an improvised causeway during his assault on the Carthaginian island-fortress of Motya. He also turned the Phoenicians' own secret weapons against their inventors. The *Katapeltes* was like a bow laid on its side, fixed to a frame and firing an arrow-shaped bolt or 3.5-kilogram stone over a range of 200 metres. The *petrobolos* was much larger, consisting of a four-wheeled waggon, in which was mounted a wooden arm embedded in a mass of twisted sinew or hair (women's hair being the longest and most resilient). The arm was wound back and a 25-kilogram stone placed in a sling at the end. The arm was released and flew forward to the top of its arc, being brought up short against a massive timber like a goal-post. One end of the sling flew free and the rock (or pot containing incendiary material) shot through the air to crash onto the target about 200 metres away. The Phoenicians had invented artillery.

During the reign of Alexander the Great and his Seleucid successors, the devices of siege warfare became more and more complicated. In the sieges of Tyre (333–330 BC) and Rhodes (about 305 BC), there are accounts of fireships and floating batteries carrying huge catapults. At one end of the scale there were furnaces for heating sand and releasing it so that it blew into the enemy's face or trickled down under his armour and clothes. At the other extreme, there were battering-rams 45 metres long each needing a thousand men to propel them. Most impressive of all was *Helepolis* (*The City-Taker*), a square wooden tower with a complement of 2,300 men pushing it along and discharging missiles in every direction. Most fantastic of all were the giant ship-lifting cranes and burning-mirrors allegedly fabricated by Archimedes during the siege of Syracuse by the Romans in 212 BC.

However, the very biggest siege-engines which did exist would only be employed against the largest fortresses, and then only when the terrain was suitable, when a causeway or ramp could be constructed, or if there were sufficient water to float a carrier warship. In many instances, the scaling-ladder was still the most significant weapon of assault – if properly made. In 327 BC one broke behind Alexander the Great during the assault on the citadel of the Malli in India (probably the modern Multan). His unit temporarily isolated, he was badly wounded and would have been killed if reinforcements had not arrived in time.

Alexander's empire broke up on his death just four years later. Already, a new power was arising in the Mediterranean, one whose own *imperium* would last for four hundred years, whose own siege techniques were efficient rather than spectacular, and whose own military architecture (representing the first steps in a trend which has been fitfully developed ever since) would stand for two millennia – Rome.

CHAPTER FIVE

Rome expanding

He fought thirty battles, conquered two powerful tribes,
capturing over twenty strongholds, and annexed the Isle of
Wight.
(Suetonius, *Life of Vespasian*)

It has often been said that the Romans never introduced anything new, merely adapting, perfecting and employing efficiently existing techniques and equipment. Undoubtedly they must have acquired considerable technical knowledge from studying at the School of Military Architecture on Rhodes. They were not even the first army to build defended camps on the march; the Persians had done that during their expeditions against Greece, and any force would have been extremely foolhardy if they neglected to post sentries and take other precautions against surprise attack in hostile territory.

The Romans, however, took the construction of temporary defenceworks to the point of obsession. Over a period of 400 years of expansion under the Republic and the early Empire, there was bound to be some variation, but what usually happened was that a legion on the march naturally enough sent out scouting cavalry (*esploratores*) ahead and on the flanks. One of the units on the intended line of march was entrusted with the task of selecting a suitable site for the next camp. Sometimes, in later years, a professional military surveyor (*metator*) was in charge, but otherwise it was under a *tribunus militum* (or politically appointed young subaltern) – officially, at any rate. In practice, most of the responsibility devolved upon the unit's centurion, who had plenty of experience and an eye for the ground. What he was looking for was a place on a slightly

sloping hillside, well-drained and fairly open, but with easy access to water, firewood and fodder for the horses. Once such a site had been located, a messenger was sent riding back to the *legatus* (commanding the legion) or to the general (*imperator*) if several legions were operating together. The Romans were quite prepared to restrict a day's march to three hours in the morning (about 9,000 double paces or 8.5 kilometres) if that brought them to an ideal camp site.

Meanwhile the survey party was staking out the centre line of the camp (*decumanus maximus*) crossed by its axis (*cardo maximus*). These two lines formed the basis of two pathways bisecting the camp, the *via principalis* about 30 metres wide. All the various *strigae* (or rectangular spaces where the tents were to be erected) were marked off, as were the corners of the square or oblong camp.

As soon as the legion arrived, the soldiers took off most of their equipment, grasped their spades and began digging a ditch (or *fossa*) as much as 3.7 metres wide and 2.7 metres deep. The excavated soil was heaped up on the inner rim to form a rampart (*agger*). Its outer face was covered with turves (*cespites*) and thorn bushes. Stouter branches were sharpened into stakes (*valli*), lashed together and rammed into the top of the parapet to form a palisade (*lorica*). From here a javelin (*pilum*) could be thrown to hit an attacker some 18 metres away. Strictly speaking, a *vallum* was only a single stake in the palisade, but in due course it came to be applied to a palisaded rampart, and eventually meant the rampart itself.

Meanwhile, the baggage train of mules and waggons had arrived, the skin tents (*tentoria*) being unloaded and pitched in their appointed places. There were eight men to a tent which the soldiers called a *papilio*, because it looked like a butterfly. The senior legionary in each mess or *contubernum* was classed as a *decanus*.

Guards were posted by day and by night, being relieved every three hours as calculated by a *clepsydra* or water-clock. Each night a fresh password (*tessera*) was issued by the commanding officer, its communication to the troops being the responsibility of *tesserarii*. In the morning, once the force had been aroused and fed, a *tuba* call gave the signal for all the tents to be struck and folded; at the second call the waggons and mules were loaded; at the third blast on the horn, the whole army moved out, leaving behind a fortification which would be known to posterity as 'Caesar's Camp' regardless of who the general actually was.

The Romans went through this tedious procedure every night in hostile territory. It should really be regarded as fieldwork construction rather than military architecture, were it not for the fact that if they spent two or more nights in the same place, it became a *castra stativa*. Steps were immediately taken to strengthen the ramparts with a wooden stockade or stone wall. There were other refinements including *castella*, wood, earth or stone redoubts attached to the *vallum*, affording elevated observation and providing flanking fire along the rampart. A *castra stativa* would have had *castella* at every corner, at the gates and at regular intervals along the ramparts. A single *castellum* could also be erected by a small detached unit to serve as a fortlet, watchtower or signal station.

A *clavicula* was a right-angled extension of the rampart which compelled enemies attacking the gateway to turn to their left and thus expose their unshielded right side to the defenders' fire.

Castra stativa served as bases for operations in the surrounding area. The soldiers left all their baggage (*impedimenta*) in the camp and went out on patrol or into battle *expeditus*, wearing and carrying only their combat gear. If the engagement did not go favourably, the legion withdrew in good order into its camp, recoiling upon its reserves of food, ammunition, and reinforcements before again striking at the enemy. This procedure was so deeply ingrained in Roman military practice that – as we shall see – their grand strategy was simply a magnification of this tactical manoeuvre.

Castra stativa were of two types: *aestiva* – still tented for summer use; and *hiberna* – with purpose-built wooden barrack-blocks insulated with skins and straw. When the Roman Empire ceased expanding and entered upon its phase of settled occupation, it was simply a matter of making permanent structures out of temporary camps; architecture out of fieldworks.

But before that, of course, the Romans were much preoccupied with defeating those native people who were unwilling to hand over the destiny of their lives and lands to the foreign invader. And for that the Roman Army maintained a massive siege train. The simplest items were *plutei*, screens or mantlets, hurdles covered with skins which were pushed forward on three rollers. They provided cover for archers firing at the entrenched enemy, and for engineers digging the *circumvallatio* all round the beleaguered city. At the stronghold of Alesia (now Alise Sainte Reine, west of Dijon in France) where the Gallic leader Vercingetorix made his last stand, the *circumvallatio* was six metres deep and six metres wide. Six hundred metres behind this trench were two more each 4.5 metres deep, one filled with water from a diverted stream. Then came a rampart and palisade 3.7 metres high, itself reinforced with redoubts or *castella* every 120 metres. It was not only continually patrolled by sentries, but permanently garrisoned by separate units each charged with intercepting sorties from the city into their particular sector. Sharp stakes and other obstacles projected from the sides of all the ditches and ramparts, others being concealed in pits in the approaches to them.

Parallel with the *circumvallatio* and additionally protecting the Romans' camps was a similar series of fieldworks entitled the *contravallatio*. Facing away from the city, it prevented a relief column or supplies reaching the besieged. The *contravallatio* at Alesia was about 19 kilometres in circumference – there is no doubt that the Romans were obsessed with digging! (Perhaps partly to give the men something to do – boredom could undermine discipline.)

Inwards from the *circumvallatio* was pushed an *agger* or inclined ramp. It was composed of earth and hurdles, reinforced with tree trunks and fireproofed with stone facing. The *agger* was designed to reach the same height as the enemy's walls. Further elevation – either separately or on top of the *agger* – was provided by *turres ambulatoriae* or *turres mobiles*. These wheeled towers could be ten *tabulata* (or storeys) high. The topmost floor carried an artillery weapon; the bottom level covered *aries* (the battering-ram). This was an enormous swinging beam, up to 55 metres long, with an iron-shod head. Other *tabulata* in the siege-tower were equipped with swinging beams of lesser size, variously headed with grapnels (*falces murales*) or iron points (*terebra*) to rip away masonry and palisades or to pierce holes in the gates. (All these devices could be employed on their own quite separately from the siege-tower.) Infantry assault from the *turris mobilis* was made via drawbridges (*sambucae*).

Lesser structures affording protection to siege engineers were *testudines* or tortoises. The lightest type was called a *vinea* or vine-arbour. It was about 2.5 metres high, 2 metres wide and 5 metres long, totally enclosed and made of planks or hurdles. The *musculus* was a solid sloping penthouse roof, reaching down to the ground. With its face towards the enemy, it could be leaned right against the wall to screen engineers tunnelling under the masonry.

All this work was conducted under covering fire from catapult artillery, which was of two kinds. The *scorpiones* were big crossbows firing metal bolts horizontally or at a slight angle. They were anti-personnel weapons, whereas the higher-trajectory *ballistae* hurled lumps of timber and stones to smash down palisades and huts. However, they did have an additional anti-personnel effect when their missiles shattered on

impact, sending lethal splinters flying in all directions. The *ballista* was also known as the *onager* (or donkey) because of its violent kick when triggered.

The Romans do not seem to have been keen on the idea of hurling dead animals or incendiary materials into the besieged fortress to spread disease and fire. This was no doubt due in part at least to the fact that the aim of their warfare was the conquest of people and property, not their wanton destruction. At the same time, they were well aware of the dangers of retaliatory incendiarism and all their mobile siege equipment was covered with water-saturated sacks or mattresses, and thick hides. Meanwhile, the defenders also employed such devices as grapnels and cranes to overturn and wreck the besiegers' towers, rams and so on.

This Roman artillery and other siege engines have been described in some detail, not because they are military architecture, but because their standardised and efficient use by the Romans, and their description in military treatises, set the pattern for all siege equipment until the introduc-

21 *The* scorpio.

tion of gunpowder and cannon. All through the Dark Ages and the medieval period, these machines and techniques remained in use somewhere in Europe, the Mediterranean or Middle East; their construction and employment were never forgotten. There were some minor modifications, variations in size and obviously changes of name, but otherwise this weaponry determined the defensive form of military architecture for the next fifteen centuries. Apparent improvements in fortress design simply represent the relearning of old lessons.

In theory the Roman legion had no siege equipment of its own. All these items, plus the personnel to operate them, and the pioneers, blacksmiths, armourers, transport and drivers, came under the *praefectus fabri*, who was responsible to the commander-in-chief, not to the legion commander. Engineer and artillery units were thus what a later period would classify as 'corps or army troops'. However, relevant personnel and equipment were attached to individual legions, and any one legion could call upon the firepower of 60 *catapultae* of various sizes.

Even so, they do not seem to have accompanied Julius Caesar on his two expeditions in 55 and 54 BC – a double reconnaissance in force. On the two occasions when they encountered British hillforts (Bigbury near Canterbury in Kent, and Wheathamstead, the capital of the Catuvellauni in Hertfordshire – both in wooded areas), the legionaries formed their own *testudo* by locking their shields over their heads. It was standard infantry training, and thus protected they smashed in the gates and stormed the *oppidum*.

It was almost a century before the Roman army came again to Britain. By then, the Britons had devised a type of fieldwork and a fresh strategy to counter similar assaults by the Romans on their strongholds in the future. These can best be seen at Colchester in Essex (*Camulodunum*) where Cunobelinus dug a series of ditches and ramparts on the approaches to the city. Some were parallel trenches and others were switch-lines. No doubt it was hoped that the Romans blundering about in the woodland would never be sure whether they had run up against the main fortifications or a mere delaying position. If they had to mount a major operation against a small rearguard each time they encountered some sort of ditch and rampart, they should eventually wear themselves out, so that they would fall easy victim to the Britons' field army when it emerged from its strongholds.

However, the Britons were not only disunited, they had misread the lessons of the earlier invasions. When the Romans came in AD 43, they came to stay – and they came with artillery and engineers. Aulus Plautius defeated the two sections of the Britons' field army under Caractacus and Togodumnus, then set about the systematic elimination of the British hillforts.

Considering the close links the British tribes had with the Continent, they must have heard how the Romans had captured Avaricum in 52 BC. Now the modern Bourges in the Département de Cher, it was then the capital of the Bituriges – a hillfort-city. The Gallic leader Vercingetorix advocated a scorched-earth policy, creating a winter wilderness. The Romans under Julius Caesar would be compelled to spend all their time foraging in small groups, which could be easily overwhelmed. The Bituriges complied with Vercingetorix' command, but dissented when he wanted them to destroy their capital with its fine buildings and well-stocked granaries. They determined to defend Avaricum, which they did resolutely, while Vercingetorix harassed the Romans in the field.

A period of hard weather helped the legions to haul their heavy equipment through the marshes surrounding Avaricum before a thaw set in with heavy rain. Even then, they managed to raise a siege ramp 100 metres wide and 25 metres high, to enable the legionaries to fight on the same level as the Gauls on the ramparts. The latter made frequent co-ordinated sorties against the *agger* and the siege-towers, simultaneously hurling flaming material onto them and digging tunnels under them, either to make them collapse or to set fire to the woodwork in the *agger*. One raid on a dry night was particularly dangerous, but Caesar's contingency plans and the legions' disciplined training paid off. Those *musculi* already well ablaze were abandoned to the flames, while the engineers pulled back the other equipment and damage-control units concentrated on putting out the subterranean fire in the *agger* and shoring it up. None took up arms themselves, trusting in their comrades assigned that duty to deal with the enemy. Meanwhile the artillery maintained a ceaseless rain of missiles upon Avaricum. Caesar describes how, in the lurid light of the flames, he saw a chain of Gauls outside the gate, passing lumps of burning tallow from one to the other until the last man threw it into the nearest Roman siege-tower. A *scorpio* bolt struck him in the right side and he collapsed. Another man stepped over his dead body, so that the fiery missiles continued without pause. He too was killed – and so was his replacement, and so on until the Gauls were driven back into the city.

It was their last effort. Two days later, the siege rampart was completed. Under cover of heavy rain – which the Gauls apparently assumed would preclude operations by either side – the legions assembled behind a screen of *plutei*. At a given signal, they pushed the siege-towers forward, swept up the *agger* and stormed into the city. Avaricum and its storehouses had been captured, but of the 40,000 inhabitants, only 800 escaped the legionaries' swords; it was a lesson to all would-be dissidents.

But even if the fate of Avaricum had been remembered it would probably not have made any difference to the resolve of certain British tribes to resist the Roman invader in AD 43. Indeed, even if the hillfort defenders had kept that lesson in mind it is unlikely that they had the resources to rebuild their defences so radically that the Roman army would find them impregnable. Slingers on triple ramparts, convoluted and palisaded gateways, hordes of chariots and well-stocked grain-pits – the very appearance and reputation of Mai Dun (or Maiden Castle) in Dorset might well have deterred charging tribesmen or enabled the defenders to sit out a long siege. In AD 44 the Romans were neither deterred nor prepared to wait. Vespasian's IInd Augustan Legion just stood off and hammered the hillfort at long range. Warriors, old men, women and children, the Durotriges fell under the bombardment, their spines and skulls pierced by *scorpio*

bolts, their huts and defences shattered by a rain of rocks from *ballistae*, crushing roofs, splintering palisades, weakening gates, scattering the dying embers of some hearth that had not been properly extinguished. As the flames spread and the smoke billowed, the Romans charged, the engineers bringing up the battering-rams and grapnels and protective *testudines*, the infantry locking their shields over their heads. The sagging gates collapsed and with them fell Mai Dun.

There was similar bloodshed at Spettisbury Rings and Hod Hill, both also in Dorset. In the north-west corner of the latter hillfort, the Romans built an overnight camp after the battle. When the IInd Legion marched away, they left behind a signal unit and police detachment, who set up permanent home in the place to maintain communications and keep an eye on the surrounding area. In due course, it developed into a stockaded fort which housed 600 infantry and 250 cavalry, plus their horses, their water requirements being met by a 9,000-litre reservoir in the chalk. Extra protection was provided by an external system of multiple ditches to break up a massed charge by tribesmen. Hod Hill was very definitely a Roman stronghold, a base from which patrols emerged to gather intelligence about subversive activities, collect taxes and punish lawbreakers. It may also have acted as a slave-trading centre for the estates in the area.

Maiden Castle, Spettisbury Rings and Hod Hill were but three of the twenty *oppida* captured by Vespasian during that campaign. Note Suetonius' use of the word 'captured' rather than 'stormed'; many of the hillforts may have surrendered without a fight – if they had learned the lesson that the Romans waged war to conquer, not destroy. Provided the Britons accepted the benefits of Mediterranean civilisation (i.e., accepted the servitude of an alien power) the Romans treated them well. Only those who resisted ran the risk of incurring Roman wrath. And for those who accepted Imperial rule and then rebelled against it, there was no mercy.

Everybody has heard of the revolt of Queen Boudicca and the Iceni, but there is evidence that that rebellion was not the only civil disorder during the first generation of Roman rule. We shall probably never know what offended the Somerset Durotriges in the 70s AD or what led them to believe that they could successfully challenge the might of Rome. Certainly the people of Cadbury Castle (with their shopkeepers' stalls just inside the main gate) had gone on living there without interruption all through the period of the Roman conquest and its turbulent aftermath. And yet, just when lowland Britain was beginning to benefit from *Pax Romana*, the inhabitants of Cadbury Castle decided to refurbish their fortification. Perhaps they refused to move to the new Roman town of *Lindinae* (Ilchester). Perhaps they were led by some religious fanatic who guaranteed death to the Romans and salvation to the Durotriges. Perhaps some local chief had decided to throw in his lot with the losing side in Vespasian's bid for the *imperium*. Perhaps Cadbury Castle was the lair of an outlaw gang, feared and hated by Britons and Romans, like the later Doones, also of Somerset. Whatever they were, they stood no chance against even a small Roman force.

The Romans smashed through the crude barricades obstructing the south-west entrance and battered down the gate. Men, women and children were cut down among the brooches and other trinkets and goods from the overturned market-stalls, their corpses abandoned to the wolves that prowled the area. In due course, another Roman unit (probably engineers) returned, set up a temporary hutted camp, and proceeded to destroy the fortifications, pulling down masonry and burning everything of wood. They did not bother to bury the mangled dead, merely allowing the flaming debris to cover them.

On the eastern limit of their Empire the Romans inflicted even greater retribution upon the Jews who rebelled in AD 66. It took Vespasian three years of anti-guerrilla operations before three legions were able to lay siege to Jerusalem itself. The garrison and citizens, totalling some 30,000 souls, were divided by factional warfare which intensified as famine and disease took hold, while anyone who tried to escape was crucified by the Romans outside. By now, Titus was in command of the Roman forces. From April to September in AD 70 ironclad siege-towers

and massive *ballistae* battered through the triple walls of Jerusalem, an assault culminating in the destruction of the Temple. 'Not one stone was left upon the other'; the Jews were massacred or dispersed to the ends of the earth – except for a few still holding out at Masada. This hilltop refuge overlooking the Dead Sea was surrounded by a curtain wall and bastioned with a rectangular tower. The place did not succumb until AD 73, when the defenders killed their wives and their children and then themselves, rather than submit to Roman domination.

The pulling apart of cities and fortresses stone by stone was not simply a brutal punishment; it was also part of a policy of recycling strategic raw materials. Massive blocks of building stone were often keyed together with iron tie-rods and lead seals, as well as being set in mortar. It was more economical to rip houses apart for the sake of the metals they contained, than it was to ship ingots and ore from one side of the Empire to the other.

By employing a double policy of ruthless annihilation of dissidents and favourable treatment of friendly factions, the Romans guaranteed peace throughout the known world for four hundred years. There were occasional periods of internal violence, but these were usually the struggles for power between rival emperors, or large-scale riots resulting from the temporary breakdown of law and order during such interregna.

It is true that cities were surrounded by walls. The former capital of Britannia, Camulodunum, was encircled by 2.93 kilometres of wall, of which over 900 metres can still be seen. Fronted by a ditch (six metres deep and three metres wide) and by a level berm, the wall itself was of rubble and mortar. Its inner and outer faces were made of courses of bricks alternating with layers of squared nodules of stone-hard solid clay (*septaria*). The wall proper was about 3.7 metres high, but above that a battlemented parapet of 1.8 metres' height afforded protection to sentries on the rampart walk. There were seven gates (including the ceremonial Balkerne Gate) and a number of turrets, but as these were constructed against the rear of the wall, they could not have provided flanking fire along the outer face. It

22 *The Roman wall around Colchester in Essex.*

therefore seems as though Roman city walls became symbols of municipal pride, rather than weapons systems of military significance. And, indeed, eventually amphitheatres, temples, workshops and houses spread out beyond the protection of the city walls, while villas were completely out in the country.

In due course, the villa – a self-contained agricultural productive unit comprising master's house, labourers' dwellings, farm-buildings, livestock, fields, orchards and vineyards – became the normal way of life in settled Roman Britain and indeed through much of the Empire. Admittedly the living accommodation of some was surrounded by a *vallum* and *fossa* of military appearance, but that may not indicate the lawlessness of that particular area at that particular time. It is easy to imagine a retired legate or centurion declaring that there were only two ways of doing things: the wrong way – and the army way. Every building he had ever lived in had been surrounded by a ditch and a rampart – and his new villa was not going to be an exception to that rule.

CHAPTER SIX

'Pax Romana'

He set out for Britannia, where he made many reforms, and
was the first to build a wall for eighty miles to separate the
barbarians and the Romans.
(Spartianus, *Life of Hadrian*)

The Romans now had their empire; the problem they now faced was how to defend it against outsiders.

The latter might seem a long way from Rome itself; they might be disparaged as mere barbarians; their occasional attacks might be mere forays by undisciplined raiding parties – but they did pose a threat to the law-abiding, taxpaying landowners and townsfolk on the periphery of the Empire.

The Romans solved the problem of the Empire's security by turning their whole realm into one titanic fortress.

To the west, the Empire was bounded by the limitless ocean. To the south, there was the sand sea of the Sahara Desert. In the east, Arabia Deserta, the mountains of Asia Minor and the narrow defiles of the Balkans afforded well-worn highways for traders, but presented inhospitable hindrances to large armies. These frontier zones could be dominated by garrisons stationed in *castra stativa*, replicas in stone and wood of the earth and tented camps of the Empire's expansion. From these remote stations horsemen swept out to gather intelligence of barbarian intention and, if necessary, blunt any thrust before it became too dangerous. In extreme cases they fell back and the legions marched out to confront the savage band, and turn it back.

Only in certain places were there gaps in formidable natural barriers. In those areas, walls were built to keep the barbarians out, although – as will be explained – the actual functioning of the Roman frontier barriers (*limites*) may not have been quite so simple.

Whether the Romans got the idea from seeing the frontier ditches some German tribes had dug around the borders of their territory is not clear, but the first *limes* was built in Germany by Domitian in AD 83. It was a series of *castra stativa* and wooden watchtowers, all linked by a woven palisade. It stretched 50 kilometres along the ridge of the Taunus mountains and partway across the valley of the Maenus (Main), thus screening the settlements around Nida (Frankfurt), and in turn being able to be reinforced by the reserve forts there.

Domitian was also responsible for the Dobrogera *limes* running for 50 kilometres across the flat land of Scythia Parva from the Danube to the Black Sea (near the present border between Rumania and Bulgaria). Garrisoned by *castra stativa*, it was an earth bank 15 metres thick, and in some places still stands almost four metres high. Some authorities believe it was constructed on an earlier tribal boundary of similar design. It also seems to have been realigned during its existence, its remains passing both north and south of present-day Constança. Domitian's attention then returned to Germany, rebuilding the *limes* where necessary and extending it towards the neighbourhood of Limburg on the

River Lagana (Lahn) in the north, and right down to the River Maenus in the south, making a total length of 120 kilometres.

When Publius Aelius Hadrianus became Emperor in 117, he personally inspected the *limes Germanicus*, realigning it in some places and ordering the construction of a massive palisade of oak on top of the rampart, with a ditch in front. In addition, he gave instructions for the building of an eastern section to begin at Miltenberg. It ran first south-south-east, then east-north-east, and finally east-south-east, to meet the Danubius upstream from Regina (Regensburg). Sweeping across river valley and mountain ridge, its total length was about 280 kilometres. Some 55 auxiliary forts were established along the line of the *limites*, with a sophisticated road system ensuring legionary reinforcement from garrison towns in the rear.

The *limes Germanicus* underwent modification several times, in particular about 148, under the Emperor Antoninus Pius, when a parallel length of fortification produced a wide no-man's-land, evidently to prohibit unauthorised entry from either side of the frontier. In its final form a wall 1.2 metres wide ran along the eastern section, being known to some later peoples as 'the Devil's Wall'.

The *limes Germanicus* was an incredible work of military architecture, but the frontier defence which has most captured popular imagination was located in northern Britain – Hadrian's Wall. It is also the one which has lasted longest and the one about which most is known.

There had been a number of attempts to conquer Caledonia and stabilise the northern frontier of Britain before the Emperor Hadrian carried out a tour of inspection. In 122 he ordered that a wall be built 'to separate the barbarians from the Romans'. It was to begin at a bridge over the River Tyne (Tina) at Newcastle, to be known as Pons Aelius after the Emperor's middle name. As far as the River Irthing the Wall was to have a foundation 3.4 metres wide made of flagstones 76 mm thick, laid down in puddled clay. The core was of whinstone rubble bound together with puddled clay and faced with rectangular stones of quartzose grit, so cut that they

bonded into the core. The mortar for the facing stones was obtained by burning local limestone. The Wall was ten Roman feet wide and 15 Roman feet high (3 metres × 4.5 metres). Above that was a crenellated parapet 1.5 metres high.

West of the River Irthing the limestone comes to an end, so that meant difficulties in mortar production, as well as a shortage of suitable stone. Accordingly, the wall from Camboglanna westwards was to be made of solid turves cut in a standard size of 18 × 12 × 6 Roman inches (345 × 290 × 145 mm). They were stacked to form a vertically faced, rearward-sloping rampart, 6 metres wide and 4.3 metres in height, with a wooden walkway and crenellated parapet 1.8 metres high on top. The western end of the turf wall was at Maia (Bowness) on the Ituna Aestuarium (Solway Firth).

In front of both turf and stone walls was a level berm of 1.8 or 6 metres' width respectively. Then – if the terrain permitted – came a vee-shaped ditch, 8.2 metres wide and 2.7 metres deep. There was a squarish drainage channel at the bottom. All the material from the ditch was thrown out to the north forming a glacis 18 metres in extent and, coincidentally, raising the outer rim of the ditch to a height of four metres above its bottom. The whole frontal approach was so designed that until he was right up against the wall, an assailant was never out of sight of the sentries on the walkway.

The actual construction was entrusted to the IInd Augustan, the VIth Victrix and the XXth Valerian Victrix Legions under the governor, Aulus Platorius Nepos. Each cohort of each legion was assigned its own length, assisted by auxiliary troops and, undoubtedly, local labour. When complete the auxiliaries who would comprise most of the Wall's patrolling garrison would be based at a number of camps nearer the River Tyne to the south. From these bases they would go up to the Wall, 32 men being accommodated in each *castellum*, occurring every Roman mile (approximately every 1.5 kilometres).

Each milecastle covered a rectangle some 15–18 metres × 20–23 metres, its walls enclosing a barrack-room, a store, an oven and a latrine. There were two gates across the track or road leading from the south, the northern turreted one piercing the Wall itself and opening out onto the barbarian land to the north.

The guards not only patrolled the walkway, but also did lookout duty at two watchtowers flanking each milecastle about 500 metres distant. These square turrets had stone walls a metre thick, providing a floor area of 195 square metres. There was a simple hearth for warmth and cooking, and a stepped platform, from which rose a ladder to a trapdoor in the ceiling. This afforded access to the First Floor and out onto the Wall's rampart walk. Three metres above that was the turret's flat roof, an observation and signal platform surrounded by a metre-high parapet. The turrets only had one door at ground level; there was no admittance from the north.

Meanwhile, the Legions themselves would be withdrawn and be stationed in reserve at the garrison cities of Eboracum, Lindum and Deva (York, Lincoln and Chester).

However, work had not been in progress for very long before the Wall's basic design was being modified. From about 124, the incomplete stretch of stone wall was built to the narrower width of eight Roman feet (2.3 metres). This alteration was possible because the Wall had reached the limestone uplands, where there was plenty of stone and mortar production was easier. Apparently the limestone was burnt in charcoal kilns before being ground down and mixed with sand and gravel. On arrival at the work site, water was added, thus producing mortar. Because it is a stronger bonding material than clay, freestanding walls using it in the rubble core as well as for facing stones did not have to be so wide to support the weight above them. If Broad Wall foundations had already been laid, they were utilised, but otherwise the Narrow Wall had its own narrower foundations set in a trench 45 cm deep.

The other alteration at this time was the decision to construct fortified camps right against the Wall. Each fort accommodated an infantry cohort (480 men) or a cavalry *ala* or wing (500–1,000 men), plus supernumeraries. There were variations, but generally fort design followed the layout of *castra stativa*, themselves derived from camps established on the march. Inevitably there was greater emphasis on ordnance workshops and granaries. They also became more luxurious, the commanding officer having his own bath-house. The one for the troops was outside the fort, and so was the *vicus* or civilian cantonment. The most significant feature of the forts was that they projected beyond the northern face of the Wall, so that columns could debouch simultaneously from the main northern and the two side gates, all of which were double-portalled.

Meanwhile a number of outpost forts were constructed beyond the Wall. Evidently the territory out there was not impossibly hostile, so reconnaissance troops would be able to give advance warning of any dangerous gathering of the clans.

Once the Wall itself had been completed about AD 126, the Legions began work on the Vallum – a ditch-system to the south of the Wall. (The Romans must have called it a *fossa*, but the Venerable Bede got his Latin wrong in AD 731 and it has been *Vallum* ever since.)

Concurrently the Wall was extended to Segedunum (Wallsend), and part of the Turf Wall was rebuilt in stone. The opportunity was taken of realigning certain stretches, allowing the original Turf Wall to decay. One part still remains west of Camboglanna, now sectioned so that the visitor can see its composition of squared turves, looking for all the world like a giant earthen Battenberg cake.

In addition a series of flanking fortlets and lookout towers was erected along the Cumbrian and Northumbrian coasts.

Still to come within a generation was the programme which built an exclusively military road running the whole length of the Wall between it and the Vallum; and the conversion of the remaining lengths of Turf Wall to a red sandstone wall of intermediate thickness (2.6 metres).

Why was Hadrian's Wall built? What was it for? The emperor's stated aim of separating the barbarians and the Romans is too facile. A simple ditch and rampart or row of milestones would have been quite sufficient as boundary markers.

23 *One of the two granaries (*horrea*) at Vercovicium on Hadrian's Wall. Joists were laid across the width of the building on top of the pillars, with another layer of planking running lengthwise to form the floor. Air entered beneath the floor and circulated by means of the square holes in the wall, thus helping to keep the corn dry and out of the reach of mice. It is just possible to see the solid buttresses which reinforced the wall against the deadweight thrust of grain stored in bulk. The buttresses also supported the slate roof, which was proof against incendiary missiles. Hadrian's Wall itself drops down to the left, before climbing the distant escarpments.*

It is a mistake to assume that all Roman soldiers on the Wall came from the sunny Mediterranean. In its heyday, Vercovicium was garrisoned by the 1st Tungrian Cohort, about a thousand auxiliaries from Germania Secunda. At least, that is where they had originated; no doubt some units prided themselves on always recruiting from their home territory, while others were made up to strength with any new men who wanted to join – and no doubt some local people were only too glad of a regular job in the Roman army. Vercovicium derives its modern name from the fact that there were a number of native buildings or 'housesteads' in a civilian village or vicus, *just outside the fort.*

If the work were intended to overawe the primitive mind, then splendid cities and majestic gates would have done just as well.

So why did Hadrian's Wall have to be the most considerable work of classical military architecture in Western Europe?

The favourite assumption is that it was defensive; that it was built to keep out the Picts. The popular picture is of hordes of yelling naked savages, maddened by lust for Roman wealth and Roman women, swarming up scaling-ladders, their battering-rams smashing through gates, while hard-pressed and outnumbered legionaries desperately struggle to preserve civilisation. Surely that imagined picture must be true; after all, Hadrian's Wall was severely damaged no less than five times in its history – and in view of that sort of record, it could not have been very effective.

Certainly the Wall, even in its heyday, would not have presented an insurmountable military obstacle to a determined force. A small well-rehearsed commando-style raid would find no difficulty in climbing over the Wall at night, overpowering the sleepy guards and . . . doing what? Maybe burning a couple of farms; driving off a few cattle, perhaps? It was good cattle country, yes – although how cattle could be got back over the Wall is another question – but there were no towns, no fat villas to plunder for miles and miles to the south. The little band of heroes might want to make a dramatic gesture like destroying a Roman fort – they could get the cattle out that way, too – but to do so they would have to eliminate its cohort-garrison, by now wide-awake.

It is therefore likely that Hadrian's Wall deterred commando-style raids simply by making them not worth the effort. But it could not have held off a full-scale army offensive. Any army of those days, even a primitive one, knew how to fill in ditches and scale walls. Hadrian's Wall and its 32 men every mile would easily be overwhelmed long before any help could come from Eboracum, Lindum or Deva.

However, such an assault would require plenty of warriors, at least a sprinkling of engineer personnel, the construction of specialised equip-ment or the accumulation of quantities of earth and wood. That in turn would mean more labour and larger stocks of food, plus a great deal of routine organisation – even if unwritten. Such an army could not be assembled out in the barren, squabble-ridden lands to the north without some sort of rumour reaching the ears of a Roman cavalry patrol. With age-old techniques of persuasion (force, bribe or jealousy) they would get the information they wanted, reports would be sent back, and by the time the tribes were ready to move, the Legions had arrived and were either solidly manning the threatened stretches of the Wall, or had sallied forth to catch the undisciplined warriors off-guard.

In fact, one theory suggests that the Wall was intended to serve as an anvil. The Roman army would march out in a great arc to round up any hostile force from the rear and hammer it against the Wall – a tactic particularly suited to the cavalry units employed in the later years of the Wall's existence. That is certainly an offensive use of fortification, but it still does not conflict with the popular concept of the Wall as a strategic defence.

It is only when we consider the Vallum that we begin to see Hadrian's Wall as something more than mere protection against outsiders.

It has been suggested that the Vallum was yet another defence-line, but neither its structure nor its positioning is particularly defensible. Another theory is that it was a civilian-manned customs barrier, separate from the military Wall. The present hypothesis – and the most likely – is that the Vallum was the southern boundary of the military zone – off-limits to all unauthorised civilians. It could only be traversed by causeways and cuttings opposite a fort. Elsewhere, anyone approaching the Wall from the south would have to climb a two-metre bank, cross a six-metre rampart, jump down two metres, walk over a berm ten metres wide, clamber down a slope three metres deep, scramble through the 2.5-metres wide ditch, up the other side, cross the next berm, up the next rampart, over that, and down the far side. No unauthorised intruder could claim he didn't know he wasn't supposed to be there. And he would certainly be visible to the sentinels up on the Wall walkway, who would make sure he was not allowed to proceed any farther.

No, the only way for anybody to pass beyond Hadrian's Wall was by openly asking permission at one of the forts – the milecastles being so linked to the Military Way that they were for army use only.

The smallest and unlikeliest gaps were closed. Where the Wall crossed the North Tyne at Chesters a grating was fixed in the culvert to prevent anyone swimming through. Such an obstacle is unlikely to be of purely military significance; it certainly was nothing to do with the prevention of cattle-rustling and smuggling. That grating betrays an obsession with security verging on paranoia. Hadrian's Wall must have been as much to keep Roman citizens in, as to keep the barbarians out. There are sound economic, political and military reasons for that proposition.

Firstly, the principal motive-power driving the industry of the Roman Empire was human. A slave educated in financial accounting, a peasant expert in taming horses, a well-built woman as capable of digging a field as any man – once they had been trained, the authorities did not want them taking their skills off to benefit some barbarian chief.

Second, it hardly spoke well of the marvels of Roman civilisation if – given the opportunity – people preferred to opt out and go somewhere else. Much better to make them stay where they were and *enjoy* being Roman, whether they wanted to or not.

Finally, Roman patrols and outlying forts could gather intelligence of barbarian intent. With no agents ever coming out to them, what could the barbarians learn of Roman intentions? All they saw was a high blank-faced wall, the occasional flash of sunlight on armour as a sentry turned in his eternal pacing. Now and again smoke signals rose into the air from one of those watchtowers, or there was a sudden blare of trumpets, or perhaps – on the still night air – the sound of foreign tongues. But otherwise, the barbarians were blind and deaf. They knew nothing of the roads and other communications networks being established between the Wall and

the garrison cities to the south. They did not know about the intermediate camps being built as staging posts, nor about the supply dumps and ordnance workshops.

To the north, everything was barren wilderness, tracks not roads, hills, and swamps and forests preventing assembly and organisation. To the south, everything facilitated the rapid build-up of forces and the pushing-forward of reserves to a prearranged timetable. Hadrian's Wall had become, not a fence to keep people out, but a springboard for assault.

And in AD 130–42, Hadrian and his successor Antoninus Pius (or rather, their governors Julius Severus and Quintus Lollius Urbicus) launched that offensive. A series of limited attacks in front of the Wall was followed by a thrust up into Caledonia itself. It was competely successful, Hadrian's Wall became redundant, and the new frontier was established between the Bodotria and the Clota (the Forth and the Clyde).

Covering a distance of 60 kilometres, the Antonine Wall was a turf or clay rampart 3.5 metres wide at its base with a wide ditch in front. There were a total of 20 forts, one the commander-in-chief's headquarters, and two others being sector headquarters, and a fourth apparently an ordnance, supply and remount depot. Apart from these four, the Antonine Wall forts were quite small, not really big enough to accommodate a cohort. They were on the usual *castra stativa* pattern, surrounded by palisaded *vallum* and *fossa*. Stone was rarely used, wood being preferred for gates and buildings. As these forts were only about three kilometres apart there was no need for milecastles and turrets, merely the occasional signal platform. There was a military way, but there were no flanking fortlets along the river estuaries, nor any reserves nearer than Hadrian's Wall, 130 kilometres of rough track away to the south. Evidently the Roman authorities were so confident after the defeat they had inflicted on the Caledonians that they did not expect further trouble from that quarter for a good many years to come.

There are suggestions that the land between the two Walls was either largely depopulated or it was treated as a protectorate. Either way it was kept under strict supervision. The troops employed in such work – in all ages – are often described as gendarmerie, not 'proper soldiers'. In fact their paramilitary status does not necessarily make them any less efficient nor more loved by the people they policed. It is worth remembering that the twentieth-century Nazi SS were technically 'gendarmerie'.

The Antonine Wall was evacuated during the Brigantian rebellion of 158–65, Hadrian's Wall being recommissioned first as the northern frontier again, and then as the linear base for the reconquest of Caledonia and the reoccupation of the Antonine Wall. Thus, of those five occasions mentioned earlier, when Hadrian's Wall was damaged or slighted, two resulted from its being decommissioned as part of government policy, a strategic policy which reflects the *castra-stativa* tactic of using the fieldwork camp as a base for aggressive operations and recoiling back into it when faced with possible defeat, regrouping and attacking again. The other occasions were as a direct result of the Romans' own power-politics.

In AD 197 Clodius Albinus shipped the entire garrison of Britain over to Gaul in his bid to become emperor. Denuded of troops, both the Antonine Wall and Hadrian's Wall were overrun by the Maetae and the Caledonians, who dismantled every empty Roman fortification they encountered as far south as the Midlands. However, they had neither the leisure, the hate nor the equipment to do anything about defended places. City walls manned by local militia (many of whom would have had Roman army service) they left alone, and when the civil war was over and Severus became emperor, the barbarians withdrew.

Severus rebuilt Hadrian's Wall as the final solution of the frontier question, but in 296 the Roman army was again taken overseas to play politics. Once again the untended gates of Hadrian's Wall were stormed by barbarians. Once again they retreated before the return of Imperial government. In 367, Hadrian's Wall was betrayed to the enemy in what was called the Barbarian Conspiracy. Again rebuilt, its defence was entrusted to local militia. As already pointed out, many of them would have been ex-soldiers

and quite capable of organising a successful defence. But with the break-up of the Roman Empire – as much due to local independence movements as to foreign invasion – Hadrian's Wall ceased to have any significance, except as a simple boundary and as an easily workable quarry for building stone.

It is worth remarking that there is almost a century between each of the dates when Hadrian's Wall was overrun from outside. There cannot have been many systems of fortification which have guaranteed the security of its citizens for such long periods of time – and even its failures were due more to governmental or internal political fault.

The Count of the Saxon Shore is a name which becomes increasingly significant in the later years of Roman Britain. It seems that from about AD 200 onwards there were spasmodic attacks on coastal shipping and on isolated settlements on both sides of the southern North Sea (*Oceanus Germanicus*). Whether these were piratical forays by freelance sea-bandits outlawed from the Roman Empire, or whether they were organised assaults by barbarians from beyond the Empire, is not clear. For about 150 years the British Fleet's (*Classis Britannica*) main base at Dubris (Dover) had proved sufficient for the exercise of Roman seapower in the area, detached squadrons being stationed as required at commercial ports.

However, about AD 220–30, purpose-built forts were established at Branodunum (Brancaster) and Regulbium (Reculver) covering the approaches to the Wash and the Humber, and to the Thames Estuary. Such measures were not enough and about AD 285 it was decided to establish more bases on both sides of the Channel, supreme command being invested in Marcus Aurelius Mausaeus Carausius, a Menapian or native of the Low Countries. These new forts were at Othona (Bradwell), Lemannis (Lympne), Gariannonum (Burgh Castle), Rutupiae (Richborough) and Portus Adurni (Portchester – although some authorities consider this last was at Walton Castle), Marcae (Boulogne), Grannona (near Le Havre), possibly at Oudenburg (near Bruges in the territory of the Menapii), and

perhaps at Carisbrooke on the Isle of Wight (Vectis).

All these forts had to be big enough to provide shore barracks for naval personnel (officers, fighting men and rowers) who could not be accommodated in the cramped quarters of war-galleys. In addition, room had to be found for marines (who might be employed in amphibious operations against pirate bases) and for cavalry (who could sweep out to round up such raiders as got ashore in the vicinity). Then there were workshops for shipwrights and ordnance artificers, plus granaries and stores. And then the artillerymen entrusted with the *ballista* defence of the fort had to have their own engineering facilities and huts. Altogether, it added up to a considerable complex of buildings (mostly wooden huts) quite apart from the beaching hards and jetties that must also have been necessary.

24 *The interior of Portchester Castle looking north-east, showing that the Roman bastions were hollow. They were roofed over to support catapult artillery, although in medieval times some were filled with earth for the same purpose. This spacious area would have been filled with Roman hutted accommodation and workshops. In Norman times it was the Outer Bailey of the castle, while during the Napoleonic Wars it was used as a prisoner-of-war camp.*

Its land sides surrounded by a ditch, Portchester fort was almost exactly square. Each wall was about 180 metres long, 3 metres thick and 5.5 metres in height, with a 3 metres high parapet screening the walkway. The walls were built of flint rubble with occasional courses of red tile or stone. There were two main gates and two posterns, plus 20 bastions projecting out from the curtain wall and about a metre higher. These were

25 *The Roman walls and bastions of Portchester Castle. The ditch was also dug in Roman times and periodically recut at subsequent dates.*

roofed over, providing mountings for light *ballistae* and *scorpiones*.

Carausius proved an efficient admiral and administrator. He dealt with the pirates and reorganised British provincial government, but was accused of complicity with the sea-raiders, whereupon he proclaimed himself emperor. His troops were trapped in Boulogne when Constantius dammed the tidal approach to the fortified port and Carausius was assassinated by his chief financial assistant.

After Carausius there are few reports of events in the Channel, which implies that the *Classis Britannica* was ruling the seas. But from AD 340

the number of attacks again increased. Fortifications were built at a number of commercial ports in Gaul right round to Blabia (Blaye on the Gironde). New forts were established at Lancaster and Cardiff and on the 'Saxon Shore' proper at Anderita (Pevensey) and Bitterne near Southampton.

Carausius had held the title *Comes Litoris Saxonici per Britannias* which may mean that he was commander-in-chief of the coastal area most likely to be raided by the Saxons; or, it may be that Saxon mercenaries were hired to man the ships hunting down an international brotherhood of pirates. There is some evidence at Portchester for believing that the garrison was not subject to regular Roman discipline. Excavation has indicated the piling up of rubbish in a way that a Roman legionary would never have tolerated.

CHAPTER SEVEN

The Dark Ages

In old times, the country had twenty-eight noble cities, which
also were guarded by walls, towers and barred gates.
(Bede, *A History of the English Church and People*)

The Dark Ages lasted for four hundred years. Undoubtedly, during that period, some people could live out their entire lives and never witness a barbarian assault. Other areas, through some freak of geography, lay on the route of every raiding party making for Rome or other wealthy target. And not all formations on the move were barbarian; self-styled emperors sought to revive past glories and reimpose their idea of law on barbarian neighbours. Some tribes and cities experienced a continuity of ordered administration, organised from within some ancient, but still impregnable, citadel. Other territories became the hunting-ground of adventurers, opportunist warrior-politicians, bandit-gangs, all promising to defend farmers and monks in return for the payment of taxes – virtually a primitive but effective protection-racket as far as most of the client-subjects were concerned.

Precisely where the shadowy figure of King Arthur fits into this situation is anybody's guess. Equally problematical is the location of his main base of Camelot. However, what has been revealed by excavation is that about AD 500 somebody decided that the long-abandoned Iron Age fortifications of Cadbury Castle would make a suitable stronghold in those troubled times. The ramparts were not recut, but the topmost one was surmounted by a series of vertical and horizontal timbers, the framework containing rubble and earth. The secret of mortar manufacture seems to have been temporarily lost, so the fortification was faced with a dry-stone wall and crowned with a wooden battlement. The gateway was of wood, with inner and outer double-gates, and was probably surmounted by a defensive and lookout tower. Fifth- and sixth-century Cadbury Castle was evidently a place of some importance, as archaeologists have uncovered the foundations of a Welsh-style feasting hall, measuring 19.2 × 10.4 metres.

The amount of work involved in refortifying Cadbury Castle implies that the organiser was a forceful personality, a *dux bellorum* or supreme commander of several kingdoms. It all suggests that Cadbury Castle could well have been the stronghold of King Arthur during his campaign which resulted in the defeat of the Saxons at Mons Badonicus. The remetalling of the approach road through the gateway about 570 indicates that the site was still being used as the main British base during the successful Deorham campaign.

Many of these conflicts in Dark Age Britain were followed by some sort of treaty or oral agreement, whereby one side or the other promised to keep within their own territory. This is probably the origin of such features of the landscape as the Wansdyke in Somerset and Wiltshire. A corruption of Wodensdyke or Wodnesdic, it is a ditch and rampart some 25 metres in total width and 7.5 metres from bottom of the trench to the top of the bank. It is in two sections, both built in the fifth, sixth or seventh centuries AD, but probably at different times. Both lengths face north, but experts disagree as to whether they were constructed by the British to mark the limits of Saxon power, or – if later – by the Saxons of Wessex against their rival Saxons in the Midlands.

Of greater renown and of more precise dating is Offa's Dyke, named after the king who ruled Mercia from 757 to 796. With the ditch on the western side of the rampart its various lengths extended 130 kilometres between the Severn and Dee estuaries. It was originally believed to have been an 18 metres wide barrier to keep Welsh cattle raiders out of England, but there are indications that its construction was the result of negotiation rather than conquest. In that case, the provision of a visible frontier would have secured the stability of disputed territory to the advantage of both sides.

Obviously Offa's Dyke could not have been a defensive work, to be manned for its entire length by warriors standing shoulder-to-shoulder – the population was simply not big enough. But it may still have had some military significance as it does link a number of hilltop strongpoints. It could have happened that if relations between neighbouring kingdoms deteriorated to the point of armed conflict, the rival forces could have met at a spot on Offa's Dyke, nominated by the most aggrieved party, and their cause put to the test of battle. The sporting nature of war must have appealed to the Anglo-Saxon and Celtic warrior-heroes; it is a theme which runs all through subsequent British and English military history (even thermonuclear civil defence exercises are given sporting terms as codenames) and there is no reason to assume the absence of such attitudes from the eighth century.

Other dykes ascribed to the Devil, Grim and other legendary characters – of both Saxon and Celtic date – may also have been ceremonial boundaries. Perhaps pedlars and shepherds could cross them in time of peace, but if a warrior band traversed ditch and rampart with drawn sword, in front of witnesses from the rival kingdoms, then that corresponded to handing-over an official declaration of war in more literate eras. Perhaps that is the concept which these mysterious linear features of the landscape – in other parts of the world besides Britain – represent.

One of the strange ironies of history is that having established a reputation as fearsome sea-raiders, once they had gained a foothold in Britain, the Saxons immediately settled down and became farming landlubbers. Or perhaps that is another of the myths of history; perhaps only a few were ever adventurous sailors, the arrival of their families abruptly curbing their roving habits. Certainly another of the earlier tenets of history – that the Saxons shunned all cities as haunted, and preferred to live in isolated farmsteads – has recently been shown to be more mythical than real. Some cities did indeed fall into disuse, but their decay had already set in under Roman rule. Many other towns experienced some sort of continuity of existence. That is shown by the fact that some Roman towns, such as Colchester, kept their walls more-or-less intact until the Middle Ages and even later. Indeed, the Anglo-Saxon Kings of England laid such importance upon defended sites that they decreed that no place could serve as a royal mint unless it were properly fortified. And so, once again, the fortifications of Cadbury Castle were rebuilt; it became a *burh*.

The idea of the *burh* or fortified town was to protect trade and culture, and to provide a base from which royal cavalry and, on the coast, longships could operate against Viking raiders. *Burhs* probably derived their name from the Latin word *burgus* or watchtower, many of which had been erected along the German boundary of the Roman Empire. It is significant that the Holy Roman Emperor Henry I (the Fowler) was also of the Saxon dynasty, ruling from 918 to 936. He, and other German rulers, organised the construction of purpose-built fortified cities in their eastern territories where the danger came from Magyar and Slav invaders. Henry the Fowler established nine knights in each of his fortresses, encouraging the local villagers to regard the *burgen* as centres of government, by making them the sole places of entertainment and festivity in the area. (No doubt there were other, more direct, methods of ensuring peasant labour in the construction of these strongholds.)

In England, *burhs* were first noted in the reign of King Alfred the Great (871–99). If they had no existing Roman wall, they were usually encircled by a ditch and earth rampart, plus a quickset hedge or stockade. Later on, stone was employed; Towcester in the Midlands being the first to be so treated in 917.

The reign of Ethelred the Redeless began in 978, and two years later – after a long period of peace – the Danes commenced another offensive against England. Ethelred decided that the *burh* of Ilchester in Somerset was too vulnerable to attack and in the winter of 1009/10, the royal mint was moved 11 kilometres to the east to the abandoned British hilltop settlement of Cadanbyrig (Cadbury). By now, masons again knew about mortar, so the new wall on the topmost rampart was properly set. It had a total thickness of six metres, comprising a mortar-bound core of rock-rubble and a facing of lias slabs. The gateway was a long passage about nine metres by three metres.

In 1016 the period of Danish invasion and civil war came to an end with the accession of Cnut the Dane. The Cadanbyrig mint was transferred back to Ilchester by 1019, and the wall and defences of Cadbury were levelled to the ground to prevent the place being employed as a stronghold by English dissidents or new waves of Viking raiders. For the latter did not cease their depredations just because one of their number had become King of England.

Ever since the latter days of the Roman Empire the Northmen had been raiding, trading and adventuring – but mostly raiding, or so their hapless victims record. All round Europe, fortifications had been erected, not as strongholds, but as refuges where frightened people could hide while the tide of Viking fury washed around them and – hopefully – abated.

Such places were not exclusively of Viking period. Indeed, some sites believed to date from that time have now been shown to have been inhabited and abandoned long before the Vikings came. But many which were refuges from the Northmen did date from the Iron Age, or represented continuations of Iron Age ideas of fortification.

In Scotland and Ireland in particular, crannogs, vitrified forts, brochs, round towers and pele towers were all employed in more or less mysterious circumstances and dangerous times over a thousand years or more.

The earliest in date – perhaps 800 BC – is the vitrified fort. Imagine a traditional hillfort encircled not by earth ramparts, but by two dry-stone walls, each 6 metres thick and 7.5 metres high, the individual boulders and slabs kept in position by a complicated network of internal timbering. It has been estimated that the work would involve shifting 25,000 tonnes of rock and three kilometres of woodwork. The completed result would not be all that different in appearance from some of the palisaded and timber-faced hillforts described in an earlier chapter. Fire was always a danger to timbered structures, but never on the scale which seems to have been inflicted upon seventy forts on wet and windy Scottish hilltops, ranging in size from Ord of Kessoch near Inverness (275 metres across) to small sites (or duns) just 15 metres in diameter. For within twenty years, while the timbers were still unrotted, a fierce fire swept around whole sections of these ramparts, the space between the two walls acting like a huge blast-furnace, cooking the integral woodwork to charcoal, which burnt so fiercely it reached temperatures unachieved for another two millennia. It was so hot it melted the stone to glass.

Some authorities say that these conflagrations were accidental, but experimental archaeology has shown that 2,500 tonnes of brushwood would be needed to start and keep such a blaze going, so it must have been deliberate. If so, who did it – and why?

Did the inhabitants want to produce a sealed and smooth surface to their walls? Hardly – or if they did, they could have done so with a lot less effort. And if they did use this method, they would have treated all the walls, and not just certain sections, in particular around what appear to be entrances. It also seems unlikely that attackers would have done it. There were plenty of ways of destroying walls without going to so much brushwood-piling effort, which could not have gone unmolested by the defenders. In any case, if the forts were so vulnerable to fire, why did they go on building them until 350 BC, if everybody knew they were likely to be destroyed within twenty years? Actually this last theory is the most unsatisfactory of arguments against their being of military significance; it would not be the last time in history that a people have clung to a prestigious weapons system long after its inefficiency has been disastrously demonstrated.

One hypothesis is that unknown attackers ritually purged the site with fire *after* its capture by more conventional means. Perhaps – and this is an idea for which I have no present archaeological or geological evidence whatsoever, merely the thought as I write – perhaps the vitrified forts of Scotland were not military architecture at all, but industrial structures, the homes and workplaces of a widespread metal-working clan, who could only achieve the high temperatures they required by this clumsy but effective technique. The space between the ramparts could have been intended to be a forced-draught blast-furnace, designed to obtain full advantage of the wind whistling round the hilltop. Smelting was carried out in one section after the other until over a period of years the whole structure had completely disintegrated or until the ore in the area had been worked out, whereupon the clan moved on to the next suitable site.

Whatever their function, the vitrified forts had long since disappeared before the Vikings came. Not so the brochs, one of which at Mousa in the Shetlands was besieged by the Northmen. The broch-builders are as mysterious a folk as the inhabitants of vitrified forts, although the brochs' purpose as refuges seems indisputable. The earliest were built about 500 BC, a date obtained by Carbon-14 dating a wooden structure which was replaced by Dun Mor Vaul Broch on the island of Tiree. (Note the name; some authorities consider duns to be the link between vitrified forts and brochs.) The brochs themselves, being entirely of dry-stone walling, cannot be Carbon-14 dated, and only an occasional later

wooden artefact suggests that they were already ancient when such an item was dropped in their ruins.

When building a broch masses of stones were systematically piled up to form a smooth-faced solid circular wall up to five metres thick, enclosing a central floored area five metres in diameter. As it rose, the wall became hollow, thus enabling it to rise to a beehive-looking height of 14 metres. There were floors and platforms at various levels, including a defensible roof, all being reached by internal wooden ladders.

The lowest part of the wall was so solid it could hardly be affected by the sort of primitive pick or battering-ram available to non-Roman forces. When the Romans themselves encountered brochs (as at Torwoodlee near Galashiels in AD 140), their artillery pounded them very badly.

Brochs varied somewhat in design – some were ground-galleried, not solid-based. Some were encircled by outlying walls. Some had guard-rooms beside the incredibly constricted entrance, which was only 1.5 metres high and 60 centimetres wide. This tunnel was surmounted by another chamber with holes in the floor, through which the inhabitants inflicted various unpleasantries upon the cramped invaders trying to get through the solid door at the end of the tunnel. If they were successful, the attackers could only emerge one at a time, and were compelled to turn to the left to ascend the ladder, thus exposing their unshielded right side to the defenders' missiles on the verandah-platform (or scarcement) above.

It was all very crafty, but the dimensions of that tunnel-like entrance provide the main clue for the existence of brochs. It shows that they were indeed places of refuge and not true strongholds, bases for military operations of offence. It would hardly be in keeping for any chief with the slightest pretension to majesty to crawl like a mouse into such a hidey-hole. Nor could brochs have been used for the storage of large quantities of possessions, grain or cattle. They were for the temporary protection of personnel existing on such portable foodstuffs as they could drag through that narrow entrance.

It has therefore been suggested that the 500 or

so brochs (mostly built in Orkney and Caithness from 100 BC to AD 200) were constructed in response to sea-raiders who were out to capture, not property, but slaves for sale to the labour market of the expanding Roman Empire farther south. If so, it would be somewhat ironic if the Roman demand for such a commodity encouraged Saxon and Viking maritime development to such an extent that it began to pose a threat to Roman civilisation itself, necessitating the establishment of the Count of the Saxon Shore to deal with raids on the wealthier targets in Britannia and Gaul. Certainly by about AD 200 the broch-dwellers were being left in peace – or perhaps there were no longer enough of them to be an economical source of slaves – and the structures were being utilised as stone quarries. Those which were still habitable at the end of the Roman

26 *Mousa Broch in the Shetlands.*

Empire were again pressed into service.

Although of a much later date than brochs, the tall thin towers which dot the Irish landscape were also refuges rather than strongholds. Built of mortared stone and presenting an occasional window-slit to the outside world, their entrance was several metres up the smooth face, accessible only by means of a removable ladder. The local population would shelter in them until the raiders gave up trying to batter the solid foundation wall, or retreated at the approach of the local lord's army.

Pele towers were similar in principle, but more sophisticated and of an even later date (1100–1700). They were erected in Ireland and especially on both sides of the Anglo-Scottish border, doubling as combined refuges and strongholds. The practice of extorting tribute in cash or kind from small farmers and peasants in return for freedom from molestation – blackmail – was a common one. Pele towers provided fortified accommodation for the local landowner, his family and retainers. Sometimes they were provided with an adjoining enclosure bailey or 'barmkin' for the protection of tenants and their livestock. The word 'pele' means 'enclosure' as in 'The Pale', the fence enclosing the Viking settlement around Dublin in Ireland.

Of course, the landowner who one day was sheltering in his pele tower from the depredations of his neighbour, was the next day riding out on *his* own blackmail expedition, but some pele towers were entirely of refuge function; some were fortified church buildings, where the local townsfolk could shelter until the lord to whom they normally paid blackmail came to their rescue.

CHAPTER EIGHT

Northmen

From the fury of the Northmen, Good Lord deliver us.
(Anglo-Saxon prayer)

Whether called Danes, Swedes, Vikings, Norsemen or Northmen, these raiders' depredations frightened people into building towers of refuge, strong walls around their cities, riverside castles and fortified bridges, equipped with artillery, bowmen and booms to prevent longships coming upriver or to trap and destroy them on their return downstream. Yet the Vikings were themselves redoubtable fortress-builders. If, late in the season, they found themselves far from home, they tried to capture a walled town for their winter quarters. Otherwise they hauled their boats ashore and set up camp, protected by an earth rampart or wooden palisade. Expert horsemen, they rode out to sweep the countryside in wider search of plunder. When spring came, the Viking squadron moved on again – or perhaps some of them did, the rest remaining to develop their winter camp into permanent settlement.

Most of those in Britain can be distinguished by the place-name suffix of '-by', a term which has led to the words 'bye-law' and 'bye-pass'.

Vikings, Danes, Swedes, Norsemen or Northmen, they ranged the known world. They sailed westwards to England, Scotland, Ireland, Iceland, Greenland and perhaps America. They sailed eastwards through the Baltic and up the far rivers and marshes at the invitation of traders who greatly desired protection against Turkish bandits. The Vikings came in 862, seizing Novgorod as a base for their operations. Led by Rurik, the force was called the Ruotsi by the Finns of the region. Within a generation, the

territory under their control had become known as Rurikcia (or Russia), with its capital at Kiev. However, distances were so vast, the forests and swamps impenetrable away from the rivers, and communications through the winter snows were virtually impossible at that time of year. Settlements had to be completely self-contained; it was no use expecting food or tools to arrive from anywhere else. And in the campaigning season of summer, when attacks by the Tartar Golden Horde or by rival princelings could be expected, it was no good relying on the speedy arrival of friendly troops to beat off the enemy. For immediate protection cities had to look to the strength of their own walls, remote trading stations to their stockades.

To the outsider, whether foreign invader, wary trader, or winter wolf-pack, the early fortification of Russia presented a blank, impenetrable façade. It was an impression which has persisted in one way or another to the present day.

Moscow did not become the capital of Russia until 1156, and its famous walled citadel which originally enclosed the whole of the city was not built until the fifteenth century. Within the Kremlin were eventually located not only the usual offices, headquarters and barracks for the administration and policing of a mighty empire, but also an incredible variety of palaces and cathedrals of wondrous majesty and beauty. Safe behind the massive wall, they survived the destruction of the rest of the city during Napoleon's invasion of 1812, and are still preserved as

27 *A model of the Danish camp at Trelleborg in West Zeeland. It consists of a near-circular enclosure surrounded by an earth rampart, revetted with wooden boards and topped by a palisade. The rampart was high enough for the four gates to be in the form of tunnels through it, bridges leading over the ditch which lies outside one arc of the circle. That sector was further protected by another ditch. A full-sized reconstruction of one of the barrack blocks (29.5 metres long) is in the background. Note that the buildings bear a distinct resemblance to upturned boats, undoubtedly reflecting the earliest Viking encampments. Recent practical experiments have suggested that primitive buildings may not have had a hole in the roof to let the smoke out from a central hearth. It could well have produced a dangerous forced-draught effect, and there were plenty of accidental interstices in the thatch and under the eaves to allow smoke to escape. It is believed that this and other encampments were built early in the eleventh century on the proceeds of Danegeld paid by Ethelred the Redeless. By thus assembling and training their forces the Danish kings were able to launch a co-ordinated campaign against England, instead of a series of separate raids by individual adventurers. The result was that Cnut the Great became King Canute of England.*

museums and art galleries, symbolising for the Russian people the glory and craftsmanship of their predecessors.

However, for the Westerner, it is the Kremlin's enclosing wall which is itself the symbol of Russia, still seeming to present to the outside world the same blank, impenetrable façade as the early fortifications.

Some of the Vikings who advanced into Russia back in the ninth century continued their movement south-eastwards. Eventually they became the Varangian Guard, the personal bodyguard of the Byzantine Emperors. Other Norsemen of that period settled in northern Gaul, became Nor-

mans, and went on to conquer England and Sicily.

Throughout the whole of the period following the break-up of the Western Roman Empire until the beginning of the Middle Ages, the knowledge of classical military architecture had been kept alive in the surviving fortifications of countless cities and strongpoints. Each generation accepted or adapted or rediscovered existing or forgotten techniques to meet the requirements of different military situations or geographical locations. And no doubt monastic libraries contained copies of documents originally from the Rhodes' School of Military Architecture, their abbots

28 *The Russian exploration of Siberia began in 1483 and the area was first used as a place of exile in 1710. This modern photograph of a reconstructed settlement conveys something of the atmosphere and architecture of Russia during its pioneering days. The abundance of tall-growing fir trees provided a good supply of long straight timber. Apart from ensuring solid walls it also meant that beams could be an integral part of the blockwork structure and still project far enough to carry an enclosed gallery enabling defenders to drop or shoot missiles on anybody trying to gain unauthorised admission. With lookout post and rectangular loopholes, such a building is proof against all weaponry except explosive and fire. The latter is particularly dangerous in winter when water freezes before it can reach the flames. Nevertheless, incendiarism is not a practicable weapon, as Second World War Germans fighting on the Russian Front learned. It was often necessary for them to launch a winter assault with anti-personnel weapons only, on remote farmsteads, simply to gain shelter from the bitter weather; the object was to kill the people inside, not destroy the building. If the defenders could keep the property reasonably weatherproof and hold out long enough in comparative warmth, the attackers outside would die of cold anyway. In more primitive times, the only way of gaining admission to such a stronghold as is illustrated might be to pose as a friendly traveller in need of assistance. Once inside, he would assassinate the chief and open the door to his friends outside – a powerful reason for regarding all strangers with suspicion, a trait which could become deeply ingrained in a people's attitudes.*

making them available to friendly Christian princes or their monkish agents. Even without such theoretical expertise, as we have seen, there was nothing unusual about the building of strongholds anywhere in Europe during the so-called Dark Ages. There is no reason why the building of castles by the Normans should be so pointedly commented upon by their contemporaries. Quite obviously the Normans did not invent castles; and yet it is for castles that we chiefly remember them.

29 *From such beginnings as the previously illustrated settlement grew Moscow and the mighty stronghold of the Kremlin, seen here from across the Moskva River. The prominent tower at the lefthand corner of the wall is the Water Tower, with the Annunciation Tower rising from the trees and the Tainitsky Tower at the far right. The centre of the picture is dominated by the Great Palace, now bearing the letter CCCP (Cyrillic for USSR). Its right-hand end dwarfs the Cathedral of the Annunciation and the Cathedral of the Archangels, the latter with scaffolding around one of its domed towers. Behind rises the Belfry of Ivan the Great. Then comes the Kremlin Theatre, while the Spassky Gate (with its clock-face) gives access to Red Square. The Red Star-surmounted spire on the skyline in the background (between the Water Tower and the Great Palace) belongs to the Trinity Gate, while the onion-shaped dome above the roof of the Great Palace itself surmounts the Cathedral of the Assumption. In addition there are a further thirteen towers and gates along the wall, each one a self-contained fortress. Inside the Kremlin there are another two great churches, five palaces, the Arsenal, the Armoury and the Senate Building, besides what has already been mentioned.*

CHAPTER NINE

Normans

They wrought castles widely throughout the nation, and
oppressed the poor people.
(*The Anglo-Saxon Chronicle*)

The Normans brought nothing new to military architecture that had not been known before; in fact, some of their early stone construction was inferior in design to that of the ancients. In details of defensive device and items of siege equipment, there was nothing in a Norman castle or baggage train which a Roman legionary or soldier of Alexander the Great would have found unfamiliar.

However, it was to the strategic and tactical concepts which castles represent that the Normans contributed most. They saw castles not just as places for civilians to hide in, nor as simple barracks for the soldiery, but as integral units in the administration of the State and as solid bases

30 *All the elements of late-Viking/early-Norman castle-building and siege warfare are contained in this scene from the Bayeux Tapestry. Duke William and Harold Godwinson are pursuing Conan of Brittany who takes refuge in his stronghold of Dinan. The castle is of vertical timbers on top of a motte. Within the stockade is a wooden tower, the lord's more sumptuous apartments being on the upper storey. The motte is surrounded by a ditch and rampart, which is crossed by a bridge fronted by a ceremonial archway. At first, combat takes place outside the walls of the fortress, but then the Bretons retreat within. Assault infantry armed with special incendiary lances set fire to the woodwork and Conan decides to surrender; he leans out from the turret on the right, offering the keys of the castle gate on the end of his ensign-staff.*

for a very mobile form of warfare. For what the Dukes of Normandy (simultaneously the Kings of England) developed was the privatisation of law and order. When William conquered England he rewarded his accompanying nobles with grants of land, in return for which they promised to serve the king in time of war and to supply certain specified amounts of produce when required. The baron himself did not have to see to this personally; he in turn laid a share of the responsibility upon lesser knights or sub-tenants – and so on. And of course, all the actual work was done by the villeins and serfs right at the bottom of the feudal heap.

Among the routine tasks assigned to each baron was the collection of taxes for the king in his area of jurisdiction, the punishment of offenders against the King's Peace, and the repulse of invaders (if his territory abutted foreign domains). To maintain himself in proper style, the baron was also empowered – naturally enough – to levy tolls and raise taxes for his own benefit. Furthermore, he could punish offenders against his own dignity and take up arms against unlawful aggression by rival barons. The medieval lord could do virtually what he liked, provided he maintained law and order, sent the correct amount of tax money to the Royal Exchequer, and turned out to fight for the king when summoned.

In a perfect world it would have been a perfect system of government – except from the peasants' point of view (and they had nothing to complain about, because their baron defended them from the much harsher extortion of wicked neighbours). Unfortunately, like all human institutions, the binding oaths, the responsibilities, and the privileges of the feudal system could be interpreted according to who was doing the interpreting. The king could not always rely on his barons and, to keep an eye on them, he built and maintained his own royal castles, putting a royal constable in charge of each. This officer was responsible for maintaining the fabric of the place, garrisoning it with properly trained soldiery, equipping it with arms, armour and weapons of every description, and provisioning it with ample reserves of food for men and fodder for

horses. Castles – particularly royal castles – were not intended to be refuges where frightened people hid from the outside world. (In fact, during the siege of Chateau Gaillard in Normandy during the winter of 1203/4, civilian refugees were driven out of the castle as so many useless mouths. The besieging French army had no intention of feeding them either, and these hapless displaced persons were compelled to spend the winter in the castle ditch, eventually resorting to cannibalism to stay alive.)

Norman castles, especially royal castles, were intended as bases for offensive operations, sending out detachments to hold bridges or narrow valleys, preparing siege equipment to batter a rival's stronghold into submission, despatching independent tax collectors and justiciars to undermine an enemy's economy and legal system, launching a full-scale field army to meet an invader head-on, putting rival claims to disputed territory to God's test of battle.

Of course, human nature being what it is, the royal constable did not always agree with the king's policy, or even that he was dealing with the rightful king at all. Some constables were inefficient, neglecting their duties until – when the crisis came – the castle's storerooms were empty, its garrison a few elderly pensioners, and its stonework dilapidated. We always think that bygone craftsmen built to last. This was not always so; there are reports of investigations revealing that builders were paid for high-quality materials, but made a botched-up cheap job of their work. Some places were so badly constructed that it was not worth repairing them.

Others were so inconveniently situated that they were soon abandoned. Paradoxically, others proved so effective as bases for securing and pacifying an area that they fulfilled their purpose and became redundant within a couple of years. Indeed, some royal constables were so energetic, taking such an interest in their responsibilities that they came to regard the place as *their* castle, becoming openly rebellious when the king ordered them to hand it over to a replacement. To act as counters to them – and to any over-mighty subject – the king appointed shire-reeves (sheriffs) who could call out all the able-bodied men of the county (the *posse comitatus*). At first the shire-reeves were appointed from the lowlier ranks of the nobility, but as they too invariably operated from the chief town of the county, and as that usually had a royal castle as its administrative headquarters. . . .

The feudal system varied somewhat from country to country and from age to age, but all medieval kings never lacked problems with their barons and problems with the Church. And yet there was never any shortage of candidates for the job of king, even from among the reigning monarch's own family. So great was the feeling of personal insecurity among royal families and the peerage that although castles were built as operational bases, defensible against external foes, it was customary for at least one section to be constructed as a refuge for the lord and his family, keeping them separate from the hurly-burly of stronghold life and, hopefully, from the assassin's knife.

One thing the Normans could not be accused of lacking, was energy. They certainly brought tireless enthusiasm to the task of stronghold-construction and they brought a measure of standardisation. That is not to say that all Norman castles were exactly the same. Each was a unique weapons system, specifically intended to meet the requirements of that particular geographical and political situation. Nor was their network of castles systematically planned, although they saw it as a whole, a major part of their governance.

Instead, like the camps of the Roman army, the earliest Norman castles were built as temporary overnight protection for the Duke or his knight and their soldiers. However, the Normans had fewer working men at their disposal. First, the numbers involved were smaller; the Duchy of Normandy was much less in extent than the Roman Empire, so there was no chance of raising armies as big as the Romans had. Second, of those who were present on a Norman campaign, many were either noblemen – who could not be expected to soil their hands digging trenches or chopping down trees – or they were servants, who could not be spared from the vital task of making their masters as comfortable as

early medieval travel would permit. As for local peasant labour . . . they had probably run off and hidden at the approach of the Norman warlord and his retinue.

Accordingly, a Norman expeditionary force had to be content with digging a ditch, throwing the earth up on the inside and erecting a wooden wall around it. To save more time and labour, the Normans took a prefabricated castle with them – a series of stout wooden panels, fixed to posts which could be hammered into the ground. It was not impregnable, but once Harold's field army had been defeated at Hastings, such a stockade would easily keep out disgruntled Saxon peasants. The next morning, the prefabricated castle was dismantled, stowed in a waggon or on pack-animals, and the column set off again, leaving behind a mouldering ditch and a bank . . . and a local legend that once upon a time, a mighty treasure-filled castle had stood there, secret tunnels connecting it with the nearest nunnery several kilometres away.

Perhaps the Normans were forced to stay longer than they expected, or perhaps this spot was a particularly favoured one, within the territory allocated to the baron by the Duke. In that case, measures were taken to erect a permanent stronghold as soon as possible. They then sent out a party to round up all the peasants they could find. Their bodies and mortal destinies now belonged to their new overlord, and the sooner they understood that, the better. This labour force was set to work to dig more ditches and palisaded ramparts, but on a much greater scale than for an overnight site. To one side, or perhaps in the middle, the earth had to be heaped up until it formed an artificial hill. This was done in a series of layers, each of which had to be pounded into a solid mass before the next layer – of different soil or rubble, if available – was dumped on top. The mound was then covered in clay to keep out water, the whole structure being known as a *motte* from the French word for 'turf'. While the top layer was being deposited, provision was being made for foundation pits to take heavy timber posts, so that these could be an integral part of the motte. They formed the main supports of a wooden palisade and house (*domus*), where

31 *Berkhamsted Castle in Hertfordshire is a near-perfect example of an early Norman motte-and-bailey stronghold. The bailey measures 137 metres × 91 metres, while the motte is 55 metres in diameter tapering to 18.3 metres at a height of 13.7 metres. Berkhamsted was particularly significant in the Conquest of England, being the place where the Saxon supporters of Edgar the Atheling surrendered to Duke William. The latter's half-brother (Count Robert of Mortain) was the first castellan of* Berkhamsted, *subsequent holders of the fief including the Chancellor Thomas Becket. He began the reconstruction of the castle in stone. The original main gateway, bridge and barbican were to the south, near the road and railway. For most of its history Berkhamsted Castle has been royal property, remaining loyal to the Crown during the French invasion of 1216. It resisted Prince Louis for a fortnight before being compelled to surrender.*

the lord (*dominus*) lived. In due course these words became corrupted into *donjon*, which became *dungeon* (or cellar under the house).

Meanwhile, the term *motte* had been transferred to the ditch around the mound and transcribed as *moat*. The rest of the enclosed area – the greater part in fact – at the foot of the mound, was called the *bailey*. It was where the lord's soldiers lived in huts, did their training, and so on. The entrance to the bailey was via a bridge and the motte could only be approached through the bailey, usually over another bridge.

After a suitable interval, the lord began construction of a stone edifice. A different site from

32 *A typical Norman motte, erected to support a wooden castle at York in 1068–9. The existing stone King's Tower of quatrefoil plan embodied the new idea that round walls were harder to undermine than sharp corners, besides being more resilient to battering-rams and picks or bores. Note the bartizan supported on corbels to provide vertical fire over the blind angle at the join of the curved walls. This donjon derived its present name of Clifford's Tower after Edward II's victory at the Battle of Boroughbridge in 1322. Sir Roger Clifford, being on the losing Lancastrian side, was executed and his body hung in chains from this tower.*

A similar fate befell Robert Aske, organiser of the Pilgrimage of Grace rebellion against Henry VIII in 1537.

the original motte and bailey was preferred. This was partly to enable the stronghold to continue in operation while the new was under construction, and partly to avoid subsidence which might result if a massive stone tower were erected upon an artificial mound. This precaution illustrates the foresight of the Normans, and the fact that they expected their way of life to go on for ever, for such a weakness would not necessarily become apparent for several generations.

In the autumn of 1069 a Danish force came to help their relatives in Jorvik, overwhelmed the Norman garrison and dismantled the castle. William the Conqueror returned and devastated the North as retribution for this rebellion. The castles – there were two, on either side of the River Ouse – were re-erected, again of timber. The original wooden tower of York Castle was burnt down during anti-Semitic riots in 1190. Again rebuilt, complete reconstruction was undertaken from 1245 to 1270. This was when the motte was crowned with a stone tower.

The problem of subsidence would not arise for the Normans if the new masonry structure replaced a temporary wooden building upon a natural eminence with solid rock not far below the surface.

However, if there were no alternative to the

original motte-and-bailey site, foundations of solid stone slabs set vertically (like piles) into the topmost layers of the motte could help to distribute the weight of the tower. This was done at Longtown Castle in Herefordshire in the twelfth century.

Some stone towers proved too heavy for the earth mottes and suffered subsidence. However, there are other reasons for the leaning gatehouse and cracking fabric of Clifford's Tower (York) today (see figure 32). In 1315–16, a flood washed away part of the motte, but most weakening occurred after Robert Redhead became governor in 1596. At that time Clifford's Tower was being used as a prison, and he systematically removed and sold much of the stonework. But as his depredation was confined to the interior of the building, it was a long time before it was obvious that anything was amiss and his activity could be stopped. The gatehouse itself was bombarded during the English Civil War. After rebuilding, further damage was incurred in 1684 as a result of a fire and explosion when the place was serving as an army barracks.

But even if subsidence did not occur, the very fact that the stone tower was located on the apex of a narrow mound made it very cramped. More commodious accommodation was provided by the shell-keep, a simple wall encircling the top of the mound, its foundations going down into the top layers of earth in such a way that the masonry seemed to spring from the sides of the motte. This wall enclosed several one- or two-storeyed apartments for the castellan and his immediate entourage. Even so, shell-keeps were still comparatively small, their walls being but 2.5–3 metres thick and rising at the most 7.5 metres into the sky. (Compare this with the walls of the Great Tower of Rochester Castle, 3.7 metres thick and 34 metres high.)

The building of Colchester Castle was begun in 1074–6, the place always being regarded as an important royal fortress because of its strategic location on the roads from East Anglia to London and from the Thames Estuary northwards. The baronial faction and their French allies took possession of the castle during the reign of King John. The latter's forces under Savory de Meulon ('the Bloody') – and later the king himself – besieged the castle from January to March 1216. The French, including 17 crossbowmen (whose weapons were considered so barbaric that they were liable to be massacred if they surrendered), were allowed to march out, but they were all rearrested in London.

For most of its subsequent history, Colchester Castle was a prison, one of its deputy constables being William Dych who 'laid his hands illegally on Matilda Haras who was staying at the house of the aforesaid William, within the walls of Colchester, and without permission or warrant carried off the said Matilda to Colchester Castle and there cruelly imprisoned her, and placed thumbscrews on her hands till the blood oozed forth.' Presumably Matilda Haras (or Harris) was a woman of some wealth, and presumably William Dych was trying to force her to marry him, or otherwise make over her property to him.

The castle itself played little part in the Civil War siege of Colchester, which was mainly an affair of fieldworks and entrenchments. The cellars of the building served as the Armoury of the Colchester Volunteers during the Napoleonic Wars, and as an air raid shelter during the Second World War. Colchester Castle is now a museum.

Rochester is another good example of the development of a site by the Normans. The city was itself surrounded by some sort of defensive wall when the Normans arrived and built a timber motte-and-bailey castle on Boley Hill. Both city and castle were held for the king by Odo, William I's half-brother and the warrior-Bishop of Bayeux who wielded a skull-crushing mace because clergymen were not allowed to shed blood. When William I died Odo supported one surviving brother (Robert) against one of the others (Rufus). In 1087, the latter captured both the city and Odo. Old Rochester Castle does not seem to have played any significant part in these operations. Either the timbers had decayed so much that the place was untenable, or the site for a new stone castle was already being prepared a few metres to the north. Certainly by 1089 work was in progress under the direction of Gundulf, Bishop of London, who was also responsible for the construction of the Tower of London. In-

33 *Here the wall of Colchester Castle is hidden by the north-east tower, the latter's base protected against undermining by a sloping plinth or batter. Buttresses strengthen the south-east tower, which is rounded to accommodate the projecting apse of a chapel – a similar plan to that of the Tower of London. Originally 24 metres high, the keep does not now rise above ground and first floor levels.*

deed, there were similarities between that edifice and the Great Tower of Rochester Castle. However, the two projects were separated by forty years, the latter being supervised by William de Corbeil, Archbishop of Canterbury. The entrance to his tower was by means of a forebuilding, approached via a stone staircase which ended at the edge of a pit just short of the main

doorway. Further access could only be made over a drawbridge and, once in, the attacker had to turn to the right towards the portcullised entrance to the keep proper. He thus exposed his right, unshielded side to the next series of defenders. It is worth noting that many passageways in castles were deliberately narrow, so that one man could hold it against many. He would not have to stay there indefinitely – like Horatius keeping the bridge – the Norman only had to hold it long enough to kill or disable just one opponent. The casualty himself would remain jammed there and could only be removed by being dragged all the way back to the nearest wide part. (Presumably the *defender's* death would achieve the same object of delaying the enemy.)

During the Baronial Revolt of 1215 Rochester Castle was held against King John by William of Albini and 95 knights, plus 45 men-at-arms. They rushed in with hardly any stores but with all their horses. King John arrived with an army of mercenaries on 13 October. Under covering fire from catapult artillery and crossbows his engineers undermined the south-east tower of the curtain wall and broke into the bailey (or outer ward). The barons' field army of 700 men on the other side of the River Medway made no attempt to interfere with the assault. Now the engineers began tunnelling under the south-east turret of the keep, removing its masonry and shoring up the foundation. King John had already organised the supply of food and wine for his force, requisitioning stores from as far away as Sandwich. Now he demanded 'with all speed, forty of the fattest pigs of the sort least good for eating, to bring fire to the tunnel.' It is not clear whether entire carcases were pushed in, or whether they were rendered down and the jars of grease or lumps of fat stacked around the wooden shores. When first ignited the fire must have merely smouldered because of the lack of draught at the far end of the tunnel, but at the same time a fierce heat must have been generated. And when the stonework began to crack, the sudden inrush of oxygen would have produced something like an explosion. The charred timbers burned through in a matter of seconds and the lower part of the turret collapsed. King John's assault troops

34 *The Norman tower of Rochester Castle was begun by William of Corbeïl, Archbishop of Canterbury, in 1127. Built principally of Kentish rag (a coarse sandstone), it was completed in 1137–42. It is 21 metres square and 34 metres high, with the four corner turrets adding an extra 3.7 metres. The solid projections running the full height of the wall between the turrets are pilaster buttresses to strengthen the tower. Note the holes at the alure (walkway) level of the walls and turrets for a timber hoarding (also known as a hourd or brattice), which could be installed to permit vertical fire upon the enemy at the base of the keep. The battlements show up well against the sky; the solid portions are merlons; the gaps between are crenels (or embrasures). The technical term 'to crenellate' (which private owners could only do under special licence from the king) shows that the earliest Norman stone castles were built with solid parapets, which subsequently had gaps made in them; rather than having extra courses of stone added to the top. The number of largish windows indicates that Rochester Castle was intended as a residence and administrative centre as well as a military fortress. Although at a good height, they would still have been boarded up in time of war. This photograph of Rochester Castle in Kent was taken from the south-east corner. It shows how both the turret of the donjon and the south-east angle of the bailey curtain wall (wrecked during the Baronial Revolt of 1215) were rebuilt with circular turrets, so that there were no corners from which individual stones could be dislodged by battering ram or bore.*

rushed the breach and stormed the castle.

The capture of Rochester Castle on 30 November 1215 was a feat of organisation and generalship for which King John has never really been praised. But one wonders what the outcome would have been if the castle had been properly provisioned from the very beginning; or if the barons' field army had played a more active part at this juncture.

The wrecked masonry was subsequently rebuilt in circular form. Thus strengthened, Rochester Castle was successfully defended by Henry III's constable, Roger de Leybourne (together with Earl Warrenne, the Earl of Arundel, and the king's nephew, Henry of Almain) against Simon de Montfort in 1264. The latter mounted an amphibious assault across the river under cover of a fireship and in co-operation with an advance towards the city from the east by the Earl of Hertford and Gloucester. Within three days (17–19 April) they had captured Rochester, sacked the cathedral and stormed the castle's bailey. The Great Tower proved more difficult, and was still holding out on 26 April when the rebel barons moved off at the approach of the king's field army under Henry III himself and his son, the future Edward I.

Although the square tower became associated with Norman architecture, they were not the first to use it. That honour is accredited to the Count of Anjou. Anjou was centred on the Loire valley south-west of Paris and bordered by Normandy and Britanny. It was a very lush region, its fertility enhanced by being left fallow for several years during a series of bitter campaigns by rival invaders during the later Dark Ages. None of them could hold the valley, but neither were they prepared to let another have it. But eventually there arose a leader who did achieve dominion over that coveted territory. His name was Fulk Nerra – Fulk the Black.

Fulk Nerra had already evolved the strategy of establishing wooden strongholds to exploit each newly won patch of Angevin territory, and to serve as springboards for the acquisition of the next area of land on his programme, and he had inflicted fire upon other people enough times to know the destructive power of that element and to realise the advantages of building a military fortress of stone. And so it was that, about 995, Fulk Nerra founded the castle of Langeais, west of Tours, which was then occupied by the Count of Blois. Langeais was a simple rectangular tower 16 × 7 metres in plan. Its walls were of smallish, roughly hewn masonry, but the floors were wooden. Entrance was by means of a small tower which projected in such a way that anyone approaching the door would have to expose their right, unshielded side to missiles from the top of the walls. (And lest the reader think that there is unnecessary repetition of this architectural feature, it is a deliberate reminder to the modern castle-visitor to look round to see the direction from which danger threatens – it is not always obvious!) Once inside the little turret at Langeais the attacker had to climb up a stone staircase to reach the first floor where was located the entrance to the castle proper.

As the Dukes of Normandy shared a common frontier with Anjou it was inevitable that in time they, too, should erect castles of stone for practical military purposes as well as to symbolise their own proud strength.

And it is with the erection of stone castles by the Normans that we enter upon the great period of medieval strongholds.

CHAPTER TEN

The medieval castle

Men of Harlech on to glory
See your banner fam'd in story
Waves these burning words before ye
Britain scorns to yield.
(Thomas Oliphant, *March of the Men of Harlech*)

Certain trends in castle-building can be discerned as the Dark Ages progressed through the medieval period towards modern times.

For the people of Europe, the Dark Ages began in AD 410, when the army of Alaric the Goth captured and looted Rome. How could the Eternal City have been subjected to such humiliation? Was it not at the centre of the whole world, far removed from the wild frontiers? Even if the barbarian hordes did manage to cover such a great distance without defeat, was not Rome itself impregnable? After all, it was encircled by a tile-faced, volcanic tufa-cored wall 4 metres thick, 6 metres high (17 metres in places), and 18 kilometres in circumference. There were 18 gateways, each guarded by two towers, some round, some square. And there were a further 381 towers, all solid-based, but with defensive rooms and roofs rising some 4.5 metres above their flanking walls. The construction of this wall had commenced in AD 271, being laid out on a completely new line and officially finished about 281. However, there was spasmodic rebuilding when fresh ideas were incorporated, and in time of crisis such repair and refit was speeded up. The walls of Rome had certainly held against rebel forces during the civil war of the reign of Maxentius (307–12), but the object of that strife had been the control of Rome, not its destruction. And so when the decisive test came between Constantine and Maxentius, the two armies met

in the field. Thereafter, Constantine's architectural attention was concentrated on the establishment of his very own new city of Constantinople in the East.

It was not until the Ostrogoths and Visigoths, driven from their homelands by the Huns, first requested and then demanded and finally conquered their own territory within the Empire, that there was any attempt to refurbish the Walls of Rome. By then it was 395 (the reign of Honorius) and the work principally consisted of rebuilding some of the gate towers square instead of round, completely blocking up six gates and narrowing the others, further obstructing them with a portcullis.

In that form the Walls of Rome had withstood siege by Alaric the Visigoth in 408. Honorius had found shelter in the smaller, swamp-protected garrison-city of Ravenna, leaving the citizens of Rome to their own devices. Thousands of them died of starvation rather than surrender, for the Goths were more to be feared than pagan barbarians – they were heretics. The Goths were Christians, but Arian Christians – on the wrong side of the doctrine of the Trinity. Alaric might promise to respect the shrines of Roman Christendom, but could the word of an Arian be trusted? But in the end, the invaders had agreed to go away on payment of '5,000 pounds of gold, 30,000 pounds of silver, 4,000 robes of silk, 3,000 pieces of scarlet cloth and 3,000 pounds of pepper.'

Their appetites whetted by such a morsel and their leader's ambitions aroused by the lure of Imperial politics, the Goths returned to Rome in 410. Still abandoned by their emperor, the citizens of Rome once again prepared to withstand the rigours of sectarian conflict. But at night, disgruntled servants, with no affection for their harsh masters, opened the Salarian Gate, and the Goths stormed in.

Although the Walls of Rome had themselves not been overthrown on this occasion, the consequences of a breach being made either by force or by fraud highlighted the disadvantages of a single-perimeter wall. No matter how strongly built, once an enemy was in, there was nothing to prevent him rampaging all through the city.

In Constantinople about 413 the architects of the Byzantine Emperor Theodosius II proposed solving the problem by constructing concentric fortifications on the landward side of the city. First there was a ditch 18 metres wide and 6.5 metres deep, the water which normally flooded it concealing a variety of stakes. Then there was a wall 5.5 metres high, while 55 metres beyond that, there came another wall. This was 2 metres thick, with projecting towers every 55 metres to provide flanking fire. That fortification was paralleled by yet a third, 4.6 metres thick and 27 metres high, its concrete core faced with stone and reinforced with courses of bricks. It, too, was equipped with projecting towers, each strong enough to mount catapult artillery, and so placed that their field of fire was not obscured by the bastions on the outer wall. In fact, the whole system was so constructed that men on the higher walkways could direct missiles over the heads of the soldiers on the lower outer ramparts. If the enemy gained a footing on the outer wall, he would be an easy target; if he broke through altogether, he would have to mount another full-scale assault or settle down to another prolonged siege to capture the next wall – only to face the third line of fortification. And having done all that, the invader still had to seize whichever one of the great towers or palace-fortresses the emperor was still holding out in. It was only with his person – dead or alive – in their custody, that the assailant could finally

claim that he was now ruler of Constantinople. who knew what sort of assistance – divine or military – could come to the help of the emperor in that time? Not that the Byzantine emperors relied entirely on the protection of stone walls. Their fleets and armies ranged the Mediterranean and Middle East, keeping enemies at bay, stabilising the far distant frontiers with traditional Roman forts. In addition, the Byzantine emperors resorted to a variety of diplomatic tricks and psychological warfare to disarm their foes. In 1014, Basil II (Basil the Bulgar-Slayer) captured 15,000 Bulgars in battle. He ordered that they all be blinded, except every tenth man, who only had one eye put out, so that he might lead the other nine back home. Such policies might have been effective militarily, but they aroused such hatred that Constantinople became a symbol of terrible oppression as well as of fantastic wealth. Every emperor knew that one day fearful retribution would come to Constantinople itself; his military and foreign policy was devoted to putting off that day for as long as possible. And when that day did come – if it came in his time – he was determined that the city would hold out as long as possible, the last place to fall being the emperor's own refuge. Everything was designed to kill so many of the enemy that their entire army might be bled to death while the emperor survived.

Machicolation was re-invented, projecting stone walkways with murder-holes through which all manner of missiles could be dropped upon the attacker trying to undermine the wall, or batter down the gateway. Solid parapets and walls had arrow-slits made in them, the internal embrasures so shaped that the archer could traverse his weapon through a wide arc of fire as well as down and up – somebody might be climbing a scaling-ladder outside. Periodically the walls of Constantinople were extended or reconstructed, Manuel Comnenus II being notable in this work in 1143–80.

Vikings from the north, Romanised barbarians from the west, Mongols from the east, all beset the Byzantine Empire – and each other. To them was added – from 622 onwards – the Arabs from the southern desert, fired with religious zeal

And if each operation took several months,

for the expansion of Islam. By 750 their civilisation extended from India to the Atlantic, and from the borders of Gaul to equatorial Africa. Only the city of Constantinople itself seemed impregnable against their advance, withstanding two sieges. The first was a desultory affair compared with what was to come, although of course the Byzantines were not to know that. In 655 a projected offensive against the city was frustrated by disagreements among the Muslim leaders, but in 668 their fleet made its way through the Hellespont in a direct assault on the walls of Constantinople. The Saracens went into winter quarters at the end of each campaigning season, but disease and combat resulted in their force losing some 30,000 troops; in 675 they were compelled to withdraw. (Incidentally, the importance of the summer for warfare was not because the soldiers of those days could not stand the cold, nor even because they might find it difficult to obtain food; warriors were expected to be hardy. The chief problems of winter campaigning were the shortness of daylight hours, and the impossibility of guaranteeing

35 A late nineteenth-century view of the Golden Gate and the Seven Towers Palace, the latter incorporating four of the towers of the Land Walls of Constantinople. The fortified palace (Yedikule) was built by Sultan Fatih Mehmet in 1457, after the Turkish capture of Constantinople. The Golden Gate had been blocked up long before that; according to tradition, it could only be entered by the emperor; the last time it had been used had been in 1261, when the Byzantines had reclaimed their city from the Latin usurpers. Though showing signs of age due to damage by earthquake and unauthorised squatters when this photograph was taken, both palace and wall still convey an impression of solid majesty. It is also possible to see how the inner walls overlook the outer fortifications.

good grazing for thousands of horses. If fodder were available and the battlefield so close at hand that troops could get into position, fight the engagement and if necessary disengage all in the six hours of good daylight during a midwinter day, then battles were fought in the winter.)

The Saracens came again to Constantinople in 717. While their army encamped outside the

36 *The ruins of one of the strongholds built in Jordan by the ancient Arabs to control an oasis or desert crossroads. Very often they utilised the dilapidated walls or foundations of an even earlier fort. During the First World War such places were frequently used as bases by Arab and British forces operating against Turkish lines of communications.*

Land Walls, their fleet attempted to blockade the city from both the Aegean and the Black Sea. In spite of the accumulation of foodstocks, the Byzantines eventually suffered severely from starvation, some resorting to cannibalism to stay alive. However, the walls – which had been strengthened and re-equipped – held, and in 718 Byzantine seapower and an army from Christian Bulgaria imposed such defeats upon the Saracens that they retreated. It was another seven centuries before a Muslim army next stood before the gates of Constantinople.

Elsewhere the Arabs seemed unchallengeable. Like many other conquerors, they made use of existing fortifications as bases for controlling and exploiting the areas they had occupied. Where suitable ones did not exist – in Spain, for example – they built their own strongholds. Being in a hurry and usually men of the desert with little experience of masonry, they did this by erecting shuttering to take a primitive form of ready-mixed concrete – mortar reinforced with stones.

Inevitably the resulting structure had to be rectangular in plan, with square towers at each corner and protecting the gate. The walls were crenellated with pointed merlons. Within the walls were constructed living quarters of simple austerity and a mosque.

In due course some of these *alcazabas* were enlarged and rebuilt in stone to become *alcazars*, serving as defended palaces for regional military governors.

While these developments were taking place, the peoples of Europe were busy with their own feuds and troubles. The Northmen's conquest of what became known as Normandy and of England has already been mentioned, and so has how they established first motte-and-bailey, and then stone castles as bases for the exploitation of their domains.

Central Europe and Italy, however, presented a different picture. The personality of Charlemagne had so stamped itself upon his contemporaries that he had been generally accepted as the successor of the Emperors of Western Rome. Because he had been crowned by Pope Leo III on Christmas Day 800, his dominion was termed 'The Holy Roman Empire'. It was in fact a loose federation of independent States, only held together by force of character and fear of anarchy. Nevertheless, it continued to exist as a viable political unit, stable and comparatively peaceful. Only on the remotest fringes was there any need for towers of refuge.

But in 1073 Hildebrand became Pope Gregory VII. Influenced by the new movements within monasticism and by his own personal ambitions, his zeal for Church reformation became an attack on the Holy Roman Emperor. The point at issue was the question of which was legally responsible for the mortal lives of men: the spiritual authority of the pope, who represented God; or the temporal authority of the emperor, who represented . . . what?

Inevitably there was conflict, the result being the excommunication of the Emperor Henry IV. With such a curse laid upon him, all his subjects were automatically freed from their oath of allegiance to him. For his friends, that did not matter. His enemies saw it as a heaven-sent opportunity to enrich themselves by seizing Imperial territory and that of the emperor's allies. The result – a near-frenzy of castle-building in Germany, the strongholds doubling as bases for offensive action and as hiding-places for noble refugees in time of crisis.

It was in this atmosphere of religious and political strife that the Crusades were launched. Officially they were intended to recover the Holy Places of Jerusalem from the Seljuk Turks; effectively, it represented the backlash of Christendom against Islamic conquests. The real reason for their instigation was that the Byzantine emperor wanted Western assistance in ex-panding his territory and in stabilising his frontiers. Meanwhile Holy Roman Emperors and popes both saw the organisation of these expeditions as bringing some measure of unity to Christendom – under their respective control – and the First Crusade set out in 1096.

It did indeed recover Jerusalem and found the Frankish kingdoms of Outremer ('Beyond the Sea'). For almost half a century the Crusaders lived a life of comparative peace and increasing comfort, either in captured fortresses of ancient foundation or in newly built square castles of Norman appearance similar to those in their homelands. These were indeed strongholds for the governance of a conquered land.

But from 1144 onwards there arose a succession of Saracen leaders who rekindled the missionary zeal of Islam and organised Turkish energies for war. For them, Crusader castles became symbols of Frankish domination, of infidel pollution. They could not be ignored or bypassed by the Muslim army in complicated manoeuvres which might end on a favourable battlefield. They could not even be invested, the defenders demonstrating their prowess by putting up a stout resistance and then surrendering honourably. No, each and every Crusader castle had to be stormed and either destroyed or purified in some way, preferably with the blood of its inhabitants – unless they chose to become Muslims. And that was impossible for the Crusaders were dedicated to exterminating their Islamic foes, both sides being equally assured of eternal life if they fell in battle.

And so the castles of the Holy Land became sophisticated killing-grounds, weapons systems designed to enable a few defenders to hold out as long as possible, while selling their lives as dearly as possible. Usually located on some inaccessible mountain-top, each massive keep was now encircled by two or three concentric walls, so arranged that the inner higher defenders could fire over the heads of their comrades on the lower outer ramparts. Each of the curtain walls was reinforced with projecting towers or bastions, usually round in plan – it had been learned that these were more difficult to undermine or dilapidate than square ones. In spite of the seasonal

37 *The onion-shaped dome, in this old illustration, suggests that the town or castle being captured is in the Holy Land. Both curved scimitars and straight-bladed swords are being wielded. Note that one man is steadying a scaling-ladder, while others undermine the walls. A defender throws up his arms in the universal gesture of surrender, but his fellows and their womenfolk continue to hurl down stones as the flames roar up around them.*

38 *Looking up at a murder-hole in front of the portcullis slot in the entrance to the shell keep of Farnham Castle in Surrey. This part of the building dates from the twelfth century. Farnham Castle belonged to the Bishops of Winchester.*

shortage of water, surrounding ditches could be flooded – an effective deterrent to tunnelling. Further strength was provided by giving the lower portion of the walls and tower a great sloping apron or plinth. Technically known as a batter or talus, it was not only too wide to be tunnelled under and weakened, but it also stabilised the walls in the event of an earthquake – quite common in that region. (Such a natural catastrophe did not unite the combatants in mutual anguish, but proved to the besieger that God was personally fighting on *his* side.)

The talus also inhibited the use of scaling-ladders. They could not be footed upon its angled slope and if placed on the nearest level ground would either be too short or would be resting at such an oblique angle that they would inevitably be weakened to the point of collapse if several armed men tried to ascend at the same time. (One at a time, and they would be killed individually as

they reached the top of the parapet.) Yet another advantage of the talus was that when the defenders dropped stones upon it they splintered and ricocheted with a shrapnel effect. To enable the men on the parapets to do this without exposing themselves stone verandahs were built out from the top of the walls, with holes in the floors. This was officially designated machicolation. The Franks had a more succinct word for it – *meurtrières* or murder-holes! They became a feature of all subsequent castle-construction, being located in all the obvious places – and in quite a few unexpected ones, too. There were portcullises and drawbridges, dead-end corridors and covered ways, so that the outer curtain walls could be reinforced or evacuated in safety. The outer, middle and inner wards could be further subdivided by walls. And very often the alures or wall-walkways were only accessible via the doorways in the flanking towers; which meant that if the attacker did gain a foothold on the curtain wall, it did not get him anywhere. The doors into the towers on either hand, though weak compared with those at ground level, could easily withstand anything the assailant could carry up a scaling-ladder – and all the time he was exposed to missiles from the inner walls as well as from the flanking towers.

It was about this time that a new type of siege-engine – the trebuchet – was introduced, although it is not clear whether it was originally developed during the Crusades. It relied for propellant-power, not upon the elasticity of sinews and twisted rope, but upon a solid, heavy weight of several tonnes, which was fixed to the short arm of a huge pivoted beam. The missile was slung from the end of the long arm which was winched down to the ground and then released. Its range was about 450 metres, but one of its great advantages was its very high trajectory, enabling it to clear the tallest wall. The other advantage was its accuracy, the counterweight being slid up and down the short arm to vary the range. It could of course be used by people inside the castle just as effectively as by those outside.

For more direct action against the besiegers Crusader castles were provided with a number of small, heavily fortified gateways, known as sally-ports (or posterns, which are more properly simple doorways for peacetime use by foot travellers, to save opening the main gate). From these sally-ports the defenders could take advantage of the besiegers' off-guard moments, rush out, strike and recoil within the walls before the attackers could react.

The Crusader castles were well munitioned with plenty of stone, arrow and combustible missiles, as well as with the artillery for projecting them. Careful attention was paid to reserves of water (almost ten million litres in the stone tanks of Sahyun) and food. In that climate there were problems with the storage of meat; even keeping animals alive in cramped conditions and on reduced rations until required for slaughter was not a satisfactory solution. Perhaps only doves and pigs could be reared in that sort of situation. (And if pork were consumed, it was no doubt spiced with the knowledge that the very act of

eating it was somehow insulting to the Muslim besiegers outside.) Stored food, therefore, was usually in the form of grain, which could be expected to keep longer than flour. Of course, the corn would have to be ground into flour before cooking, and to do this some castles (like Krak des Chevaliers) were fitted with a windmill. It has been calculated that Krak des Chevaliers could have fed a thousand troops for a whole year – two years if there were only 500 in residence. Of course, a two-year diet of unflavoured, gritty pasta would have seemed as burdensome to the spirit as any of the devices of the enemy. There must have been provision for the container-storage of spices and sauces, sweetmeats and oils, dried fruits and herbs.

Not that the Saracens were prepared to wait for the Crusaders to die of monotony. Savage assaults were interspersed with psychological, chemical and bacteriological warfare. Catapults launched pots of quick-lime and Greek Fire, shattering on impact, sending their contents flying in all directions. The medical experts of the day might not have been fully cognisant of the means by which disease was spread, but they knew it was something to do with dead and rotting flesh. Accordingly the decomposing corpses of men and animals were among the projectiles shot by besiegers (of both creeds) into the fortresses they were attacking. It is recorded that on at least one occasion, beehives were similarly employed. The effect of a swarm of angry bees under the armour can well be imagined.

More subtly, the defenders' morale could be attacked by parading the captured survivors of a defeated relief column in full view of the garrison, then massacring them and hurling their heads into the castle. (A variation was to speed the living prisoners on their way to their intended destination by catapult.)

Or a Muslim of Frankish appearance and manner would pretend to be a messenger who had somehow got through the Saracen lines, bearing forged instructions from Crusader headquarters for breakout or surrender or whatever was most advantageous to the besiegers. That was how Krak des Chevaliers was captured in 1271.

39 *An old print of the Crusader castle Krak des Chevaliers in Syria. The talus can be seen just beyond the bridge over the moat.*

A century earlier, however, two thousand Knights-Hospitallers (one of the orders of warrior-monks) had put up such a defence for a month in 1188 that Saladin himself had been compelled to abandon the siege; he had to maintain the momentum of the Saracen thrust against other, more vulnerable Crusader territory.

Things were different in 1271. Krak des Chevaliers was designed for efficient defence by a few, but 200 Knights-Hospitallers (plus serving men) were *too* few. Certainly they could not man the whole circumference of the outer wall. And once in possession of the Outer Ward, the Saracens undermined one of the towers of the inner wall. Now the Hospitallers were confined to the keep, itself an integral part of the inner curtain wall. But with each retreat, they found the reduced perimeter easier to defend. Sultan Beibar's force had suffered enough casualties in the previous three weeks for him to appreciate that storming the Hospitallers' final refuge would be far too costly. That was when the idea of tricking the survivors into surrender was put into effect – and successfully so.

Three years later St Jean d'Acre fell to an Egyptian force after six weeks' siege. The adventure known to posterity as 'The Crusades' was over.

A similar order of Knights Templars had been founded in 1191 for the protection of pilgrims travelling to and from the Holy Land. Like all such Orders, they took monastic vows of poverty, chastity and obedience, but were also warriors. However, because of the wide-ranging nature of their particular duties (which involved operations throughout Christendom), the Templars were made independent of all authority except that of the pope. They soon acquired considerable wealth through the benefactions of grateful pilgrims. The failure of the Crusades should have brought their activities to an end, but they still had to journey extensively to administer their vast estates. They did so secretly, staying at their own lodging houses, unlike other travellers who were accommodated in monasteries, castles or inns depending on their social class. In due course, to do something with their wealth, the Templars became the bankers of Europe, money-lenders to kings of all nations. Inevitably they aroused considerable resentment when they reminded monarchs about repayment. In every land they were eventually accused of espionage, witchcraft and unnatural vice. By 1312, the Templars had been persecuted into extinction and all their property seized by the royal borrowers who owed them money.

Religion, political power and wealth were also the main factors in the campaign against the Albigenses. They were an austere Christian sect who portrayed Jesus as a rebel against the cruelty of God the Father. They existed in southern France from about 1120 onwards, sending out wandering preachers – and assassins – to other lands. They became so numerous that a Crusade was proclaimed against them in 1209. The campaign not only restored papal authority, it also extended royal power over areas where the king's writ had previously been weak, and it enabled crusading barons like Simon de Montfort to amass great wealth. Thousands of alleged Albigenses were slaughtered – 'Kill them all! God will know his own!' – as, one by one, their places of refuge were overwhelmed.

Carcassonne was one of their missionary strongholds and was besieged in 1209. Trencavel went under safe-conduct to negotiate an honourable surrender, whereupon Simon de Montfort put him in prison, where he died soon afterwards. Leaderless, the people of Carcassonne could only hold out for another fifteen days. Later Carcassonne survived another siege, this time by the Albigenses, who made great use of tunnels.

40 *This building may not look particularly militaristic, but in its day it was regarded with as much loathing as the Gestapo headquarters in a Nazi-occupied country during the Second World War. It is the central lodging-house of Temple Manor near Rochester in Kent, all that remains of the Templars'* curia *(or court). Ignore the later seventeenth-century additions at each end, but note the distinctive shape in the background of an ex-army Nissen hut of the twentieth century.*

However, these were countermined by the defenders and the Albigenses eventually withdrew at the approach of the crusading army, which went on to exterminate the last of these religious and political nonconformists.

Subsequently, in 1260–70, King Louis IX ordered the construction of concentric walls around the city of Carcassonne itself, making it a firm base for future operations by the royal army. The view in figure 41 gives a good indication of the fortifications which enabled the defenders to fire over the heads of those below and in front. Note that the merlons have arrow-slits in them, giving added fire-power if there was not enough time to erect the brattice.

It was not only in France that the Crusaders found martial activity in Europe. In Spain the Moors were on the defensive, being ejected by knights and dukes who established their own strongholds for the exploitation of newly liberated (or newly conquered) territory. In Eastern Europe the warrior-monks who made up the Knights of the Teutonic Order were carving out virgin territories for themselves – virgin, that is, except for the existing inhabitants who had to be administered by a network of strongholds. In Germany itself, the rivalry between pope and emperor simmered and occasionally boiled over into open conflict, in which dukes and bishops took sides according to their worldly ambitions.

And in every country kings strove to extend their boundaries and curb the power of the barons, while the latter fought for the freedom to be absolute dictators within their little patches of territory.

In all these lands square towers gave place to octagonal, polygonal and round towers. Concentric castles became common. Curtain walls became stronger and some castles dispensed with keeps altogether, one of the corner towers or a massive gatehouse serving as the principal accommodation and administrative headquarters, and as final refuge for a beleaguered baron or king. (If he was also an impecunious baron or king, he might have as much to fear from his mutinous soldiery, as from the enemy.)

Although of asymmetric construction, Harlech Castle in Gwynedd was designed as a concentric castle, allowing the inner defenders to fire over the heads of men on the outer walls. Harlech could thus be defended most efficiently by very small numbers of soldiers, well-filled store-rooms and well-equipped armouries enabling them to hold out for a very long time. The arrival of seaborne supplies and reinforcements – in medieval times, the water covered what is now flat land below the castle – could prolong a siege almost indefinitely.

Harlech Castle was built in the summer months of 1283–9, a thousand labourers being employed at any one time – pressed men, volunteers and contractors from all over the kingdom. The man in charge of the new castles in North Wales was Master James of St George. When the work was completed, he was appointed Constable of Harlech, holding the post until 1293.

Harlech was one of Edward I's strongholds for the pacification of Wales. During the peace it was intended to enforce it served as a base from which royal officers rode out to collect taxes, gather information about possible sedition, and arrest suspects before they actually struck. In time of war it accommodated a cavalry force which could

41 *The citadel of the walled city of Carcassonne in the Languedoc region of France was built by the Trencavel family in 1130–50 on the site of a Visigothic and Moorish stronghold. The citadel consists of a number of very solid, independently defended towers linked by a curtain wall, but without a separate donjon. The gatehouse is the most formidable feature of the design. Its devices include two portcullises worked from different floors; a lone traitor might be able to raise one, but the other would still be in loyal hands. The holes for the projecting beams which supported the brattice can be seen below the battlements of the city.*

Carcassonne was largely restored by Violett-le-Duc from 1844 onwards.

42 *Brattice being employed during the siege of a city. On the ground a crossbowman makes use of the shelter provided by his pavise or mantlet. Note the rosette of small holes, so that he can select his target before discharging the weapon. A statue of the Virgin and Child is bringing divine fortune to the city, but the pikeman to the left of the figure does not look too happy about his chances.*

Castle roofs often had lead guttering and flashing. This was quite likely to melt if the building were set on fire, which must be the origin of the common, but erroneous, belief that castle defenders often poured molten lead down upon the besiegers – the metal was too valuable to be used in such a manner, but even if accidental it would still be just as uncomfortable for somebody ten metres up a ladder.

43 *Orford Castle in Suffolk was a link between the square towers of the Normans and the round towers of the later Middle Ages. The Great Tower of Orford Castle was polygonal in plan, with three square corner turrets. Begun in 1165, it was completed just in time to act as a base for maintaining Henry II's authority in Suffolk. Note the use of dressed stone (known as ashlar, a term given to any masonry which was cut and shaped instead of being left in a rough-hewn state) for the plinth (or batter), the quoins, the dressings around the window openings, the string-courses and the battlements. The castle is seen here undergoing repair before being opened to the public.*

Perhaps the strangest story connected with Orford Castle concerns the shaggy wild man of the sea, caught in fishing nets and imprisoned in the castle during the reign of Henry II. 'Although oft-times hung up by his feet and harshly tortured', he refused to talk, nor did he show any signs of respect for or faith in the church. Eventually the Orford Merman escaped back to the sea.

sever the lines of communication of any army – rebel or foreign – passing through the area. Therefore, it could not be left to wither on the vine and would have to be neutralised by capture or siege. Either operation would inflict casualties on the enemy without and would delay him, by which time the king's field army would be ready to do battle. Besides, such a symbol of Anglo-Norman conquest could not be ignored. The very fact that Harlech Castle was there reminded patriotic Welshmen of defeat, and challenged them to overthrow it.

Harlech has been besieged five times during its history.

In 1294 Prince Madoc rebelled against Edward I's rule. Thirty-seven men kept him out of Harlech Castle and prevented him campaigning elsewhere. Madoc was forced to abandon the siege when relief arrived by sea for the defenders of Harlech.

The besiegers were successful over a century later when Owain Glyndwr raised the standard of Welsh independence. Although the building was not in good repair it still took from 1401 to 1404 for Glyndwr's forces to subdue the fortress. He promptly made it his headquarters, but he was absent conducting guerrilla warfare in the mountains when Harlech Castle was again besieged in 1409. This time, the thousand men outside were well supplied by Anglo-Norman logistics, while the Welshmen inside – having been unable to build up a reserve of provisions and munitions – suffered terribly from starvation. The gaunt survivors were forced to surrender.

Similar trials beset Dafydd ap Ieuan, who supported the Lancastrian cause during the Wars of the Roses. For seven long years the siege dragged on until the garrison yielded to the Earl of Pembroke. One of the people in the place was Henry Tudor, the future Henry VII of England. It is said that his experiences so etched frugality into his soul that he became one of the most tight-fisted monarchs of history. Be that as it may, the heroic Lancastrian defence of the castle inspired the march *Men of Harlech*, which has become one of the anthems of Wales.

Finally, in the English Civil War, Harlech Castle was held for the Royalists. By now it was dilapidated and poorly equipped. And yet it took the Parliamentarians' army a year's siege operations before those inside agreed to capitulate on 16 March 1647, the last Royalist stronghold to do so – and after the official close of hostilities. Total of garrison, officers and other ranks – 42!

The turreted curtain wall was much favoured by the merchant princes of city-states throughout Europe. Massive walls not only warded off jealous rivals and predatory armies, but were also symbols of civic wealth and achievement. Indeed, it is ironic that the trading cities of Italy had secured much of their riches by overthrowing the walls of Constantinople.

In 1198, the Venetians wielded so much influence with the leaders of the Fourth Crusade that all that military zeal was diverted against the capital of the Byzantine Empire. The emperors themselves involved the Crusaders in Byzantine politics. At the behest of a dethroned claimant, the Crusaders stormed the city from the Venetian fleet on 7 April 1203. Just over a year later, the Crusaders, tired of awaiting payment for their services in reinstating the emperor, assaulted the city again from both land and water. This time they breached the walls, plundered the place, and then established one of themselves as Emperor Baldwin I.

Medieval castles may today appear terribly bleak and depressing places, but even the best-preserved, unruined ones are but empty shells of their former selves. In their heyday they would have had wooden floorboards at every level, probably even covering stone flags. Partitions would have provided a measure of privacy, while blazing fires gave off light and heat. There would have been glass or curtains at the windows, and thick hangings preventing draughts around the doors. Stone walls would have been plastered and painted, with statues and heraldic devices adding interest to the scene.

Nor is there any reason to suppose that castle-dwellers were particularly squalid in their habits. Sanitary and washing facilities may have been primitive, but they did exist. Tales of great halls ankle-deep in soiled straw for the whole of the winter can be discounted as untypical. Such conditions might have existed in the household of the inefficient or eccentric or after a particularly merry feast, but there were plenty of servants to clean up the mess. Besides, straw would be a dangerous fire hazard (especially during a siege). It is more likely that floors were left bare – they would certainly be easier to keep clean. It is difficult to imagine a great master accepting filthy living conditions; servants would have to be found jobs to do, if for no other reason than to keep them busy. And no lord would tolerate a hound-handler who could not even teach a dog to be house-trained.

Every stronghold requires considerable stores of water, food, munitions, fodder for animals and fuel for heating, lighting, maintenance and vehicles, if it is to withstand a prolonged siege or act as a springboard for offensive operations. In broad-based fortresses these reserves can be accommodated in separate buildings; during the Middle Ages it was customary for them to be accumulated in the lower storeys of the castle. Such rooms would have been fitted out with shelves and racks, and kept as clean and cool and dry as possible. Once the castle had ceased to be of military significance, basement store-rooms soon showed signs of neglect, until today, bare of fitting, dank and dark, they give no indication of their original function. The commonest assumption is that these gloomy places were dungeons, prison cells for the punishment of the guilty and the mocking humiliation of the innocent.

However, although the majority of below-ground chambers were for storage purposes, there is no doubt that most castles had – and most modern fortresses still have – at least one room serving as a prison cell. It is unlikely that they would have been used to imprison rebellious peasants; even feeding them on bread and water would have been considered a waste of resources. A public flogging would be more effective as an immediate punishment and a deterrent to future recalcitrants. Castle cells were most likely for the temporary incarceration of retainers or soldiers who had infringed some garrison rule. Trained mercenaries – or *routiers* (a medieval word meaning highwaymen) – were expensive commodities, and it was a waste of good money to execute them, or even cripple them with a

44 *The garderobe chutes at Hadleigh Castle in Essex. It was originally believed that latrines were so called because people hung their clothes there so that the smell would keep the moths away. It is more likely that garderobe was yet another of those euphemisms for a necessary facility, no doubt much politer in Norman society than some harsh Anglo-Saxon word.*

Hadleigh Castle was founded soon after 1231, although this round tower probably dates from about 1350. There was no keep as such, each tower acting as a self-contained defence work along the curtain wall.

flogging. It was much better to lock the offender away until he sobered up or otherwise saw the error of his ways.

A completely different category of prisoner was the prince or knight being held for ransom. In this case, it was no good shutting him away in a noisome dungeon, where he might sicken and die; that, too, would be the waste of a valuable asset. Such prisoners often lived a restricted, but otherwise comfortable, life in the residential part of the castle.

It was something else if the high-born prisoner had some claim to the territory held by the custodial baron. Then he could well find himself dropped into an oubliette, a bottle-shaped hole in the foundations of the castle. He – or she – would be left there until they withdrew their claim . . . and if he did not, but chose to be left there until he starved to death, no man could be deemed guilty of shedding his blood or laying a hand upon him. Instruments of torture could be used to obtain similar recantations or to obtain information about fellow-conspirators. Escape was well-nigh impossible. Castles were designed to keep people out, but they also kept people in so effectively that when their military significance declined, many found employment as national or local gaols.

Often, part of the defence relied upon the castle's position in relation to the natural landscape. Both Chepstow Castle and Conway Castle are examples of this. Because of its location on a narrow, precipitous cliff high above the River Wye, Chepstow Castle is a natural linear fortress, having a Lower Bailey, a Middle Bailey and an Upper Bailey (containing the Great Tower) with

a barbican beyond that. It was originally founded by William FitzOsbern, created Earl of Hereford soon after the Battle of Hastings in 1066. Because of its strategic location it spent most of its life either as a royal castle or in the hands of barons whose loyalty to the king was unquestionable. During the Civil War of 1642–6, Chepstow Castle was held for the king, but, by October 1645, there could be no hope for the Royalist cause and the garrison (which only totalled 64) surrendered.

A larger number of 120 men under Sir Nicholas

45 *Massive and austere, Marten's Tower of Chepstow Castle symbolises Anglo-Norman dominion over the Welsh Marches. Note how the round tower, already an improvement on earlier square designs, has been given additional protection and strength by the two integral spur buttresses. At their level, the storage basement is unlit, but two of the arrow-loops covering the ditch and illuminating the ground-floor room can be seen. Each has three oillets (or spy-holes) at top, middle and bottom of the slit. The rectangular window of the first floor was added in the sixteenth century, but the arrow-loop on that level is original as is the lancet window on the second floor. These two storeys were the personal living room and bed chamber of the lord of the castle. Arrow-loops are also provided in the merlons on the battlements, giving additional fire-points for bowmen without reducing their protection. Note the roll on the merlon coping, to prevent the enemy's arrows glancing over the battlements and into the defenders on the roof of the tower. The figures crowning the merlons are apparently purely ornamental, but they may also have helped to deceive distant attackers when attempting to estimate the strength of the garrison. The battlemented north turret served as a lookout post, access-point between the east curtain wall and Marten's Tower, and as a chapel – into part of which was raised the portcullis protecting the flat-faced entrance from the Lower Bailey into Marten's Tower. The small square holes in the curtain wall were for the installation of wooden hoarding (or brattice), when the castle was put on a war footing. The flagpole is modern, but no doubt there would have been medieval provision for displaying the Lord's personal standard whenever he was in residence.*

Kemeys reoccupied the place in November 1647, when hostilities broke out afresh, but their heart was not in the fight. When a battery of four guns smashed a breach in the curtain wall, the Cavaliers began running out through the hole to surrender. It is said that when the final assault was made, Sir Nicholas Kemeys – deserted by all his men – was shot and killed in the breach, trying to hold the castle all by himself. That may have happened where slightly different colour stonework to the right of Marten's Tower indicates signs of rebuilding. The tower derives its name from Henry Marten, one of the Parliamentarians who signed the execution warrant of Charles I. He was imprisoned – fairly comfortably – in this tower from his trial after the Restoration of Charles II in 1666 until his death in 1680 at the age of 78.

Marten's Tower is 12.8 metres in diameter and 19.2 metres high, and was built about 1285–93. Richard Bigod III (Earl of Norfolk) then held the Lordship of Striguil (the Welsh name for Chepstow). He initiated this particular rebuilding and ensured that the castle was fully equipped for service as a well-defended base for Edward I's Welsh policies. This included the installation of four springalds (or giant catapults) on selected towers of the castle. At the same time Roger Bigod III encouraged traders to come to Chepstow, the security of new town walls being among the inducements. Spiritual control over the local people was attempted by the foundation of Tintern Abbey farther up the Wye Valley.

There were not only strategic reasons for Edward I's siting of Conway Castle in North Wales, but also tactical and psychological ones. Together with the walled port of Conway itself, it

46 *This photograph of Conway Castle was taken on 8 May 1929, when the flag was being flown at half-mast to denote a period of State mourning. It is easy to see how a prearranged combination of banners on different towers could convey quite a lot of information to a relieving force.*

Notice how nineteenth-century industrialists did their best to create railway buildings in keeping with the adjacent medieval grandeur. Thomas Telford's suspension road bridge is just visible; both it and the railway bridge and Conway Castle have now all become works of historic interest.

would serve as the administrative capital and as a base of operations to maintain English rule over the land. Its catapult artillery and its bowmen could interdict hostile traffic along the coastal road where it traversed the Conwy Estuary and met the route coming down the valley. And it was intended to impress the Welsh.

In this last function, it was not immediately successful; certainly in the winter of 1294/5 Prince Madoc ap Llywelyn refused to be impressed. He organised an independence movement, stormed the incomplete castle at Caernarvon, and laid siege to Conway Castle. Edward I was himself in the fortress, having hurried ahead of his main army, and now cut off from them by the floodwaters of the Conwy. The king was also ahead of his supply train which was ambushed. Edward and the garrison were compelled to survive on bread and water and a single cask of wine. However, Prince Madoc was also short of provisions; after a fortnight he was obliged to take a large proportion of his force off on a foraging expedition. While so engaged he encountered part of the English field army and was defeated; both Conway Castle and Edward I had been saved.

Conway Castle was built in five summer seasons (1283–7). It has no separate keep, each of its drum towers being a self-contained defensive work, simultaneously covering every part of the inner wards. Note how the towers rise from the living rock, which thus acts as a natural batter or talus. The Union Flag is flying from the North-West Tower. Between it and the South-West Tower (nearer the camera), can be seen the low fortification of the West Barbican, protecting the approach to the main entrance. The next tower (working in an anti-clockwise direction) is the Prison Tower, matched on the north side of the Outer Ward by the Kitchen Tower. The four towers with crow's nest lookout turrets form the four corners of the Inner Ward, which is itself a castle within a castle. Out of sight to the right is the East Barbican. The windows along the upper floor of the south curtain wall illuminated the Great Hall and (within the Inner Ward) the Royal Apartments.

Conway Castle has survived the ages with neither cannon nor gunpowder being able to breach its defences.

CHAPTER ELEVEN

Gunpowder

They were planted against the walls of a town with such
speed, the space between the shots so little, and the balls flew
so quick and were impelled with such force, that as much
execution was done in a few hours as formerly, in Italy, in
the like number of days.
(Contemporary account of the cannon used by King Charles
VIII of France)

For half a century, until 1261, Constantinople was the capital of a Latin Empire. Then Michael VIII Palaeologus again took possession of the city for the Orthodox Faith.

The city was to change hands once more in 1453. A major factor in its capture then would be a weapons system unknown to the Crusaders – gunpowder and cannon, although the first published reference to guns had appeared in 1320.

One of the myths of history is that the twin inventions of gunpowder and cannon rendered all castles obsolete. This just was not so. Admittedly early gunners did achieve some successes against fortress walls. The Scots besieged the castle of Estrevelin (presumably Stirling) with engines and cannon in 1342, and in 1377 French cannon breached the walls of Ardres near Calais. Three years later two Venetian bombards smashed down part of the campanile at Brondolo, with weapons which would have a maximum range of 2,500 metres compared with 275 metres of a trebuchet.

It seems obvious now that cannon were the weapons of the future. However, these achievements were noted simply because they succeeded. What chroniclers did not bother to record was the failure of early cannon to accomplish anything – except frighten the horses. This was partly because their ineffectiveness was so common, and

partly because it was not wise to criticise the king's new toy. The number of cannon-breached holes in late medieval siege pictures may represent wishful thinking on the part of the artist, or perhaps a desire to illustrate the latest weaponry, or perhaps it was simply because guns are easier to draw accurately than catapults; certainly flames and smoke are more dramatic (as any small child with a pencil will know).

The trouble with early cannon was threefold: those big enough to do damage to castle walls at a safe distance were too big and cumbersome; all cannon had to have a special propellant, and they had to have special shot. It was better to use a specially cut spherical stone in a trebuchet or mangonel, but if such were not available, then any large rock, jar of Greek Fire or dead horse would do. No gunner could take such liberties with a cannon; every ball – whether carved from stone or latterly cast in iron – had to be as round as possible and had to fit the bore as perfectly as existing technology would permit; too large and the shot either refused to enter the piece or jammed on firing and exploded the gun (that is how James II of Scotland was killed when besieging Roxburgh Castle in 1460); too small and it lost range and accuracy. That meant that a field army had to cart loads of special cannon-balls around with it and each might weigh up to

200 kilograms.

That was in addition to waggons carrying barrels containing the separate ingredients of gunpowder – saltpetre, sulphur and charcoal. If mixed before setting out into what was called serpentine, the inevitable jolting around on rough tracks – or on no roads at all – gradually sifted all the grains back into three layers. Obviously, it was not a precise separation, but it was enough to make sure that when the gunpowder was ladled into the gun, it did not do what it was supposed to do. So artillerymen preferred to transport the constituents separately and mix them on arrival in the siege lines – not an easy task on a wet day, and positively hazardous on a dry, breezy one, with the occasional flaming arrow or pot of Greek fire coming over from the castle walls, quite apart from the careless cook who would insist on trying to roast an ox close by. Even if conditions were perfect, the serpentine could still ignite through the very friction of the mixing process.

The subsequent invention of corned gunpowder about 1425 did not solve all the artillerymen's problems overnight, although it did make things somewhat easier. Corned gunpowder involved mixing saltpetre, sulphur and charcoal into a soggy paste and then sieving and drying it, so that each individual grain or 'corn' contained the correct proportion of ingredients. The process not only obviated the need for mixing in the field, it also resulted in more efficient combustion, thus improving power, range and accuracy. But being more violent in action, it was now more likely to explode the gun. Of course, it was still subject to accidental ignition while being handled in the siege lines and it was still susceptible to damp – and many castles were situated overlooking rivers or swamps.

The cannon or bombards could themselves weigh up to 664 kilograms. They had no wheels, so they had to be transported on waggons and erected in position on timber-framed beds. That meant that they had to be manhandled across rivers, through marshes, even up cliffs to get within range of the target.

How much easier it was for the castellan to employ his cannon. He could import them in peacetime, the waggons crossing local natural hazards and arriving at the castle gate via bridges and a proper road – which in time of siege would be either destroyed or dominated by the fortress artillery. Once mounted on the strongest ramparts of the castle, they could be left there until required. All through the years of peace, a regular contract steadily accumulated a stockpile of stone or iron shot, sufficient for any emergency. The same applied to gunpowder, which could be kept safe and dry in magazines, and only taken out in small quantities when actually required. Of course, supply was not always such a smooth procedure, and there were plenty of opportunties for corruption of officials and the sale of inferior products, but generally the acquisition of the new munitions could be more easily accomplished by people inside a stronghold than by those who attempted to besiege it.

In the actual storming of a castle, too, the advantages of gunpowder lay with the defenders. All the devices of merlon and embrasure, murderhole and machicolation, portcullis and concentric curtain walls, all worked just as well for firearms as they did for hand-propelled missiles. The man up a scaling-ladder was in no position to reload his piece once he had discharged it, while one marksman behind the battlements could keep firing away as fast as comrades reloaded and handed fresh weapons to him. Meanwhile, the altitude of the cannon on the castle towers enabled them to outrange the artillery at ground level, the solid shot dismounting enemy pieces, smashing into beffroys (the belfries or siegetowers), shattering scaling-ladders placed against a neighbouring tower and tumbling a score of men into a rocky ditch or swampy moat far below. And if the besiegers did gain a foothold on the curtain wall, they could be swept from it by a single charge of grapeshot or langridge (small balls, nails or miscellaneous hardware) which killed and maimed, but left property intact.

Obviously not all castles were suitable for mounting cannon; their curtain walls might be too narrow to permit safe recoil, or the stoutest roofed or most easily strengthened part of the building might not command a good field of fire. Arrow-loops had to be adapted to permit the

discharge of firearms (either pistols or long-barrelled musket-type weapons). This usually took the form of a round hole at the base of the arrow-slit, which – if already serving both long-bow and crossbow – invariably became known as a 'cross-and-orb'. For larger artillery the arrow-loops were opened out into full-scale embrasures. Blocked with shutters when not in use, the inward part had to be made splayed very wide, to enable the gunners to traverse their weapon.

Bodiam Castle was designed to make defensive use of the new invention of gunpowder. It was of late construction, Sir Edward Dalyngrigge being granted licence to build and crenellate by Richard II in 1385. It was also designed to inhibit the attackers' employment of gunpowder. The moat ensured that no undermining tunnels could be

47 *A row of gun-loops above longbow arrow-loops in the Byward Tower. There are two theories regarding the origin of the name of this part of the Tower of London. It was either 'By-the-Ward' or it was the place where the 'byword' or password was given before entering the fortress.*

48 *With lily-covered moat, crenellated towers and leafy prospect, Bodiam is everybody's picture of a medieval English castle. In fact, it is one of the least typical of British fortresses.*

The position of the chapel is denoted by the large decorated-style east window. The small watchtower just visible above that window belongs to the gatehouse over the postern gate and bridge to the south. That range of buildings from the chapel right round to the obscured south-west tower, made up the lord's quarters. They contained the Lord's Hall and Great Chamber. The flues from the latter's fireplaces were led up through the square east tower, thus helping to heat the upper rooms in that section. The Lord's Quarters were fortified as a separate unit within the castle, the wall, kitchen and food stores being accessible only to his personal servants.

The separateness of the Lord's Quarters is assumed to have been because of the uncertain temper of mercenary retainers when they were not paid. In fact, it is possible that that extra fortification might have been to keep out the non-resident refugees if they felt that the lord and his entourage were getting more than their fair share of the available rations.

dug, while the near-miss splashes of rocks thrown down from the battlements must have drenched any gunpowder being carried by the assailants. Nevertheless, wet moats could be something of a mixed blessing. They were inconvenient in peacetime, which meant that unofficial bridges were often erected – with subsequent argument and indecision about the best moment to chop them down in an emergency. And unless the moat were fed by a fast-flowing river it could freeze over in winter and present an all-the-year-round health hazard in both peace and war.

Access to the north-facing main entrance was via an artificial octagonal island and barbican just off the right of the picture. The linking drawbridges and causeways were originally laid out in dog-leg fashion, so that an attacker had to make his approach with his right side exposed to fire from the battlements. The massive gatehouse is composed of two square towers, the door itself being protected by a portcullis. At the foot of these towers can be glimpsed the gunloops, round holes for gun barrels, with vertical sighting slits above. Any hope of cover in the dead ground between the towers was denied the enemy by murder-holes in the arched machicolation supported by corbels high above his head.

Bodiam is an impressive-looking castle, its walls rising 12.5 metres above the water, with the towers 5.8 metres above that. However, its construction does betray certain weaknesses. Its walls were only two metres thick, and contain too many angles, which concealed dead ground and were vulnerable to battering rams. The machicolation should have been carried all the way round to have been effective against rafted engineers attacking the walls. Bodiam, therefore, could not have withstood a serious siege, but it was not intended to do so. It was not a royal or baronial stronghold, a base for operations, but a refuge affording temporary shelter for the local people and their valuables during French raids on the Sussex coast and up the River Rother. Such corsairs carried little in the form of siege equipment, and every minute they were held at bay gained time for a relief force to come to the rescue.

However, the new weapon of cannon and gunpowder was not only employed in the defence of castles, but could also be used to cover sorties by the garrison, while the castles themselves could be utilised as armouries for the peacetime storage of gunpowder, cannon and firearms for the king's field army. The invention of gunpowder in no way diminished the role of the medieval castle or fortified city as a stronghold, a base for operations.

Both cannon and gunpowder improved as the fifteenth century wore on, and it was in the Siege of Constantinople in 1453 that the new weaponry achieved its most spectacular success.

The city had been attacked in 1422 during the Turkish invasion of Europe, but the Ottomans sustained heavy losses in two months of assault and counter-attack. Eventually their leader (Amurath II) had to take his army off to put down a revolt elsewhere in his empire. But on 6 April 1453 the Great Siege began when 60,000 Turks surrounded Constantinople. Well-stocked with provisions and water, the 7,000 Byzantines expected to hold out almost indefinitely, but the Ottomans made great use of cannon. Often only capable of seven rounds a day, because they overheated and burst, these bombards fired in rotation to maintain a ceaseless horizontal hammering of the weakest points in the Land Walls. The first breaches were made on 18 April – and were repulsed.

One of the factors in the successful defence of Constantinople on previous occasions had been Byzantine sea power. On a large, strategic scale, that had prevented the enemy simultaneously blockading both the Dardanelles (from the Mediterranean) and the Bosphorus (from the Black Sea). Tactically, the peninsula on which Constantinople stands was protected by a series of booms, chains and blockships across the entrance to the Golden Horn. This time, the Turkish ships and coastal fortifications controlled the sea approaches to Constantinople, and in late April 1453, the Ottoman leader (Mehmet II) ordered a road to be built around Galata, the fortifications on the shore opposite Constantinople itself. It was eight kilometres in length; greased rollers were laid down, and the Turkish fleet dragged overland, so that the ships

could be launched into the Golden Horn. Now the Turks could deliver an assault on the city from that direction, as well as from the Sea of Marmara, and from the landward side. These commenced on 29 May, but even these failed until a commando party of Janissaries (the élite Christian bodyguard of the Turkish Sultan) discovered a long-forgotten passage which led under the walls into the city – and Constantinople was doomed. The last emperor, Constantine Palaeologus XI, was killed in the battle. His head was cut off and taken to various parts of the Ottoman Empire, so that everyone should know that the last emperor was no more.

The bombards employed by the Turks against the walls of Constantinople were unwieldy weapons. The contribution of Charles VIII of France to siege warfare was the introduction in 1494 of wheeled artillery of lighter weight and higher muzzle velocity, with barrels which could depress and elevate, firing iron cannonballs. The wheels not only made for easier transportation, but also

49 *Although the Dardanelles Gun was not cast for Sultan Mehmet II until 1464, it is typical of the breechloading bombards employed in the Siege of Constantinople. It was presented to Queen Victoria in 1867 and can now be seen at the Tower of London.*

Note the entrance to the White Tower in the background, the staging being a modern equivalent of the original wooden approach to the Norman doorway several metres above ground level. On the batter (or sloping plinth) of the White Tower, to the left of the Dardanelles Gun, can be glimpsed one of the Tower ravens.

enabled gunners to traverse their pieces and to trundle them around the siege works to take advantage of any fleeting opportunity. This mobility, plus the accuracy of depression and elevation, enabled all the artillery to concentrate on just one spot on the curtain wall, delivering an uninterrupted series of horizontal hammer-blows, which eventually disintegrated the stone-work.

50 *Renaissance thought devoted to military study produced a variety of devices, such as these two instruments of escalade invented by Capitaine Ambroise Barchot in 1587.*

To use the one on the right, the soldier put his feet in the stirrups and raised the handles. Locking them, he pulled his feet up, utilising his knee to lock and unlock the stirrups. He then repeated the manoeuvre until he reached the top.

To use the one on the left, the soldier knelt on the

pads and hoisted himself up by the pulley. The author has not personally tried the efficacy of such a device, but he suspects that such a feat may be contrary to the laws of physics.

Whether feasible or not, such gadgets could only be used by one man at a time and such a method of gaining access could only be employed by a small and stealthy commando party. It is unlikely that wideawake defenders would have permitted the undisturbed operation of such complicated machines.

Conversely, wheels were of no particular advantage to the artillerymen on the castle walls. Even that refinement would not permit them to move their guns from one place to another in a hurry, not up and down stairs and from one tower to another. However, the defenders were better able to make employment of another use of gunpowder, which came into service about this time.

One of the standard methods of breaching a fortress wall was to dig a tunnel under it and remove the foundations, shoring up the space with timbers which were then set on fire. When they collapsed, so did the wall. Now kegs of gunpowder could be detonated at the end of the tunnel to let the explosion blast away the solid foundations instead of excavating them by hand. It was a double-edged weapon, for the defenders could dig a counter-mine tunnel under or alongside the enemy's work and thus entomb the miners and seal the mine. That was done by John Vrano during the Turkish siege of Belgrade. A sophisticated refinement was employed by the Venetian defenders of Padua in 1509, when they tunnelled under their own walls at the exact point where the Holy Roman Emperor Maximilian I's guns were concentrating. In due course, the walls collapsed and as the victorious Spanish and Germans swarmed in to loot and kill, the Paduans detonated the mine, annihilating the attackers.

But in most cases the explosive mine was a means of breaching – not defending – fortress walls. In fact, it was so frequently employed that in the terminology of war, a 'mine' eventually came to be regarded as the explosive device, rather than the hole in which it was laid.

A specialised refinement of the explosive mine was the petard for use above ground. It was a conical cask or other container of gunpowder. Some valiant soul had to rush forward and place the wide end against the enemy's gate. Having survived everything the people on the walls could fire and throw at him, he had to decide upon the best length of fuze to ignite. The right length and he was able to run back through the gunfire, while the petard's cone focused the force of the explosion onto the gate and blew it in. Too long – and the enemy could extinguish it by pouring water down through a meurtrière above the gate. Too short – and the attacker would be literally hoist with his own petard.

The high-trajectory mortar was another weapon developed in the gunpowder age. It was a short, fat cannon of near-vertical elevation, which enabled projectiles to be lobbed up over the highest wall, to come plunging down into the fortress. Stone cannonballs shattered like shrapnel, but iron cannonballs merely buried themselves in the castle's parade-ground. It was not until the development of the explosive shell, which could be ignited before firing, that the mortar came into its own as a siege weapon. From then on, no place in the fortress was safe from plunging fire.

By now it was obvious that something would have to be done by castle-builders if they were to stay alive. The first attempts involved thickening the walls of existing castles, a measure which soon reached practical limits. Another idea was to thicken and curve the merlons on the battlements, this area being particularly vulnerable to near-horizontal fire (which was how cannonballs arrived at the top of their trajectory, if the gun had been elevated correctly). The stonework of towers and walls could also be shaped either with curving or oblique faces. But these were temporary measures. Special castles would have to be constructed to take account of all the aspects of the development to date of gunpowder, cannon and small arms – and the formation of large, standing armies.

CHAPTER TWELVE

Renaissance and Reformation

With all speede and without sparing any cost, he builded
castles platfourms and blockhouses in all needful places of
the Realme.
(Lambarde, of Henry VIII)

King Henry VIII of England was blessed with many accomplishments and fired with many enthusiasms, one of which was his fleet. Great seagoing ships armed with great guns, they would both impress foreign ruler and subject, and serve as a floating weapons system, keeping the invader far away from the coasts of England. (Any distance beyond three miles was then considered far away. That was the extreme range a cannon-ball could reach, skipping across the waves on a favourable day; which was why territorial waters were limited to three miles – or about five kilometres.)

However, every ship has to put into harbour some time, and that was when fleets of sailing warships were most vulnerable. In restricted waters, their masts and yards struck down, they could not manoeuvre, even if there were room to do so. Their gunpowder was sent ashore because of the fire hazard while refitting, so they were in no state of self-defence. And all round them were warehouses, magazines and offices full of gunpowder, tar, wooden spars and masts, cordage, sailing instructions, flags and bunting, documents and drawings, navigational instruments, food, clothing and money, not just for the ships at present in dock, but reserve stockpiles for many years hence. An enemy attack on any one of the royal dockyards could ruin Tudor foreign policy and lay England open to invasion, certainly for the rest of Henry's reign and perhaps for the duration of his dynasty – if it survived such foreign aggression at all.

The threat of invasion was very real in 1539. Four years earlier, Henry VIII had declared himself Supreme Head of the Church in England. His suppression of the monasteries and rough handling of opponents to his measures demonstrated that this was no passing enthusiasm for religious disputation. Nor could there be any hope of Roman Catholic revival in England; only external action could guarantee that. Besides, Catherine of Aragon, whose divorce from Henry VIII had started the whole affair, was the aunt of the Holy Roman Emperor Charles V.

In December 1538 the pope excommunicated Henry VIII, which meant that all faithful Englishmen were bound by conscience to rebel against their monarch. At the same time, Charles V and Francis I (King of France) joined forces in preparing for the invasion of England.

Henry VIII therefore ordered the construction of a series of castles to dominate the sea approaches to the most vulnerable harbours and likely landing places. The significant word is 'dominate'. With an artillery range of five kilometres, a ship trying to sail past one of these forts, could be under fire for ten kilometres – at least an hour, and very probably much more. Admittedly the ship could fire back, but unless it obtained a direct hit on one of the cannon, the castle would appear unscathed. The ship, however, could easily be dismasted and wrecked with the loss of all her crew and the troops on board. Even if the enemy task force managed to land the assault troops, their movements would be circumscribed or delayed by the new forts and by existing castles – and they would still have to deal with Henry VIII's field army. And at any time the fleet would appear to attack the enemy supply ships upon which the French and Imperial armies depended.

Henry VIII's coastal forts not only took account of the new weaponry, they also represented a new concept of military defence. There had to be living accommodation of greater or lesser comfort for officers and soldiers, but these buildings were not royal or baronial residences, in which the high-born castellan shared the rigours of siege with his own personal bodyguard, servants and their families. These forts were intended to be garrisoned by professional soldiers. There might only be a few in peacetime (perhaps a governor and 23 men), but they would all be full-time experts in artillery, engineering and logistics, a select cadre who could be relied on to discipline and train volunteers and pressed men in time of crisis. Meanwhile, the king himself would be in residence at his capital, directing the grand strategy of the whole war, hard-riding messengers ensuring that his army and fleet were in the right place at the right time. The forts marked out the board upon which the great game was played.

Whether or not Henry VIII actually saw his forts in those terms is immaterial; that was the practical effect of his strategy. It was certainly part of his character to take a personal interest in the details of things military. He was accustomed to studying relevant information from all over Europe. Architects, engineers and artillerists were among those who had either been persuaded to come to England or – unwittingly – had had their work reliably observed and reported by knowledgeable agents.

They had plenty to describe, particularly from Italy. Castle-builders such as Filippo Brunelleschi and Francisco di Giorgio had reintroduced the ancient idea of the bastion. It projected from the curtain wall or from the corners to fire anti-personnel shot at assault parties hard up against the curtain wall or the base of neighbouring bastions. Unlike medieval towers the bastion was usually the same height as the curtain wall and perhaps even lower. The caponier had an even lower profile and was virtually a fortified corridor running at right-angles across a dry ditch, so that musketry fire could be directed against any enemy crawling about at the very bottom of the wall. (The term 'musket' is being used in these chapters to include arquebuses and all other early long-barrelled small arms employed in these centuries.) Wide-diameter round bastions enabled several cannon to be moved around to deal with the enemy, but there was still dead ground in front of each bastion. Some bastions were ogival in shape, their plan view being like a pointed arch with the apex towards the likeliest direction of hostile approach, to deflect shot.

By now, the Renaissance had made military engineers well aware of mathematics and geometry and all the other sciences necessary for their trade. It did not take long for generals and draughtsmen to figure out that bastions with a vee-shaped ground plan were the most effective. With guns mounted in the base of the vee, no assault party could approach the wall without being fired at from the side. A development was to site the guns in a recess, so that they were screened from direct fire. This resulted in a bastion of arrowhead plan.

All these were Italian concepts of fortress design and they were the ones which would gain widest acceptance in Europe, but for the time being German experts were the dominant voice at Henry VIII's court in England. Albrecht Dürer's name – and that of Leonardo da Vinci in Italy – is often mentioned in the evolution of fortification. Certainly Dürer produced a treatise on the subject in 1527, but it is not clear whether he had any real influence on fortification. It is known, however, that the Bohemian Stephan von Haschenperg did. He came to England to work for Henry VIII – or rather, to work *with* Henry VIII, the king being well able to hold his own in any consideration concerning the governance, defence and welfare of his realm. The result of this collaboration was a castle which in plan form has often been compared to a Tudor rose – which if not a deliberate similarity, nevertheless must have taken the fancy of that proud monarch.

51 *A picturesque covering of dense trees may have grown up around the citadel of Spandau near Berlin, but they still fail to conceal the distinctive shape of a sixteenth-century Italianate arrowhead bastion. The castle was built on the site of a twelfth-century fortification, of which only the Juliusturm (a typical German Bergfried) remains. Casemates of a later period can also be seen. For part of its later history Spandau Citadel was utilised as a prison, its last occupant being Rudolf Hess, the last of the Nazi war criminals in custody and now confined in Wilhelmstrasse Military Goal. The Citadel is now a museum.*

In both plan and elevation, the coastal forts of Henry VIII and Haschenperg displayed a remarkable symmetry. There was a central stone column containing a spiral stone staircase leading from the basement and affording access to every floor. Daytime illumination was provided by a cupola at the top, with candle-lanterns being used at night and in the depths of the fortress. The items stored down there included gunpowder. To lessen the risk of explosion, the lanterns were positioned behind fixed glass windows which illuminated the magazine, but could not be

touched by the men working in that room. The lanterns were only accessible via a separate passage or lobby. Ventilation holes in the lantern-alcoves prevented the build-up of excessive heat and maintained a flow of fresher air to keep the candle burning. Even so, the illumination was very faint, but after a while eyes became accustomed to it, at least sufficiently well enough to cope with the issue of sixteenth-century gunpowder. Better a slightly short measure be weighed out than the whole fortress be blown up.

The spiral staircase was the vertical, central axis of a round tower comprising basement, ground floor, first floor and roof. The three upper levels were strengthened to carry cannon whose muzzles projected through embrasures in the walls. These latter were composed of smooth-faced, thick stone blocks, while the keep's circular plan meant that no flat surfaces were presented to cannonballs. The battlemented parapet was of much thicker construction than in medieval castles and was rounded vertically to deflect cannonballs up and over the heads of the gunners serving the artillery mounted on the roof.

The central tower or keep was surrounded by six semi-circular bastions of slightly lesser elevation, but of similar construction to the central structure. They were only accessible from the tower's first and ground floors. The roofs of these semicircular bastions each mounted more cannon, while their lower walls were pierced with embrasures to enable musketeers to shoot at anybody who tried to approach their base. Flues drew off the smoke and fumes of firing from these enclosed spaces.

This whole central complex of tower plus chemise of bastions, was enclosed by yet another six semicircular bastions, so positioned that their roof guns covered the arcs of fire where the upper cannon could not bear. An underground tunnel connected the ring of outer bastions to the central keep and the basement magazine.

The whole fortress was enclosed within an artificial ditch, wide and deep, and covered by musket ports from the lower levels of the outer ring of bastions. The ditch itself was surrounded by a low wall to prevent accidental falls in peacetime and to provide yet another obstacle to a storming party. There was only one entrance, over a drawbridge spanning the ditch and into one of the outer bastions through massive doors and a portcullis, while exposed to fire from embrasures and meurtrières. Even if the attackers broke through that bastion, they would still have to face similar obstacles when assaulting the central keep.

For these coastal forts were not only intended to exchange cannonballs with a fleet offshore. They had to withstand traditional investment, repelling infantry assault while their land-facing guns broke up siegeworks and smashed enemy artillery. Every minute the fort held out enabled the seaward guns to keep firing at the main body of the enemy's fleet, preventing it landing the principal assault, and gained time for Henry VIII's field army and warships to come into action. That was the plan, and in 1538, it had better be implemented immediately.

Henry VIII ordered his commissioners to report on the state of the nation's defences, analysed their findings, decided what had to be done, and told the relevant authorities what to do; whereupon they did it. Completely new forts were built at Sandown, Deal, Walmer and Sandgate in Kent, at Calshot and Hurst on the Solent, and at Portland in Dorset. Blockhouses (simpler structures often mounting just one cannon with a couple of musket-embrasures) were erected at Tilbury (two), and Gravesend (three) to protect the Thames, two at Cowes on the Solent, and one at Sandsfoot opposite Portland. Three new batteries were added to existing fortifications at Dover, while an old tower at Camber in Sussex was expanded into a full-sized fort – all that had been done by 1540.

It was an incredible achievement, even making allowance for the fact that Henry VIII's newly acquired monastic wealth meant that he could afford to spare no expense in implementing a crash programme of construction. But even if high wages gave them the incentive for working fast and skilfully, there was still the problem of organising such armies of labourers, making sure the materials were in the right place, switching gangs and shipments to new projects – all without benefit of telephones, photocopiers and calcu-

52 *An aerial view of Deal Castle taken on 6 September 1946. The square crenellation is not original; the faces of the merlons of 1540 being rounded in the vertical plane. Another later addition is the square strongpoint built under similar threat of cross-Channel invasion 400 years later. Battlemented to harmonise with the rest of the castle, it is clearly visible on the bastion at the top of this photograph. To its left repairs are being carried out to damage caused by a German air raid in the Second World*

War. Access to Deal Castle was via the drawbridge at the bottom of the illustration.

During its history Deal Castle suffered from coastal erosion and was also besieged by the Parliamentarians in July and August 1648. The Royalist garrison was well-provisioned and conducted a number of successful sorties, but eventually surrendered after the total defeat of an amphibious relief force.

lators. To a large extent, the Crown simply nationalised all that expertise which had previously been engaged in ecclesiastical construction and maintenance. Certainly much stonework came from that source. The country learned very quickly that religious allegiance had to take second place to the demands of the State, while those workers who tried to take advantage of the king's emergency by going on strike for more money at Deal Castle in June 1539 were put in prison.

After 1540, the immediate danger of invasion diminished, but there was no guarantee that Charles V and Francis I would not again make common cause against England. Accordingly, Henry VIII ordered the building programme to continue as a high priority. In fact, he personally visited a number of sites. Blockhouses were erected on Brownsea Island in Poole Harbour and at Harwich, but most attention was devoted to the construction of fortifications much farther west and north than previously. This was not just a matter of covering the flanks of the main network of south coast forts. Henry VIII's own father – Henry Tudor – had invaded England through Milford Haven. In 1497 (only a generation ago) the Cornish had tried to reject Tudor authority. And as recently as 1536 there had been the Yorkshire rebellion known as the Pilgrimage of Grace. Who knew what disaffection still smouldered in those areas? A Roman Catholic fleet at any of those places might perhaps rouse their local co-religionists to open rebellion again. The invader might even be invited to come!

Whatever the reason for his appearance, an invader would not get much of a welcome from the fortifications and loyal garrisons which Henry VIII decided to establish in those areas. St Mawes and Pendennis Castles denied access to Falmouth in Cornwall, while two blockhouses at Dale and Angle guarded the entrance to Milford Haven. The Humber was protected by a fort and two blockhouses at Kingston-upon-Hull.

Although all these Henrician forts involved some variation on the semicircular bastion idea, not all of them were as complex in plan as the basic design of Deal Castle described earlier. Not all of them were surrounded by an artificial ditch;

their low-level bastions could be pierced by splayed embrasures, enabling cannon to be traversed for aim against a passing target. Walmer and Sandown Castles were completed with simple central towers surrounded by a separate complex of four semicircular bastions. St Mawes Castle had a trefoil-chemise of three bastions, while Portland (which cost £5,000 to build) dispensed with separate bastions, two wings joining the keep to a curved battery pierced by five embrasures. Pendennis Castle was composed of a keep completely encircled by one continuous battery. Sandgate Castle's chemise of bastions formed what can best be described as a three-pointed ellipse. Camber Castle had five semicircular bastions, the connecting curtain walls forming shallow vees, with their apexes towards the enemy. This was taken a stage further at Hull, which was a square castle with two ogival bastions on opposite sides of the structure.

It can thus be seen that what Henry VIII was trying to achieve was the means of providing fire along every inch of the walls exposed to the enemy. And it did not seem that von Haschenperg's ideas could accomplish that. Even without practical considerations, there was no doubt another reason for Henry VIII's abandonment of the round compact castle which had been advocated by Haschenperg. He had divorced Anne of Cleves in 1540 and the king was temporarily dissatisfied with all things Germanic.

Henry VIII's acceptance of the mainstream of Italian fortress design is evident at Southsea Castle, begun in 1543. It had a square keep surrounded by a bailey, also square but at right-angles to the keep. The north and south curtain walls thus formed angled bastions in the Italianate fashion. The east and west corners were formed into rectangular gun platforms composed of solid earth and capable of mounting the heaviest cannon. A dry ditch surrounded the whole complex (or enceinte).

The last two purpose-built castles constructed under Henry VIII's programme were occasioned by the abortive French invasion of 1545. In spite of the tragic loss of the *Mary Rose*, Henry's strategy worked. His field army stood by to deal with the landing, but the French task force was unable to force a passage through the English fleet and its supporting forts. The French drew off and contented themselves with harrying the Isle of Wight before sailing away altogether. To forestall the use of the island as a permanent base Henry VIII ordered two more castles to be built. The one at Sandown had a vee-shaped angled salient; the other at Yarmouth was given an arrowhead bastion. Subsequent additions to existing fortifications had similar bastions, usually made of earth to absorb the smashing impact of cannonballs. Impressive façades of brick or stone were simply thin retaining walls to keep the ramparts in position.

The British development of arrowhead bastions was continued in the last year of the reign of Mary Tudor (1558) and completed under Elizabeth I. These fortifications were located at Berwick-upon-Tweed, the English bridgehead on the Scottish side of the border-river. The whole town was ringed by a polygonal wall, with the arrowhead bastions projecting from the corners. The cannon mounted on them covered all the approaches to the walls; and without storming them, no army could could gain access to the bridge and thus cross the Tweed on the East Coast route to the south. Conversely, Berwick could act as a defended base – a springboard – for English offensives against Scotland.

CHAPTER THIRTEEN

The age of formalism

Walled towns, stored arsenals and armories, goodly races of
horse, chariots of war, elephants, ordnance, artillery and the
like; all this is but sheep in a lion's skin, except the breed and
disposition of the people be stout and warlike.
(Francis Bacon, 1561–1626)

In military architecture as in landscaping and
social behaviour the late seventeenth century was
a time of codification and formalism. From now
on the story of military architecture becomes a
babel of technical terms and bizarre geometry, as
can be seen in the accompanying illustrations
from an old work on fortification.

Most land campaigns during the late seventeenth and early eighteenth centuries and, to a
certain extent, those at sea as well, were influenced by rules as complex and as formal as those
which governed military architecture. The guard-
ing of flanks and lines of communications,
march, withdraw and countermarch, all preceded
the actual battles.

Some of the bigger fortresses were urban
strongholds, centres of weapons manufacture or
places where armies were billeted and administered. Very often, these cities were ringed about
with other forts, so positioned on the major road
and river systems that no army could advance
into disputed territory without encountering at
least one of these strongpoints. To deploy against
it, the invader had to first reduce its neighbouring
fortresses – and so on.

Yet even the mightiest stronghold could be
surrendered honourably if presented with overwhelming odds. In the previous century's wars of
religion, the aim had been to exterminate the
enemy to save his soul and prevent his canker

spreading through your own people. Now, the
aim was the calculated exercise of power over the
chessboard of Europe. It could be done by
marriage alliance, by bribing other monarchs,
through commercial sanction, or by war – war
which could be halted at any time if one of the
other ploys seemed more advantageous. Fortresses were captured, only to be exchanged at the
conference table for some far-distant colony,
repossessed from a token garrison, dismantled,
and then rebuilt. Warfare of the late seventeenth
and early eighteenth centuries might not have
seemed much like a civilised game to the survivors of a storming party blown up by the
explosion of a mine, nor to villagers watching
their pillaged homes burn. But to their rulers it
was as orderly as the formal gardens which
surrounded their well-regulated palaces.

There were some exceptions who chose to
make an effort to be particularly close to their
armies, but most kings were now completely
remote from non-ceremonial military life. After
all, it was but one of the many affairs of state.
Kings had experts to deal with finance, agri-
culture, food, entertainment, everything. So generals were accepted as military experts and, provided they won the right battles and did not get
too high an opinion of themselves, they could be
left to get on with their job. And so the late
seventeenth century saw the rise of non-royal

Fig. I.
FORTIFICATION
Irregular

PLATE V

FORTIFIED PLACE

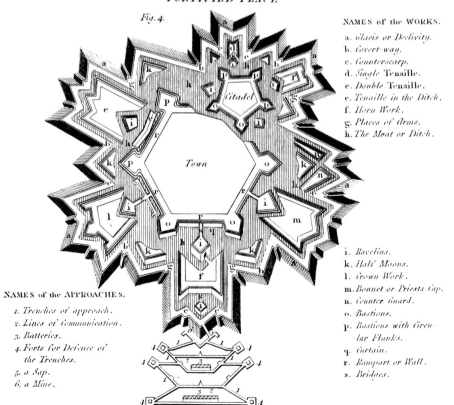

Fig. 4.

Citadel

Town

NAMES of the WORKS.

a. *Glacis or Declivity.*
b. *Covert-way.*
c. *Counterscarp.*
d. *Single* Tenaille.
e. *Double* Tenaille.
e. *Tenaille in the Ditch.*
f. *Horn Work.*
g. *Places of Arms.*
h. *The Moat or Ditch.*

i. *Ravelins.*
k. *Half Moons.*
l. *Crown Work.*
m. *Bonnet or Priests Cap.*
n. *Counter Guard.*
o. *Bastions.*
p. *Bastions with Circu-*
    lar Flanks.
q. *Curtain.*
r. *Rampart or Wall.*
s. *Bridges.*

NAMES of the APPROACHES.

1. *Trenches of approach.*
2. *Lines of Communication.*
3. *Batteries.*
4. *Forts for Defence of*
    the Trenches.
5. *a Sap.*
6. *a Mine.*

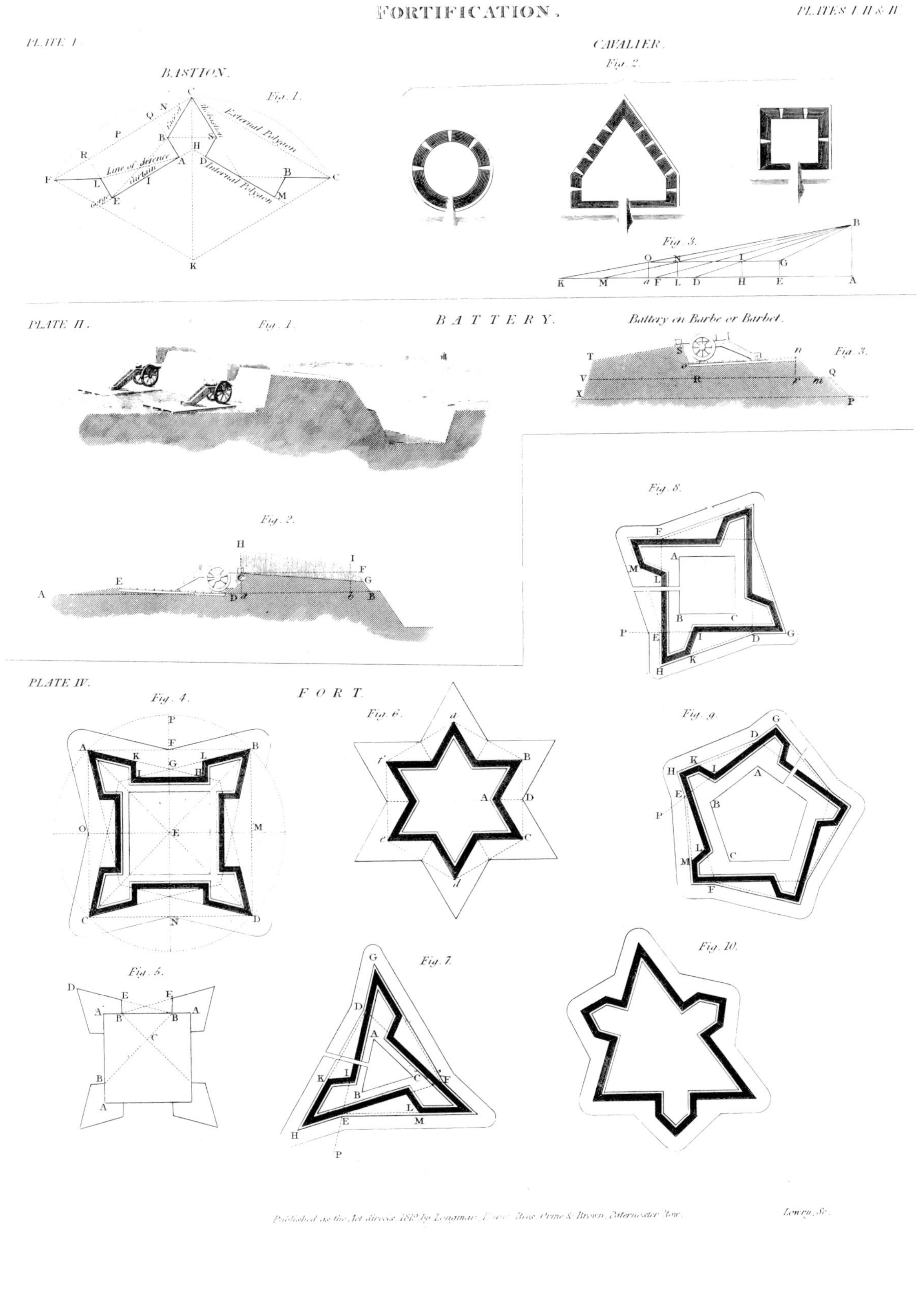

FORTIFICATION.

PLATE I.

BASTION.

Fig. 1.

CAVALIER.

Fig. 2.

Fig. 3.

PLATE II.

Fig. 1.

BATTERY.

Battery en Barbe or Barbet.

Fig. 3.

Fig. 2.

Fig. 8.

PLATE IV.

Fig. 4.

FORT

Fig. 6.

Fig. 9.

Fig. 5.

Fig. 7.

Fig. 10.

Published as the Act directs 1812 by Longman, Hurst, Rees, Orme & Brown, Paternoster Row.

Lowry Sc.

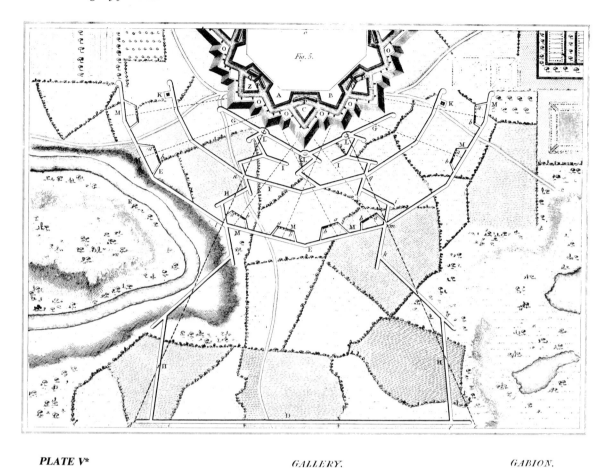

Fig. 5.

PLATE V*

GALLERY.

GABION.

Fig. 8.

A.B. *Bastions.*
C. *Ravelin.*
D. *Line of Communication of the Attacks.*
E. *First Parallel.*
F. *Second D?*
G. *Third D?*
H. *The Approaches.*
I. *Places of Arms.*
K. *Square Redoubts to prevent Sallies.*

L. *Traverses in the third Parallel.*
M. *Batteries a Cannon b Mortars.*
N. *Glacis.*
O. *Places of Arms in the covert way.*
P. *The Ditch.*
Q. *Bridge of Communication.*
R. *A River.*
S. *Rising Ground.*

53 *Technical terms of military architecture during the age of formalism.*

Plate V *shows a fortified place.*

A glacis *or declivity was a bare slope on which the attacker was completely exposed to fire.*

A covert-way *was a level pathway in front of the ditch, but lower than and covered by a parapet, where infantry could wait to break up an assault.*

Places of arms *were rallying points or command posts.*

A counter-scarp *was either an isolated caponier in the ditch running parallel with the wall, or a gallery let into the reverse slope of the ditch. Either location (reached by tunnel) enabled the defenders to fire on the rear of anybody in the ditch trying to attack the wall.*

A ravelin *was an island or isolated outwork in the moat or ditch, and in front of a gate into the fortress. It was accessible either by drawbridge or – if purely defensive and not part of the town's road system – by underground tunnel.*

Tenailles, hornworks, half-moons *(*lunettes*), bonnettes, counterguards, and* crownworks *were all species of ravelin, all designed to break up general assault, cover the approaches to each other, and, when finally abandoned to the enemy — leave him completely exposed to even deadlier fire.*

Cavaliers *were towers, or bastions, or other outworks of some larger fortification.*

Redoubts *were completely independent fortlets.*

Note that Plate II *shows the difference between a battery firing* through *the embrasures and one firing* over *the parapet and glacis, which is said to be* in barbette. *(A barbette was originally the tight scarf or neckerchief worn under the chin.)*

Plates V *and* V* *also show how such a fortified place was besieged. First a trench was dug to encircle the fortress, or as much of it as was necessary. Then trenches were pushed out at night in a series of* traverses *or zigzags, to prevent a single cannonball coming right along the trench. The front sapper was protected by a wheeled* mantlet, *while overhead cover was provided by a* gallery. Gabions *(baskets filled with earth) raised the height of parapet and parados along both the approach and the trenches which were pushed out on either side running parallel with the original encirclement. The besieging force then moved forward to the new positions and the whole procedure was repeated until close enough for a sap to be driven under the walls and a gunpowder mine installed. The* cannonade reached a climax, the walls crumbled, the gunpowder was detonated blowing the ramparts sky-high, and the assault troops stormed the breach and captured the fortress. Or, at least, one part of it. The whole operation might have to be repeated to deal with the next strongpoint or ring of defences.

generals like Marlborough.

In the specialist subject of military architecture, there was the Dutchman Baron Mennoe van Coehorn (1641–1704). One of his contributions to military architecture was the counterscarp gallery located in the reverse slope of a dry moat. Usually accessible from the keep or citadel by underground tunnel, it brought fire to bear upon attackers who had got into the ditch.

Another Dutchman, Sir Bernard de Gomme (1620–1685) was serving in England. And there was Sebastian le Prestre de Vauban (1633–1707). All these men benefited from the work of earlier engineers such as Francesco Paciotto d'Urbino, who built the citadel at Antwerp in 1567–8.

But it is the name of Marshal Vauban which is most famous. This is as it should be. He was not necessarily a greater engineer than his contemporaries, but he was a marshal of Louis XIV's France, the greatest power in Europe and able to command all the resources necessary to see any project through to completion.

Vauban joined the French cavalry at the age of eighteen. At that time, the minority government of Louis XIV (dominated by Cardinal Mazarin) was dealing with a rebellion of disaffected French noblemen supported by Spanish troops. Much of the campaigning (both then and in subsequent conflicts) took place in the territory bordering what is now Belgium, but was then the Spanish Netherlands. While still a cadet Vauban saw service on the walls of Clermont-en-Argonne and in the siegeworks of St Menehoud. By the time he was 22 Vauban had commanded the engineers repairing the captured fortress of St Menehoud, and the forces besieging four other towns (including Clermont-en-Argonne, which had changed hands). He was then appointed Engineer-in-Ordinary to the king in 1655.

Hostilities against Spanish forces did not end until 1659. Between that date and Vauban's death there also occurred the War of Devolution

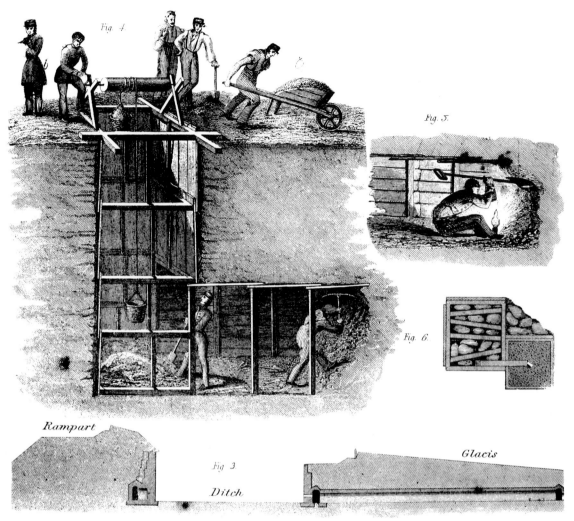

Fig. 4.

Fig. 5.

Fig. 6.

Rampart

Fig 3

Ditch

Glacis

54 *And as the activity illustrated in fig. 53 was going on the defenders were conducting their own offensive, rushing out from hidden sally-ports or digging their own mine under the besiegers' lines, as is shown in this picture. Admittedly these sappers are in nineteenth-century uniform, but the technique was the same from the fifteenth century to the First World War.*

over the Spanish Netherlands (1667–8), the Dutch War (1672–8), the War of the League of Augsburg (1688–97), and the War of the Spanish Succesion (1701–13). During all these conflicts

Vauban brought discipline and planning to the French Army's siege operations conducted under his direction. He co-ordinated the bombardment of individual batteries, deliberately employed ricochet fire to reach targets behind ramparts, and introduced the systematic application of 'sap-and-parallel' trenches, as illustrated in this chapter. These fieldworks enabled the besiegers to get closer and closer to their objective in comparative safety, until the time appointed for a full-scale assault. Such methods resulted in Vauban's capture of Maastricht after just thir-teen days of siege in 1673, similar success attending others of his operations.

Obviously, the enemies of France were not slow to realise the advantage of such techniques. To ensure that they did not rebound against their inventor, Vauban used the peaceful interludes between the wars to rebuild French fortresses in such a way that they could withstand, or at least delay, the type of siege operations he himself practised. Theoretical studies in geometry and mathematics established the best form these new fortifications should take, before practical construction began. This ensured that every angle of wall, ditch and approach was covered by defensive fire, mowing down the attackers as they struggled through a maze of outworks, and often just when they thought they were in safe shelter. It is said that 150 citadelled towns and lesser fortresses owe their defences to Vauban. That does not mean that he personally traced their lines and supervised their construction, but it is certainly an indication of his authority and of the wealth of resources available to the French Army under Louis XIV.

Vauban's successors, even in France, could not be so liberal with money, men and materials. In any case, Vauban and his contemporaries had built so well, while muzzle-loading solid-shotted cannon had reached the limit of development and the frontiers of Europe had become more-or-less settled, that there was hardly any need to design new types of military architecture. Besides Vauban was 'The Master'; it was heresy to suggest improvements on his work.

However, occasionally some fort required repair after bombardment, or a fresh strongpoint had to be erected in some newly acquired territory, which sometimes involved amendment to Vauban's ideas. The most significant was suggested by another Frenchman, the Marquis René de Montalembert (1714–1800). He wanted to mount guns in casemates instead of on exposed battlements.

Nothing came of his plans and it was not until the beginning of the nineteenth century that there was a new development in military architecture – in Europe, that is. Colonists in the savage wilderness had already been compelled to construct defensive strongholds much simpler than

55 *The magazines at Tilbury Fort date from 1716 and were strengthened with brick buttresses. Subsequent alterations included the protective blast wall on the right. When first erected in 1746 its door was opposite the magazine entrance, but later a staggered approach was adopted as further safeguard. The roof of the 1812 stables for the commandant's horses is just visible to the right. The huge mortar shells in this illustration were for the giant Mallet Mortar of 1855. Designed for the Crimean War, it was too big even for garrison employment. However, the use of smaller mortar shells meant that magazines had to be protected against plunging fire, the measures taken including brick and stone arches supporting a thick roof with grass-covered earth to absorb the initial detonation.*

56 *The officers' barracks in Tilbury Fort were built in 1772 and are typical of that class of domestic architecture of that period. They have undergone minor alterations in accordance with individual fashions and improvements in living standards. For example, in the nineteenth century, each was provided with a brick-built privy at the back, instead of a communal 'bog-house'.*

anything Vauban had ever contemplated. But that story is still to come; on 8 February 1794, it was a rather primitive dilapidated round tower on the cliffs overlooking the Gulf of San Fiorenzo in Corsica which was occupying the attention of the officers and men of *HMS Fortitude* and *HMS Juno*.

CHAPTER FOURTEEN

The Napoleonic period

I have taken upon myself to authorize Mr. Adam to engage
as many as two Millions of Bricks, and a number of
Bricklayers, and to proceed in forwarding Bricks to the
places mentioned in Brigr. Genl. Twiss's letter, without delay.

This I have done under the strong impression that all
possible dispatch was required.
(Lieutenant-General Robert Morse, 1804,
PRO/WO/55/778)

The tower on Mortella Point was about 12 metres high and 13 metres in diameter. It had a parapet fringed with loopholes and looked very much like a rook on a chessboard. There was nothing unusual about it. There were scores – perhaps hundreds – of such watchtowers scattered about the Mediterranean wherever Barbary slavers were likely to raid. Bonfires ignited on their roofs at the approach of the corsairs gave the locals time to run and hide in the hills. Indeed such towers existed all over the world. Some were square; some were round. Some were a century old and in reasonable condition. Those in the Channel Islands had only been in existence for 15 years or less, the earliest having been erected during a previous war with France. Some towers were of medieval construction, the Genoese being particularly prolific in their building, the largest of the type being the Galata Tower in Constantinople. Other towers were long ruined, dating from Roman times. They all represented a theme of architecture dating back to the Roman watchtowers on the German frontier (the *burgi*), the Celtic brochs of Scotland, and the lookout towers erected by the ancient Hebrews in the fields of Canaan. They served as sentry posts in time of war or when pirate raids by sea or land might be anticipated. When the violence of the enemy did descend upon the little community, some towers were big enough to serve as refuges for the villagers and their portable valuables.

These towers were therefore not considered as strongholds or bases of operations. Lightly armed corsairs might not be able to undermine the walls or bring with them a siege-tower capable of reaching the entrance halfway up the smooth wall or batter through masonry 4.5 metres thick. But poor mortar and stone put together by primitive labour was hardly likely to withstand a hammering by modern eighteenth-century artillery. Even if those walls did not crumble straightaway the undisciplined locals inside would soon surrender under that nerve-shattering cannonade.

Indeed, this same tower on Mortella Point had capitulated after only two hours' bombardment by the 32-gun frigate *Lowestoffe* the previous September. Since then the Corsican guerrillas entrusted with its defence had been ousted by the French, so the line-of-battle-ship *Fortitude* and the frigate *Juno* would have to repossess it again. The two vessels would sail past, battering it with a combined broadside of sixteen 24-pounder, twenty-nine 18-pounder and eight 12-pounder guns. They would then go about and deliver the other broadside, repeating the dose as necessary.

By the end of the day, *Fortitude* and *Juno* had been so badly damaged that they were sailing away with six of their complement dead and 54 wounded. Apparently the French had installed furnaces for heating shot in the tower. Red-hot cannonballs lodging in the ships' timbers were obviously unwelcome, but their use could also be hazardous for the gunners. The cannon was charged with gunpowder which was blanked off by means of sopping wet wads. The shot was removed from the furnace with special carrying tongs and handles, and rolled into the muzzle of the cannon – if it had not expanded so much that it jammed in the bore. The gunners then tried to take aim and fire their piece before the red-hot shot burned through the wad and ignited the charge. At best that would result in a miss; at worst a dismounted cannon with its crew lying dead and injured around it.

But the stouthearted gunners of Mortella Point knew their trade. The Royal Navy was driven off, so the army had to be called in. They found that the tower was invulnerable to infantry attack because the only entrance – naturally barred by a solid door – was halfway up the smoothfaced tower, only accessible by a vertical ladder – also naturally removed by the defenders. It might be possible to place a ladder against the wall, but only one man could present himself at the door at a time, and he could not get enough leverage to batter at the door without pushing himself backwards off the ladder – that is, if he had been able to get close enough through the defenders' fire.

Accordingly four cannon were emplaced just 135 metres from the tower. Their bombardment lasted forty-eight hours, the sole effect being to start a fire in temporary wooden breastwork built into the parapet. This, however, proved so hazardous to the gunpowder stored in the tower that the defenders agreed to surrender – all 38 of them. Their total armament had comprised two 18-pounder guns mounted on traversable slides firing over the parapet, and a single fixed 6-pounder firing through an embrasure.

Many of the senior British officers engaged in this operation subsequently took up posts whose responsibility included the *defence* of harbours, not their assault. Remembering the impregnability of the Mortella Tower they recommended the use of similar strongpoints for such purposes. This was the case at Simon's Town in South Africa, where two such blockhouses were begun early in 1796. Six months later another round tower (one of three) was commenced at Halifax in Nova Scotia. This modest programme was followed by a total of fifteen constructed in 1798 on the island of Minorca, a vital staging-post for British fleet and troop movements in the Mediterranean.

It is hardly surprising, therefore, that when Napoleon threatened to invade England in 1803 the admirals and generals charged with coastal defence promptly advocated the use of towers as 'Sea-Fortresses'. There were two main areas of danger: Ireland, with a possibly disaffected population at the same time as its garrisons were reduced for overseas service; and the Sussex and Kent coasts, nearest to Boney's Army of England encamped at Boulogne.

In many ways, the situation was similar to that in 1539–40, but . . . in 1803 the country was ruled by Parliament and not by a dictator, while the processes of bureaucratic administration had become as well-entrenched as any military strongpoint. The Royal Military Canal could be excavated by civilian labour under Sir John Rennie to obstruct the movement of French troops if they did get ashore. It was nine metres wide and was intended to be armed with cannon every 400 metres of its 42-kilometre length from Shorncliffe (near Hythe) to Cliff End (near Winchelsea). Most of the Royal Military Canal was completed soon after its proposal in September 1804, but that was because it was deemed an emergency 'fieldwork'. The crisis atmosphere in Ireland meant that the same category of 'emergency fieldwork' could be applied to the Mortella Tower-type of construction there, but permanent fortifications in England were quite a different matter. By the time all the various committees and boards had had their say, plans had been drawn up, submitted, altered, redrawn, approved subject to certain amendments, and confirmed, it was the spring of 1805 before the first 'Sea-Fortress' was begun, a total of six being completed by the summer of 1806.

Napoleon had long since given up hope of securing temporary command of the Narrow Seas, and the Army of England had marched eastwards, abandoning all plans for a cross-Channel invasion. Nevertheless Martello Towers (note how the name changed over the years) continued to be built until 1814, by which time a total of 103 had been completed in England stretching from Seaford to Folkestone on the South Coast, and from St Osyth to Aldeburgh in Essex and Suffolk. They were so sited that the single, long-ranged 24-pounder on each roof overlapped the arc of its neighbours. No craft could approach the shore without coming under fire. In addition there were three more in Jersey and a possible total of 56 in Ireland, plus two in Orkney in case American frigates tried to enter the convoy anchorage of Longhope Sound.

One of the puzzles must be why this massive building programme (costing perhaps half a million pounds or more) still went ahead when the reason for it had been overtaken by events. The obvious answer is that nobody could be absolutely certain of that until the end of the war. Even if agents had established that no full-scale French invasion were contemplated, it was still possible for commando-style raids to be launched – and Ireland was always a sensitive area; rebellion in sympathy with a foreign invader could never be discounted by the English authorities, no matter how loyal their Irish subjects actually were.

The second reason for the continuing building programme is allied to to the delay in its origination. The very bureaucratic process which took so long to set in train could not be easily halted or diverted to some other project. After all, contracts had been signed, people's livelihoods and industrial profits were at stake, and work had been put in hand – work which could not be abandoned after everybody had said how important it was.

One of the definitions of a Martello Tower is that its entrance (on the landward side) must be at first-floor level, about six metres above ground. Accessible in most cases only by ladder those Martellos which were surrounded by a dry ditch were equipped with a drawbridge. The Wish Tower at Eastbourne was one of these, although its doorway is now approached by a modern stairway. The windows were deeply recessed to prevent shot entering them from the seaward side, there being no openings facing the shore; they would have been barricaded over in the event of a French landing.

The water cistern, powder magazine and shot store were located on the ground floor of a Martello Tower. Down there all the fittings were of wood or non-ferrous metal to prevent explosion. Today a modern stairway makes things easier for visitors to the Wish Tower, but originally the only means of access to the magazine level was via a trapdoor in the first floor, where one officer and 24 men lived. In action, most of the soldiers would have been employed passing powder and shot from the magazine, through the trapdoor and up through the narrow staircase in the wall. It was finally handed out through a hole in a wooden door on the roof.

The Eastbourne Redoubt was constructed about the same time as the Martello Towers, but to a completely different design. It was in fact a brick-built circular fort, the curtain wall being made up of 24 casemates, only accessible from within the fortress. These storerooms, magazines and barracks were separate compartments, whose arched vaults supported a massive roof strong enough to resist exploding mortar shells and absorb the stresses caused by firing eleven heavy cannon.

It does not seem that the Eastbourne Redoubt was specifically intended as the linch-pin of the Martello system in the area, but its size inevitably resulted in its employment as a local headquarters. Although its garrison included infantry, these were for defensive musketry and skirmishing, not for wider-ranging patrols. Like the Martellos, the Eastbourne Redoubt was designed as an artillery firebase, not as a stronghold for offensive operations. The whole object of this coastal defence line was to delay and obstruct a French amphibious assault long enough for the British field army to engage those troops who had already struggled ashore, while the Royal Navy arrived to sink, take, burn or

57 *Martello Tower No. 73 at Eastbourne in Sussex, popularly called the Wish Tower, because it was located near a swampy area known as the 'Wash'. There were some variations in design, but the Wish Tower is a typical example of the South Coast type. It is about 10 metres high and 19 metres in diameter at the base, tapering to 12 metres at the top. Martello Towers were virtually solid lumps of brickwork, with hollowed-out spaces left for accommodation and stores. The thickness of the walls varied from 4 metres to 1.8 metres, depending on their height above the ground. Each Martello could contain as many as 500,000 bricks, coated with a cement and sand stucco to prevent assault infantry gaining any purchase for their grapnels or picks. The doorway is to the left of the photograph. The Wish Tower was originally equipped with a 32-pounder cannon, somewhat similar in appearance – though much smaller than – the 68-pounder of 1858 at present in position. The rear end of the slide would have been raised so that it rested on the pivot of the central traversing pillar. The gun could be traversed through 360 degrees. Its muzzle pointing downwards over the glacis slope of the parapet, the piece was said to be 'in barbette'.*

58 *This shows how the rear of the slide was raised so that the gun could be checked in its recoil for reloading and then slid into position for firing. It could thus be laid (vertically) onto the target, while training (or traversing) was accomplished by the back swivel gun platform. This 24-pounder is said to be 'in embrasure' at the Eastbourne Redoubt in Sussex. Beyond the gun can be seen the banquette or*

firing-step, which enabled infantry to fire over the parapet if the enemy had got that close. The garrison reached the top of the curtain wall via internal staircases from the barrack-casemates below, so that they would not be exposed to mortar shells falling into the open area in the middle of the fort. Today, the Eastbourne Redoubt is the home of the Sussex Combined Forces Museum, the only one of its kind in England.

59 *A total of 350 soldiers could be accommodated in Eastbourne Redoubt. This is a reconstruction of the*

appearance of one of the barrack casemates. Note the folding bed, overhead shelves and special stand for rifle or musket.

The soldiers living in Eastbourne Redoubt were kept warm by stoves, each casemate having its own. Underfloor ducting and wall louvres provided the draught and an early form of central heating. Each casemate also had its own food store and water supply, underfloor cisterns being filled by rainwater piped from the roof. Although the casemates were linked by internal corridor, each was virtually a self-contained barracks.

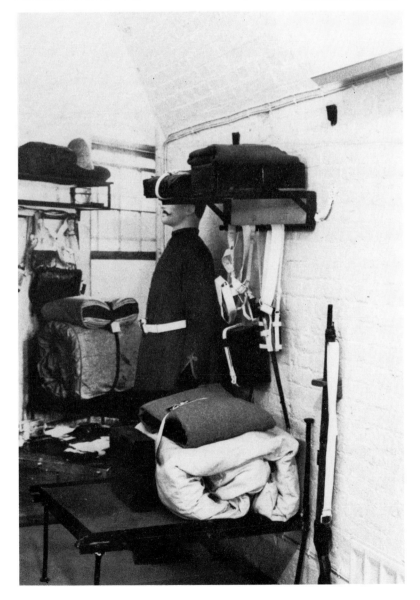

60 *The exterior of Eastbourne Redoubt is a single, massive, circular wall, devoid of all openings except for a single gateway and drawbridge over the ditch. Note the angled parapet (or glacis slope) at the top of the wall on the right, so constructed that it deflected shot up and over the heads of the defenders. Although now largely obscured in this photograph by modern buildings, the earth outside the encircling ditch was heaped up to form another glacis slope, exposing attackers to fire from the top of the Redoubt. The ditch itself was defended by five*

caponiers, fortified corridors projecting from the Redoubt. They had seven musket embrasures on each side, two of which were low down to cover the very base of the wall. Note the vent to allow the escape of fumes and smoke from inside the caponier.

61 *The interior of one of the caponiers at Eastbourne Redoubt. The square object at lower right is a modern heater installed as part of museum conservation.*

destroy the transports and landing barges off-shore. As strategic plan and tactical weapons system, it is an example of combined operations by two separate armed forces which is rarely achieved even in unified defence ministries.

Even further organisation was involved in the deployment of part-time militia units. Under the British system auxiliary defence forces were not state-administered, but belonged to – and were

paid for – by the county authorities. In peacetime, they were often regarded as nothing more than social clubs, but in wartime they were drilled to a high standard. Some Martellos were manned by regular troops, but it was the sort of employment in which the local militia proved very suitable, releasing regular army units for service overseas. Rotas ensured that somebody was always on watch, while every militiaman reported for weekly training and, of course, in emergencies. In effect the Martello system of coastal defence turned the whole realm of Britain into one great stronghold, a base of operations for launching fleets and armies against targets all round the world.

Another duty performed by British militia regiments during the Napoleonic Wars was the provision of guards for prisoner-of-war camps. Prisoners had been taken in previous conflicts, high-born ones being held – usually in some comfort – until a ransom had been paid. Common prisoners, though, were either stripped and abandoned to find their own way home or join parties of brigands, or were press-ganged into joining the victorious army. If they belonged to some heretical or infidel religion they could be slaughtered without hesitation. However, when wars started to be fought for specific objectives, not the extermination of the opponent, a more humane attitude towards prisoners of war was encouraged. At the same time, the growth of nationalism and the delineation of established boundaries made it more difficult for people to change sides even if they wanted to.

At first the numbers of prisoners involved was comparatively small; they could be accommodated in old warships, empty forts, or even billeted in private homes, any expenses being met by the 'home' government forwarding cash via intermediaries to the 'host' country. But this system collapsed with the advent of massed armies and navies of conscripts during the Napoleonic Wars. Every ship that could float was at sea, every fort was occupied, and nobody wanted hordes of Frenchmen billeted on them, especially when Bonaparte's administration refused to pay any contribution towards their maintenance.

Accordingly, purpose-built prisoner-of-war camps came into being. Most were wooden huts, arranged in avenues radiating from a central point where stood a square or hexagonal blockhouse. This was of solid timber, pierced with loopholes for muskets. Its upper floor mounted a cannon with a 360-degree traverse (like a Martello Tower). Charged with grapeshot, it made a formidable deterrent against rioting prisoners. Similar, but usually square, blockhouses could be erected at the corners of the camp.

However, the French and Dutch prisoners incarcerated at Norman Cross near Peterborough refused to be intimidated by any such device. They once staged a mass breakout by gathering quite peaceably at one side of the camp and then all leaning on the surrounding palisade, which gave way under their weight. Such incidents could be curbed by the introduction of what Americans later called 'deadlines'. These were light cords on small posts running parallel with the fence on the inside. Prisoners would be shot if they entered that forbidden perimeter zone without permission, which might be granted in such instances as retrieving a ball during a game.

But the only sure way to confine prisoners of war was in something like a stone castle, with all its fortifications preventing violent exit instead of hostile entrance. Such purpose-built structures were expensive and very rare – there are other things to spend money on in wartime. Dartmoor Prison is the most well-known of such prisoner-of-war institutions. Like the earlier hutted accommodation, all the cell blocks radiated from a central point which could be defended in the event of a riot, the whole complex being surrounded by a high curtain wall, patrolled by armed guards.

In later decades the blockhouses became lower in profile and more protected with earth. Eventually they were made of ferro-concrete, becoming the familiar pillboxes of two world wars.

CHAPTER FIFTEEN

A world of strongholds

I shall never forget the exhilaration of that moment, the men
firing and shouting like madmen.
(Ensign Walter Wynter describing the storming of the
Abyssinian fortress of Magdala, 1868)

The European wars of the sixteenth, seventeenth and eighteenth centuries were fought for reasons of princely prestige, religious freedom, national honour, community survival and economic rivalry. None of these conflicts were fought *in vacuo*, neighbours and allies being dragged in or bribed to keep out until eventually campaigns were conducted wherever rival subjects encountered each other. Traders or missionaries, their interests were defended and advanced by armies and fleets until every part of the globe became a battleground. The result was that European influence and power extended over the whole Earth. There was no people, no territory, whose natural resources were not developed and exploited by European industrialists; and no society whose culture was unaffected by European civilisation. This was particularly so in military affairs, foreign rulers of every kind, from Stone Age Red Indian Chiefs to the mighty Moguls of India, being quick to appreciate the advantages of European weaponry and organisation. Not that these other warriors were lacking in their own forms of armament, valour and discipline. And in the subject of military architecture the European soldier found much to marvel at in the alien environments he was forced to journey through and fight in. The most impressive of all such structures, indeed the largest man-made creation in the world – capable some would say, of being seen from the moon – was the Great Wall of China.

It has a rubble core of earth and small stones pounded into a compact mass and held in place front and back by a stone facing wall, rough-hewn at the 9.75-metres wide foundation and dressed stone above. Its height varies from 7.5 to 12 metres, with a crenellated parapet rising a further 1.5 metres above that. In some places, the parados – a backwards-facing parapet, and in this case, of lower height – was also crenellated.

In those respects the Great Wall of China was quite conventional in Western eyes, but what made it extraordinary was its length – 2,694.4 kilometres still standing. Its eastern end rested on the Gulf of Pokai near Chingwangtao; its western terminus was at Kiuchuan in the northern foot-hills of the Tibetan Plateau.

In 247 BC King Cheng began to reign in Ch'in, one of the seven feudal States which then made up what is now China. By 221 BC, Cheng had gained ascendancy over his rivals and had proclaimed himself emperor with the name of Shi-Huang-Ti. He reigned until 210 BC, an absolute dictator claiming total power over every man, woman and child, every soldier, administrator, trader, priest and peasant, every city, village, field, tree, lake and river. It all belonged to him, to the state.

It was during the reign of Shi-Huang-Ti that the Great Wall of China was built. Its accepted purpose was to bar the path of Hun invaders coming out of Central Asia. The Wall itself was broad enough for marching troops to rush to threatened sectors. In addition a network of roads radiating from the capital and provincial centres enabled reserves to be concentrated at danger-points.

There are suggestions that Shi-Huang-Ti's Wall may have been built along the line of an even earlier rampart, but all the same strategic, tactical and political factors apply to the Great Wall of China, as apply to Hadrian's Wall in Britain. Considering the totalitarian nature of Shi-Huang-Ti's rule it seems likely that the Great Wall of China was built as much to keep people in, as to keep invaders out.

Sections of the Great Wall were rebuilt under the Ming dynasty of AD 1368–1644, while what appear to be offshoots up to 500 kilometres in length may be deliberately planned switch-lines in anticipation of invasion, or fresh attempts to redefine the frontier after territorial acquisition or retreat.

Beyond China lay Japan, where the same sort of society which created the medieval castles of Europe existed for most of that country's history. At the top was the emperor, but executive power was vested in his vicegerent or *shogun*. Beneath him were the *daimyos* or local warlords, employing numbers of knights or *samurai* in their service. The rest of the feudal pyramid was composed of peasants, traders and priests.

Like European barons the *daimyos* built strongholds for themselves to accommodate their warriors and to impress their rivals. The earliest ones had simple stone ramparts like hillforts, but by the sixteenth century, they had become very ornate. Kumamoto Castle built in 1609 is a typical *hirojiro*, or lowland fortress. (A *yamajiro* was a highland stronghold of similar design, but plainer exterior befitting its harsher surroundings.)

The stone retaining wall around the base has a curving face to resist the heavy thrust of rain-sodden soil and to distribute the stress of earthquake shock. The towering levels of white walls and grey roofs appear massive structures, but in fact they were lightly built of resilient wood and plaster so that they could be shaken by earth tremors and yet remain standing. More solid walls would not have had such springiness and would have collapsed under similar shock. With-

62 *The Great Wall marches across the mountains of China. The watchtowers are clearly visible.*

in were stores for food, water and weapons, accommodation for soldiers, servants and concubines, private and official apartments. Some of the upper storeys were fortified with arrow-slits and – after the advent of Westerners – musket-loops. The base walls were laid out with bastions and dead-ends affording good firing positions and killing grounds.

Nevertheless, Japanese warfare was traditionally settled in the field, *samurai* swords and barbed arrows killing the enemy but leaving his property intact for the conqueror to occupy. As a result, sieges seem to have been rare and although very vulnerable to fire, many Japanese castles were spared military incendiarism, until the nineteenth and twentieth centuries. In 1877 *samurai* discontent with the rapid modernisation of Japan resulted in a rebellion in Kyushu, which was put down by a government army of conscript troops. During the fighting Kumamoto was besieged and badly damaged. During the Second World War many other castles suffered from air raids and a number were subsequently recreated in ferro-concrete, but otherwise in all their former glory. Kumamoto Castle was one of them.

Like Japanese warfare, Maori campaigns were conducted according to a certain code of rules which was reflected in the construction of their strongholds or *pas* in the North Island of New Zealand.

A *pa* was a fortified permanent settlement, the earliest – at Te Awanga (Hawke's Bay) – being built about 900 AD, soon after the Maori arrival in those islands. The defence reflected Polynesian origins, being a timber palisade, with interstices through which long wooden spears could be thrust to pierce attackers trying to force their way in. Then a terrace was built on the inside of the stockade so that the defenders could throw stones over the top. The earth on the outside of the palisade was scraped away, so that the stockade now stood on the edge of a steep little slope. A refinement of this ploy was to locate the *pa* on the edge of a cliff (see figure 64). Then came the idea

of rampart and ditch, similar to British hillforts. Multiple ditches and ramparts could be dug, and staging erected on top of the palisade from which missiles could be hurled upon the attackers. However effective these stages were in Stone Age warfare, the defenders were easy targets for muskets introduced after Captain Cook's discoveries in 1769. In later years the fighting-stages (*puwhara*) were abandoned in favour of solid earthworks.

Besides defensive structures, a *pa* contained storage pits for *kumara* (sweet potato), while *taro* (another root crop) was usually preserved in calabashes in *pataka*. These were store houses of various types, the most distinctive ones being on single posts and only accessible by one-pole ladders with the rungs projecting on either side.

A well-stocked *pa* would be a tempting target for neighbouring clans after a season of bad harvests. A watchtower was manned day and

63 *Kumamoto Castle in Japan.*

night, the lookout chanting watch-songs to tell the inhabitants that they were awake and to remind potential attackers that they could not take the *pa* by surprise. When danger threatened, the sentry sounded the alarm by striking a wooden gong. Those people who still remained in the *kaingo* (or unfortified village in the left foreground) would hurry into the *pa* and the defenders would prepare for battle.

When the *taua* or war party arrived, its members took up position on the open space in front of the *pa* to carry out the preliminary *haka* or war-dance, challenging the defenders to single or group combat with the *mere* (a single-handed greenstone club) and the *taika* (two-handed club). The whole affair could thus be settled without an attack on the *pa* itself. But if not, a frontal assault was carried out – a stealthy approach up the cliffs or a long siege was very unlikely. Sometimes the *taua* succeeded, some-

times it was driven off and sometimes the attackers pretended to run away, whereupon the defenders rushed out after them and a general mêlée resulted. Whatever happened, ownership of the *pa* was decided in battle without the deliberate destruction of the *pa* itself. Indeed, the very capture of the *pa* increased the victors' *mana* or moral authority, and decreased the opponents' *mana* by a corresponding amount. An additional factor in this acquisition of spiritual authority was ritual cannibalism after the battle.

Inter-tribal warfare on the North-West Frontier of India meant that most villages were walled with fortified watchtowers. The Afridi township seen in figure 65 had extra reason to suspect the jealousy of its neighbours. It contained a Pathan rifle factory producing replicas of the British SMLE, so detailed they included the manufacturer's number. The barrels were made out of old railway rails, the gunsmiths sitting on the floor

64 *A painting of a Maori* pa *by Marcus King.*

with the steel held between their toes, filing away by hand. The guns were sold to other tribes as the real thing – stolen from the British army – and were good for 200 rounds' firing.

Of much more sophisticated construction is the Red Fort at Delhi which was built in 1638–48 by Shah Jehan, Mogul of India. It was eight-sided, its walls being 33.5 metres high with a perimeter of 2.4 kilometres and faced with a ditch 23 metres wide and 9 metres deep. From its loopholes and battlements musketeers and archers could prevent any assault upon the person and the wealth of the Shah-in-Shah.

That was the theory, but in practice the Red Fort was besieged, captured and sacked in 1739 (by Persians who took the Peacock Throne to Teheran) and in 1760 (by the Marathas). By 1857, the last Mogul (Bahadur Shah) had been over-shadowed by the growing power of the British East India Company. He became the unwitting figurehead of the Indian Mutiny which began on 10 May 1857.

As soon as possible, the British army (most of whom were themselves Indian sepoys) began to besiege the city of Delhi, which was itself surrounded by walls and forts rebuilt by Sir Robert Napier at the beginning of the nineteenth century. Although the British were often outnumbered by the defenders and their external sympathisers who made frequent assaults on the British force, the besiegers held on. Reinforcements arrived, plus heavy siege artillery and equipment, but even after the city had been entered, bitter house-to-house fighting went on. However, by 20 September 1857, the Red Fort – the Imperial Palace of the Moguls – was in British hands.

65 *An Afridi township on the North-West Frontier of India.*

66 *The Red Fort at Delhi.*

CHAPTER SIXTEEN

On the frontier

It seemed almost improper, not to say illegal, to fight
without the Union Jack over our heads.
(Sir George S. Robertson, 1895)

When European adventurers began their exploration and attempted conquest of the rest of the world, it was inevitable that the fortresses they built should reflect those same functions as had characterised the castles in their own homelands. They served as bases for the military, administrative, commercial and cultural exploitation of the surrounding area; they were intended to impress and deter the local inhabitants; and they acted as refuges in time of trouble. The actual construction of these strongholds was subject to three main influences: the current trend in military architecture back in Europe; the local style of building, arrived at for climatological or other reasons; the availability – or otherwise – of materials, labour and time, for construction.

All these factors played their part in the nineteenth-century construction of small forts for the French Foreign Legion in the North African desert. Accommodating a garrison of 20–25 men, they were usually located near an oasis, itself invariably the crossroads of at least two trans-Saharan trading routes. These forts were built in a hurry by the legionnaires themselves, or by local labour, under the supervision of an infantry officer who had received basic engineering training. Even if a regular engineer officer was sent, he only followed the general guidelines he had been given; the rest was up to his own assessment of the local conditions.

These forts were about 25 metres square, and when complete were reminiscent of a medieval castle keep, with one, two, three or four corner towers. Hardly rising above the curtain walls – higher would have needed more solid construction and foundations – one was always used as a sentry lookout and combat command centre. Here waved the flag, its very existence heartening its own nationals, reminding the local people of foreign domination and forever challenging the sheikh and his warriors to put the matter to the test of battle.

Some forts were surrounded by a dry ditch, crossed by a drawbridge which, when raised, added extra strength to the door of the main gate. The approach could be further screened by a defensive earthwork.

The curtain walls of desert forts of the Foreign Legion were of rubble laced with tree-trunks (if available). This core was coated with mud, which – when dry – was given a layer of whitewashed lime plaster to repel moisture and keep the interior cool. For further habitability in such a hot climate the living accommodation was made as open-plan as possible, while the walls and ceilings were only thin lath and plaster or wattle and daub. Flowers and trees were planted inside the open courtyard to make the harsh environment a little easier on the eye. The barrack rooms, offices and stores backed up against the reverse side of the curtain walls in such a way that their roofs merged with the walkway (or allure) inside the parapet. About half a metre thick, the latter was pierced with rifle slits instead of being

67 *The wall around the Arab town of Goulimine in South-West Morocco.*

crenellated with merlons and embrasures. The latter were not necessary because the walls and roofs were simply not solid enough to bear the weight of cannon – that is, if it had been possible to move artillery across the desert. Certainly the Arabs did not possess it to any significant extent; nor were they organised or equipped for a lengthy siege. Desert warfare was a matter of fast-moving hit-and-run raids. If a tribe could not secure possession of a water-hole or prestigious property at the first rush, they usually made for an easier target before their water ran out and their camels

died. The besieged, on the other hand, either had easy access to the oasis, or had a well, storage cisterns or guttering and tanks to collect that rain which did occasionally fall. If they had enough rifles and ammunition to repel the initial assault, they had won that little battle – until the next time that the local tribe took a dislike to the alien flag fluttering over their soil.

It is probably no exaggeration in fictional films that when the rebel tribesmen do acquire artillery from somewhere, each cannonball or shell they fire produces spectacular destruction within the fort; such places were not built to withstand such punishment.

Conversely, farms, warehouses and churches

built with extremely solid walls and small windows to withstand the thrust of grain in bulk, with thick foundations to support tall belfries, or with outlying courtyards and walls for the retention of herds of stock, often proved formidable defensive structures in an emergency – remember the Alamo and Rorke's Drift!

Other residences were deliberately built with defence in mind. The Castle of San George d'Elmina was built by the Portuguese soon after their occupation of the Gold Coast in 1481–2. The arcaded gallery enables the governor's household to enjoy the cool breeze and shade. In a crisis defenders on that verandah can fire over the heads of the artillerymen on the lower wall and over infantry at ground-level rifle-slits. The whole system is a development of the medieval concentric castle. A counterweighted drawbridge

68 *This is a reconstruction of James Fort established in Virginia under Captain Christopher Newport and Captain John Smith. The stockade facing the James River was 128 metres long, the other two sides being 91 metres in length. Note the earth-filled, wood-revetted rounded bastions enabling cannon loaded with grapeshot to rake the front of the walls and the ditch. Besides the main gate, there appear to be small sally-ports at the side of each bastion. They are covered by small cannon on the inside, just in case hostile Indians force an entry there.*

There is a church, a well and small houses reflecting the simpler domestic architecture of the England the 103 settlers have left behind. Outside, the soldiers are drilling. Some are firing muskets or arquebuses, supported on stands, at practice targets. Others seem to be forming a square, but that is probably artistic licence rather than standard procedure for British troops in 1607.

69 *Castle of Elmina with its guns in position.*

completes the defensive arrangements on this side of the fort.

In 1642 the Portuguese were ousted from the Gold Coast by the Dutch. Their rivalry with England for its possession continued until the Gold Coast became part of the British Empire. By then the slave trade had been abolished and the cells in Elmina Castle where slaves were once kept awaiting export were empty. But whoever ruled and however enlightened their policy, the whitewalled Castle of Elmina remained on its hill, a perpetual reminder to the local inhabitants that

they were under foreign domination. The Gold Coast is now the independent State of Ghana.

In contrast to the Castle of Elmina are the British army's overnight perimeter camps, established when on the march on the North-West Frontier of India. These were about 30 metres square and were composed of a shallow ditch and a stone wall. The infantry battalion bivouacked just inside the perimeter; the transport and everything and everyone else within that screen of armed men. When the alarm was sounded because of a sweeping attack which was likely to storm the wall, pass right through the camp and out the other side, then the infantry manned the

70 *Castle of Elmina, showing its location above the river.*

wall without having to disentangle themselves from the rest of the camp.

To cut down on sniping, an outer ring of camp picquets (each a platoon strong) was established at places which were likely sniper positions. Besides provisions, ammunition and bedding, they were protected with a stone breastwork or sangar, plus a light trip wire.

On 21 December 1919 two companies (250 men) of the 3/34th Sikh Pioneers under four officers had piled their rifles and Lewis guns and were building a sangar on Black Hill (north of Jandola), when they were assaulted by 1,000 Mahsuds from dead ground 200 metres away. The covering troops were driven off, whereupon the pioneers grabbed their guns and took shelter in the sangar, still less than a metre high and only surrounded by a single strand of barbed wire.

Four Mahsud charges were stopped at the wire, but the defenders were running out of ammunition and the fifth attack broke into the picquet. The attackers were driven out with the bayonet. A sixth assault was another dangerous one, but it was abandoned when the covering force regrouped and screened the withdrawal of the survivors, 186 Imperial troops being killed or wounded.

A development of what was essentially a fieldwork, was the permanent picquet, as established in the Wazaristan Campaign of 1919–20, and the Mohmand Campaign of 1935. Most efficient were the 1/2nd Gurkhas protecting a road during the Razani Campaign of 1937. They had four strong, heavily wired picquets, each holding a striking force of one platoon, which patrolled the surrounding slopes by day and by

71 TOP *A view of Dalhousie Barracks in Fort William, Calcutta. From this base, soldiers were sent to garrison duty and frontier campaigns all over India.*

72 *The massive firebases laid out in Vietnam by the Americans were an updated version of the picquets established almost half a century earlier by the British army in India. Though small in size, picquets were as much stronghold bases of operations as much larger structures. This photograph of Duncon Picquet gives a good idea of what they were like.*

night, ambushing snipers or trailing them back to their village and shooting it up. If they got into difficulties, they could fall back to the picquet which was continually garrisoned by a machine-gun section plus, sometimes, a mountain artillery piece.

Of course, as the European nations etablished great empires their military architecture had to withstand the latest Western weaponry. Eventually their overseas works became as sophisticated as anything in Europe itself, although there was always improvisation in the wilder places on the frontier.

73 *Shargai Fort, a British outpost in the Khyber Pass on the North-West Frontier of India. Note that its plan is polygonal, in keeping with the forts built in Europe and America in the nineteenth century.*

74 *The Officers' Mess at RAF Station Risalpur in India, 1935.*

CHAPTER SEVENTEEN

The Industrial Revolution

Whereas, Abraham Lincoln, the President of the United
States, has, by proclamation, announced the intention of
invading this Confederacy, with an armed force, for the
purpose of capturing its fortresses, and thereby subverting its
independence, and subjecting the free people thereof to the
dominion of a foreign power; and whereas, it has thus
become the duty of this Government to repel the threatened
invasion, and to defend the rights and liberties of the people
by all the means which the laws of nations and the usages of
civilized warfare place at his disposal: Now, therefore, I,
Jefferson Davis, President of the Confederate States of
America, do issue this, my proclamation. . . .
(Proclamation by Jefferson Davis)

The Industrial Revolution began in Britain in the
later years of the eighteenth century. The har-
nessing of steam-power and its application to the
mechanical processes of manufacture resulted in
hitherto unparalleled output of all types of
weapons and equipment. Thousands of cannon,
muskets, uniforms, pulley-blocks and barrels of
gunpowder enabled the Royal Navy to keep the
seas in all weathers, continually practising tactics
and exercising the great guns, while the British
army was able to fight campaigns in every part of
the globe. There was still not enough – there never
is – and the supply system often broke down, but,
overall, the British armed forces and their allies
were much better off than their opponents.

Nevertheless, during that long conflict, British
factories were simply mass-producing existing
items of war material of proven efficiency and
quality; there was no time for experimentation. It
was not until victory had been won that the more
technologically minded officers could find time
to investigate the possibility of new types of
weapons and equipment – and to argue for their

introduction. They immediately encountered entrenched opposition. How dare anybody criticise
the wooden walls, the carronades, the Brown
Bess muskets, and the Martello Towers? They
had all beaten Boney; why throw them away for
some new-fangled gadget which probably
wouldn't work when you wanted it to? Besides
there were enormous stockpiles of weapons,
while existing fortifications were good for many
years yet. Nobody could justify the expense of
making new.

But, as the nineteenth century wore on, the
Industrial Revolution began to develop its own
momentum, especially after the widespread introduction of the machine-manufacture of ma-
chine-tools. The competition of free trade was a
forcing-house for the development of new processes in mechanics, metallurgy, chemistry, tex-
tiles, food-processing, communications and the
transmission of power. Many of these processes
had warlike spin-offs, while some industrialists
deliberately sought out military markets for their
products, making contacts among those techno-

logically minded officers who were now reaching ranks high enough to authorise the purchase of new equipment. Inevitably, these former 'Young Turks' became dedicated champions of *their* favourite weapons systems, resisting any change until they in their turn were supplanted by newcomers up the ladder of authority or until some international crisis precipitated a sudden spurt in the evolution of military technology.

For neither defeated France nor Britain's former allies felt any affection or allegiance towards the old-fashioned weapons and tactics of all-conquering England. If the new technology of the Industrial Revolution enabled them to win back what they had lost or what they considered a fairer share of the spoils, then they would avail themselves of it. This provoked a corresponding response from each nation's rivals, the race of development accelerating with each decade.

In 1815 smooth-bore muzzle-loading cannon could either fire a solid ball weighing 14.5 kilograms over a distance of 2,745 metres, or one weighing 30.8 kilograms over a range of 366 metres. By 1914, rifled breech-loading ordnance could hurl explosive shells weighing 879 kilograms over a range of 21.4 kilometres – and with a potentially greater accuracy than its predecessors of a century earlier. Small arms had developed from the smooth-bore musket firing a single ball every half-a-minute to rifled fully-automatic machine-guns spitting out bullets at the rate of 600 a minute.

The most obvious – though not necessarily the most significant – effect of the Industrial Revolution on military architecture was in the design of fortification. The problem was twofold: how to keep out the projectiles launched by the new weaponry; and how to install and operate that same equipment. As in the days of Vauban, the devices and stratagems became incredibly complex, while each new weapons system is worthy of a complete study in itself.

The end result was that by the beginning of the twentieth century the new fortresses had become artillery strongholds, bases of operations not for columns of infantry or cavalry, but for heavy shells whose delivery could destroy crossroads, bridges and railways over a radius of a dozen

kilometres or more. The targets did not even have to be within sight of the fort. Thanks to accurately printed maps, fire-control instruments and electrical communications, neither intervening hills nor the hours of darkness prevented a fort of 1914 from completely dominating the surrounding countryside – at least in theory. Properly sited, each fort helped to cover its neighbour with overlapping fields of fire. A ring of such forts could defend a city; a line of them could defend a frontier. Defence in depth, made up of a series of parallel lines of fortresses, strengthened by fortified complexes around manufacturing cities and communications centres, could turn the whole state into one titanic and impregnable stronghold.

This was the reasoning behind the French, Prussian and Dutch construction of the nineteenth century. Indeed, every European power subscribed to this strategic thinking in some way. Besides, forts, together with battleships, size of army and railway mileage, were symbols of national status. The emotive name of Verdun in France is a good example of such sentiment. Even the newly created state of Belgium, its neutrality guaranteed by all those nations which were likely to invade it, chose to put more concrete faith in solid fortifications.

From 1859 onwards Henri Brialmont embarked upon a building programme of staggering magnitude for such a small country. The whole of Antwerp was enclosed by a linked system of eleven lengths of fortification, the northern end forming a citadel with threefold function: it mounted a coast defence battery overlooking the Scheldt estuary; it served as headquarters; and it was the defenders' last refuge if the rest of Antwerp and Belgium had been overrun. Then came a ring of eighteen forts, redoubts and earthworks. Eleven kilometres beyond that came an outer ring of 31 detached fortifications, while the suspected German passage through the Meuse valley was to be blocked by 21 forts ringing Namur and Liège. The largest forts could accommodate a thousand men, plus 135 guns and mortars up to 21 cm (8.3 inches) in calibre. This means that if they were all fully equipped, something like 9,000 pieces of artillery would be

75 *The human figures give scale to the size of the ditch and double-storeyed caponier at Fort Widley. On the right is a sally-port to enable the defenders to deal with any enemy who may have survived their fall into the ditch. The latter themselves would be unable to get at the sally-port door because of fire from the caponier. Note the brick arches built into the masonry walls for reinforcement against bombs falling from high-trajectory mortars.*
Fort Widley is now a museum, open to the public during the summer months.

required, their operation needing the attention of 70,000 men, quite apart from 100,000 in the Antwerp garrison itself, plus however many were to make up the Belgian field army.

Obviously transcontinental countries like Russia and America, and the worldwide British Empire, could hardly hope to defend their extensive frontiers with continuous lines of fortification. Nevertheless, they followed the same poli-

cies of creating national strongholds, building fortresses to block the strategic approaches to vital areas of territory. Usually these took the form of coastal defences, protecting the vital dockyards and bases for those battlefleets whose success or failure would be the deciding factors in any global war.

Fort Widley on Portsdown was one of a series of polygonal forts built in 1860–71 to defend Portsmouth Dockyard from bombardment by French troops who – it was feared – might come ashore in Sussex and swing round overland instead of trying to force their way in through the harbour entrance. Everything was done to delay hostile control of Portsdown; every minute gained time for the Fleet to put to sea. Once beyond range of enemy field artillery, there was no doubt of Royal Navy victory over the warships and transports upon which the invading French land army depended.

In the event, the French never came, which caused the Portsdown Forts to be nicknamed 'Palmerston's Follies', after the prime minister of the time. The deterrent effect of such fortifications was completely ignored by his critics. In any case, they argued, seaport defences ought always to face the ocean. Exactly the opposite hindsighted argument was used after the Japanese had captured the naval base of Singapore by overland assault in 1941–2.

Of course, designers of nineteenth-century forts realised that the invader would have similar weapons to those in the hands of the defender. So, the fortress guns had to be shielded from long-range heavy artillery and from infiltrating infantry. Such was the rapidity of technological progress that each innovation was eventually shown to be ineffective, either in war itself, or through carefully contrived practical experiments, such as firing new guns at redundant Martello Towers.

Then there was Carnot's Wall, devised by Lazare Nicolas Carnot, who had been Napoleon Bonaparte's Secretary of War. This was a free-standing wall, about seven metres high and two metres thick, situated in the dry ditch surrounding a fort. It usually ran parallel with the main rampart of the fortress, which could thus be left at its natural angle of repose instead of having to be built with a vertical face and retaining wall. This latter arrangement would be better able to absorb artillery fire, while the Carnot Wall itself could not be damaged because of its location in the dead ground at the bottom of the ditch. It would thus provide excellent shelter for riflemen in the event of an infantry assault. In due course this was proved to be a vain prediction! More effective in covering the ditch were varieties of caponiers plus counterscarp galleries, with loopholes on the reverse slope of the dry ditch.

Of course, none of these anti-personnel works were any use if they could be penetrated or smashed by artillery. Thicker masonry was one answer. In addition, solid earth could be heaped up in front of the stonework and on top, to act as a burster layer (to detonate shells before they struck the fabric of the fort). Of course, care had to be taken not to obscure fields of fire. Indeed, the Crimean, American Civil and Russo-Turkish Wars showed that improvised fieldworks could be as difficult to storm as any purpose-built fortress.

And when trenches were properly laid out, reinforced with the occasional solid redoubt or blockhouse, manned by well-trained infantry with magazine rifles, and backed by field artillery – they were well-nigh impregnable.

But open-air fieldworks are not suitable as permanent mountings for heavy artillery, with their magazines, rangefinding and sighting equipment and accommodation. Such defence works have to be constructed and manned in peacetime; after all, their very existence might deter a potential aggressor from a pre-emptive strike at the very outset of hostilities. Indeed, some places were obviously impossible to defend with trenches, the seaward approaches to a naval base like Portsmouth, for example.

In 1863 the British solved that problem by building sea-forts on top of cofferdams (walls of piling forming enclosures from within which the water can be pumped out) and caissons (huge cylinders containing air at high pressure to keep the water out) sunk into the sea bed. Either system enabled labourers to dig out the subsoil and lay foundations in a comparatively dry environment. These foundations were of granite and Portland stone, forming a ring wall 16.3 metres thick and 70 metres in diameter, and enclosing a massive disc of cement-covered rubble. Upon this base was constructed a circular stone fort capable of mounting twenty-five 10-inch (25.4-cm) 18-ton and twenty-four 12.5-inch (31.8-cm) 38-ton rifled muzzle-loading (RML) guns, in two tiers. This armament could deliver explosive shells totalling 13.4 tonnes and capable of smashing through 30.5–45.7 cm of iron plate at about a thousand metres' range. The forts themselves were protected from horizontal fire by three layers of iron armour plate, varying in thickness from 4.6 cm to 6.4 cm, separated by two layers of iron concrete (a mixture of asphalt and iron filings or swarf). This energy-absorbing armour sandwich was bolted through an inner layer of wood and concrete onto the walls of the fort. The latter supported the iron gundecks without being fixed to them. The walls could thus be battered by enemy shot, without the shock jamming the guns. And, just in case the enemy should bring up high-trajectory bomb-ships, the roof of the Spithead forts was made up of concrete 1.4 metres thick.

This type of sea-fort was also built off Royal Navy bases at Portland, Plymouth and Bermuda. They were not all the same size, nor exactly of identical design. Some were planned to mount revolving turrets on the top, while others dispensed with part of the vertical armour plate if shallow water prevented warships passing by on that side.

These forts were virtually stationary ironclads, the resemblance to a warship being taken to an extraordinary degree in the construction of Fort Drum in the Manila Bay approaches to the American naval base at Cavite in the Philippines.

Beginning in 1908 engineers blasted away the upper surface of El Fraile island and honeycombed its interior with tunnels, store and accommodation spaces for 200 men. They then smoothed its top and sides, covering the entire

island with a concrete shell 7.2–12 metres thick, 106 metres long, 44 metres wide and 12 metres high. The armament comprised four 6-inch (15.2-cm) guns in naval-style casemates at the side, and four 14-inch (35.6-cm) guns in two massive,

76 *Extensions to Henry VIII's Hurst Castle (defending the western approach to Spithead) were carried out in 1870. Two huge wings were built, containing a total of 61 casemates.*

This is the western end of the complex, showing the armour plate which filled most of each embrasure. On the left, the other wing of casemates stretches away to the east, while the Needles Passage and the Isle of Wight can be seen in the right background. It was soon appreciated that the increasing range of modern artillery would have resulted in the forts on the two sides of the Passage doing more damage to each other than to the enemy warships in between. However, small strongpoints were built here during the Second World War; one can be seen on the right of the casemates, with observation and signalling positions on the roof. The angled structures carry samples of paint for weathering experiments.

superfiring naval-style turrets. Fire-control and signalling was conducted from the top of a lattice mast exactly like those installed in US battleships of the period. With a sharp end like a bow, and a blunt end like a stern, Fort Drum looked so much like a warship that it was often called 'The Concrete Battleship'.

Although Fort Drum was an army – not a navy – establishment, both it, Britain's circular forts already described, and the Maunsell anti-aircraft platforms and seaforts of the Second World War are really maritime rather than military architec-

ture; they belong more properly with dockyards, slipways, ropewalks and other buildings connected with the sea and ships.

More appropriate to this book, and more common in construction, were the casemate coastal defences, in which a battery of guns was mounted just above sea level to provide horizontal fire against ships entering a channel. Frontal protection was provided by sandwich armour, while earthen banks or the cliff itself gave overhead cover. Ramparts of soil were also a feature of coastal forts situated on higher positions to direct plunging fire down onto the decks of hostile ships, the latter finding it difficult to reply because they could not elevate their armament sufficiently.

77 *Hurst Castle is located on the end of a long shingle spit. The only access for heavy material is by sea, so the fort had its own quay. Unloaded there the ammunition and stores were trundled by hand along a light railway into the fort. This junction just inside the main gate (on the left) gives access to the magazine along the right-hand line. The track was also used for the distribution of ammunition from the magazine to the casemates, some of which can be seen on the right.*

Even so, there were always problems resulting from the need to store ammunition as deep under ground as possible, while mounting guns as high up as possible. The development of power-driven hoists obviously helped, but the time of greatest danger and complication was still during reloading, which always took longer than the actual

THE MONCRIEFF GUN CARRIAGE.

PLATE 1

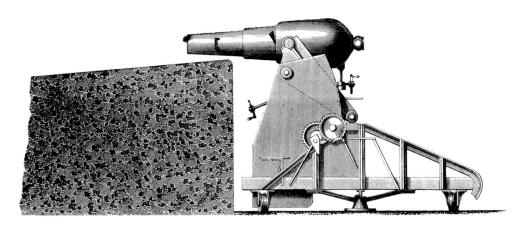

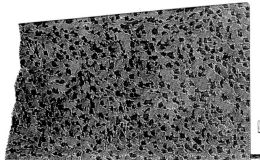

firing. This was especially true of rifled muzzle-loading weapons, when the entire piece had to be run back in and depressed below parapet level.

One answer was the disappearing mounting, in which the gun popped up, banged away and disappeared again. It certainly presented a very small target to the enemy and it was certainly very spectacular. It was the heavy artillery equivalent of the quick-draw gunfighter of the Wild West – and probably about as accurate!

Whether accurate or not, the disappearing mounting was only protected frontally; it was still vulnerable to plunging fire from mortars and from the longer range, higher trajectory artillery coming into service by the 1880s.

This may have been acceptable for coastal defence, the attackers only coming from one direction with low-angle guns; it was a different matter for artillerymen in land forts likely to be outflanked. So the Prussian Lieutenant-Colonel Schumann proposed covering the disappearing mounting with an armoured roof which went up and down with the piece, completely shielding the whole mechanism when retracted. Monsieur Mougin of the French Saint-Chamond munitions factory was also a contemporary advocate of cupolas, and so was Hermann Gruson of Krupp's. Umbrella-shaped cupolas hiding vertically retractable turrets became all the fashion in military architecture. And with the re-introduction of breechloading ordnance, cupolas did not even have to be retractable. In some types, the muzzle of the gun projected from something like an upturned metal saucer, which had all-round traverse and as high an elevation as existing mountings would allow. No matter how much it moved in any direction, the rim of the saucer was always concealed beneath an apron (or glacis) of concrete 2.5 metres thick, most of which was further shielded by three metres of earth. Indeed, the magazines, stores, workshops and accommodation were all cut out of the solid rock below and connected by tunnels. All was underground,

78 *The disappearing mounting for rifled muzzle-loading artillery, first proposed by Captain Moncrieff of the Edinburgh Militia Artillery in 1865.*

illuminated by electricity produced by internal combustion engines, electricity which also powered all the machinery necessary for living in and operating the fort. Once the scars of construction had been concealed by grass and a few bushes, the only military things visible were the low cupolas and the occasional ventilator or rifle-port. It was only if a hit were scored right on one of these very small targets that any damage could be done to Brialmont's Belgian forts. Admittedly in 1914 they were not of the latest design and were somewhat exposed, being made up of a central citadel with parapets to repel infantry attack, all set within a dry ditch, triangular in trace (or plan) and provided with counterscarp galleries. Nevertheless both armour and concrete used in their construction were believed proof against the 8.3-inch (21-cm) field howitzers which were all that could be deployed in mobile warfare at that time. Experiments suggested that a succession of shells could be placed fairly close together from a distance of 900 metres and thus gradually smash through the surface protection, but it was considered that the ideal conditions of undisturbed firing would not be likely to be repeated on campaign. During forecasts of the possibility of European war at the beginning of the twentieth century it was, therefore, confidently assumed that the forts of Liège could be completely relied upon to stop any German invasion of Belgium.

What was life like in such a fort at the turn of the century? One boy trumpeter in the Royal Garrison Artillery took part in the parade on Plymouth Hoe when King Edward VII came to cut the first sod of a new dock at Devonport. He recalls that two local infantry battalions were stationed in Crownhill or in one of the other landward forts which covered the land approaches to the naval base at Devonport. Coastal fortifications screened the seaward routes into the dockyard. The RGA headquarters was situated in the Citadel up on the Hoe. Plymouth was very much a garrison town; the Royal Navy tended to keep to itself out in Devonport, only patronising Plymouth public-houses on pay-night.

The boy trumpeter himself was posted to Fort Bovisand, on the eastern side of the entrance to

Plymouth Sound. About 120 men lived there, being responsible for the care and maintenance of a variety of calibres of guns, located in several batteries. These would only be fully manned by reservists recalled to the colours in time of war.

There were four 12-pounders mounted on the terreplein (or level area) behind the rampart of Staddon Point Battery, and backed by the then empty casemates which had been hollowed out of the solid cliff. That battery adjoined Fort Bovisand itself. Just over a kilometre farther along was situated Renney Battery, with its three 6-inch (15.2-cm) and three 9.2-inch (22.9-cm) artillery. Fort Bovisand also looked after what he remembers as the 13.5-inch (34.3-cm) guns at Penlee Point over on the western headland of Plymouth Sound. They had a maximum range of 12–14 kilometres whereas the 12-pounders were short-ranged pieces, so situated that they could deal with a hostile ship coming past on that side of the breakwater.

A small naval vessel from Devonport gave the gunners experience in training their pieces, but the big event was the occasional firing with live ammunition.

The towing-boat; She'd be coming at steam, like as if she'd worked up the same speed as a warship. She'd be towing a long line behind her. And at the end of this line, there'd be two squares of framework covered with canvas. And the distance between those two frames would be equivalent to the vital section of a ship. Anything up to say, twenty yards. And the idea was to get your shot between those two. Or knock the damn things out of the water.

Of course, it was exciting at night-time. Your battery would be in complete darkness. And there'd be the lookout. And all the searchlights would be out covering the whole harbour. And all of a sudden, the towing boat would come into the beam. You didn't take any notice of that – because you was told not to. But as soon as the target came in – all the men would be at their guns, all loaded, ready to fire – And the target would come into the beam. And you'd say 'Target in the beam, Sir.' And the OC of the battery would say, 'No. 1 Gun, Fire! No. 2 Gun, Fire!' – until you'd got the range. And once you'd got the range, perhaps 'Independent Fire!' Four guns banging off as quick as they could. Yes it

was quite exciting really – and deafening, of course. My job was to sound the 'Cease Fire!' because it was the only thing which could be heard. That's what I think contributed to my deafness; for there was nothing for the sound to go away, the twelve-pounder battery in a recess which had been carved out of the rock. Not much smoke when firing; very little smoke at all.

Apart from the fact that the men lived in the casemates, running round in a semicircle, it was

Just the same as a barrack-room. The beds were cast-iron and the biscuits were cast-iron, too. The biscuits were thin mattresses about three inches thick. Alright when freshly stuffed with coir, after being laid on a bit, they get very hard. Three biscuits to lie on and you sleep in the blankets. Sheets were coarse linen and if you had a new one, you had a rough ride because the bits of wheat would be sticking out of it. As soon as the sheets were brought up; the number of sheets to the beds in the room would be dumped on the table, you'd make a dive to get the sheet which was the most worn out. We only had the normal issue of blankets; two in summer and three in winter and could be quite cold when the weather was very cold. But apart from that you were well looked after and you're kept very healthy.

There was no cookery courses. The cook was just selected from the men in the battery. He went to the cookhouse and learned in a rough and ready manner by watching the other cooks. And of course, the usual thing in those days, was to pick a man who wasn't a good gunner. And if he wasn't a good gunner, he probably wasn't a good cook either. So the food was pretty rough. The normal ration, of course, which was meat, bread, tea, sugar, salt, and that was supplemented by purchases for which you had a grant. Very simple, very simple, indeed. And not all that enticing.

A typical day? The trumpeter had to get up first. Had to arrange with the Corporal of the Guard to get you called, say a quarter of an hour before Reveille and you'd sound 'Reveille'. And then you'd sound the calls to fit in with the day routine. Like 'Parade', 'Dress' – sound that half an hour before 'Parade'. Then the 'Quarter of an Hour', and then the 'Five Minutes', and then the 'Fall in!' 'Orderly Room' – you'd sound that, when that was on. 'Letters'. The dinner calls. And that was all. And in between that, you'd practice your calls away from everybody else. My favourite spot was along the road to Renney Battery.

It was completely free of civilians; purely military land. No fishermen living there. The boundary ran at the back of our lines; and no civilians could come beyond. And in those days of coast defence quite a lot of ground was taken up with the defence.

Your spare time wasn't organised. There wasn't so much sport in those days. What the main thing you did, was to go for walks. And that's about all. Or go into town – into Plymouth. Walk round from Staddon Heights to Turnchapel and then the ferry. No duty boat for the troops' comfort; you just had to walk round.

The nineteenth century also saw the beginning of purpose-built army camps. In the summer of 1853 the British army held a camp on Chobham Common for the purpose of exercising two full divisions of troops. This massed training operation proved so successful that it was decided to purchase over 4,000 hectares of common land which was about to be enclosed on Aldershot heath, just across the county boundary in Hampshire. This was done the following year and plans were prepared for a summer-only tented camp.

However, on the outbreak of the Crimean War in March 1854 so much of the army went overseas that the reserve militia had to be called out for home service garrison duty. They had to be accommodated somewhere and it was decided to erect temporary wooden huts on the newly acquired land. Work began in February 1855 and the first troops moved in, in the May of that year. However, in September, the war came to an end, the militia returned home and the hutted camp became permanent accommodation for troops coming back from the Crimea. At first their families lived in tents, but then they moved into spare huts in the battalion lines. Blankets were hung from the rafters as partitions between families. As the nineteenth century wore on these buildings were replaced by permanent brick bungalows, although temporary wooden huts of somewhat similar design to these have remained a feature of life in every army ever since.

The most obvious effect of the Industrial Revolution on military architecture was the simultaneous development of new weapons sys-

79 *A photograph taken in the 1860s of Aldershot South Camp, south of the Basingstoke Canal.*

80 *The United States Military Academy at West Point in New York State was established in 1802. It is a good example of the type of military architecture required for the study of war and the training of personnel, which became increasingly important after the Industrial Revolution.*

tems and of the defences against them. There was, however, another aspect of the Industrial Revolution which, though less spectacular, was undoubtedly more significant.

The increasing complexity of equipment and the speed at which new devices were introduced meant that even junior ranks had to be capable of rapidly assimilating specialist technicalities, putting their knowledge into practice and imparting it intelligently to others. Handbooks had to be printed, studied and updated; soldiers had to learn how to use them; some had to be taught how to read. Such education could not be easily undertaken on a rainswept parade-ground.

At the same time, railways and steamships meant that the opening phase of a war could develop very quickly. Time could be wasted contacting and rounding up troops scattered about in billets or half-ruined castles. Modern armies needed to be concentrated in areas where they could undertake indoor and outdoor training programmes and yet still be ready to proceed overseas at the shortest notice. Purpose-built camps had to be constructed, the ranks of wooden huts or rows of barrack blocks becoming familiar sights around newly established garrison towns. These buildings provided living, office and storage accommodation, not only for the soldiers, but also those families carried 'on the strength' of the battalion.

These camps also meant that greater control could be exercised over off-duty troops isolated behind perimeter fence and guard-room. There was less opportunity for unscrupulous traders to peddle their wares (especially bad drink) within the camp limits, thus cutting down on discipline problems due to drunkenness. For spare time activity, canteens, sports clubs and libraries were introduced. Some could be converted from redundant sheds, but it became a matter of military pride to point to the latest building contructed for the welfare of the men. This was especially true of hospitals, while as regards animals, good veterinary practices and properly run stables and remount depots were vital to any nation's war effort. Warehouses, stores and workshops all had to be designed and constructed for the accumulation and maintenance of reserve stockpiles of equipment and supplies at every level of military administration, from army command downwards.

The introduction of barracks accommodating a standing army was a great improvement on the earlier practice of billeting out regular soldiers on civilian households. It strengthened discipline by ensuring that troops were always available for duty and training; it reduced the opportunities

81 *The Armory and Gymnasium at Madison in the American State of Wisconsin. Soon most cities in the industrialised world – even those which were not garrison towns – boasted a drill hall where local reservists and volunteers could meet for part-time training.*

for fraud in the payment of allowances; and it lessened the chances of friction between military and civilians. In Ireland, however, these new barracks became the symbols of foreign occupation, the bases from which soldiers were sent out to enforce English laws. Not intended to present more than a token defence in the form of a couple of ceremonial sentries, they eventually had to be fortified with sandbags, strongpoints and barbed wire.

What would determine the wars of the first half of the twentieth century would be what the Germans called *die Materielschlacht* (the Battle of Material). For also significant in military architecture was the mass-production of items which would make temporary fieldworks of greater worth than any fort. Spade-excavated trenches and dugouts, strung with barbed-wire and reinforced with an occasional concrete structure, all manned by determined riflemen and machine-gunners, backed by massed field artillery and with a system of communications which could rush reserves forward to plug any gap in the line, were soon to prove as impregnable as any titanic fortress of metal and stone.

The British army learned that in the South African War of 1899–1902, but it was the Boers who were eventually defeated by the mass-production methods of the Industrial Revolution. Barbed wire and blockhouses had originally been erected along the South African railway lines to protect them from Boer commandos. Lord Kitchener decided to employ this defensive weapons system as a static but *offensive* weapons system.

Thousands of posts were erected beside railway lines, linked by many strands of barbed wire. Blockhouses were established at frequent intervals, often close enough to have overlapping fields of rifle fire, but always within sight of their neighbours. These blockhouses were of various types, curved corrugated iron and sandbags being common constituents of their construction. They were only proof against small arms fire, but that was virtually all the Boers possessed from 1901 onwards.

Once the railways had been thus treated,

82 *This wooden building was designed by Isambard Kingdom Brunel as a prefabricated hospital for use in the Crimea. There are suggestions that two were completed, one actually being despatched for overseas service. This one was erected in Aldershot in 1856 as the temporary Garrison Church of St Michael and St Sebastian.*

83 *The Cambridge Military Hospital in Aldershot was named after the Duke of Cambridge, Commander-in-Chief of the British army from 1856 to 1895.*

84 *On parade outside Cork Barracks in Ireland during the late nineteenth century.*
The building is typical of Victorian institutional architecture – of brick or local stone, with windows, doorways and corners picked out in lighter masonry. Note the clock and the bell, both vital in an age when few people carried their own timepiece.

85 *A blockhouse of the Boer War, garrisoned by the 24th Regiment of Foot (The South Wales Borderers).*

similar lines of barbed wire and blockhouses were used to flank the roads. Finally they were constructed right across the open veldt, the longest being 480 kilometres from Victoria Station West, to Lambert's Bay on the Atlantic.

Then the 'Mechanical Phase' began. At irregular intervals mobile British columns (totalling as much as 17,000 men) set out in carefully planned and co-ordinated 'drives'. The Boers might choose to fight delaying actions, but they were rarely more than a thousand in number and usually only a hundred. In the end, they always had to retreat. The British moved across the veldt, depriving the Boer commandos of local support by burning their farms and shipping off their women and children to St Helena and other islands in the Atlantic and Indian Oceans. They were all interned together – or concentrated – in purpose-built accommodation known as 'concentration camps' – then a perfectly respectable term, but which first gained opprobrium during that period.

Meanwhile the Boer commandos had been pinned up against the barbed wire, blockhouses and armoured trains, and were either killed or compelled to surrender. Sometimes a few managed to cut through the wire and escape into the next sector. In due course, another great 'drive' was mounted there, pinning the Boers against the next line of barbed wire, blockhouses and armoured trains. Then there was another 'drive', and another, and another, and another . . . until there came a day when there was nowhere left to go, and no Boers free to go there.

CHAPTER EIGHTEEN

The Great War

I shall manoeuvre France right out of her Maginot Line
without losing a single soldier.
(Adolf Hitler)

In military architecture, as in so many other aspects of history, the double conflict known as the First and Second World Wars is more of a single transitional period, rather than two separate events. It saw the Industrial Revolution turn warfare into a static slogging match and then transform it into fast-moving parry and thrust. Both phases developed their own forms of military architecture, while the era as a whole opened with the discrediting of the traditional type of land fortress.

The Belgian forts at Liège were believed capable of surviving bombardment by 8-inch (21-cm) guns, assumed to be the biggest practicable field artillery. Admittedly, the Japanese had employed 11-inch (28-cm) howitzers against the Russian forts at Port Arthur. These guns were in fact redundant naval equipment, their 318-kilogram shells fitted with delayed action fuzes so that they could pierce armoured decks before exploding. That was how the Russian battleships still in harbour were sunk in a single day's bombardment. The reduction of the forts, on the other hand, took from 1 October 1904 to 2 January 1905, which was hardly an indication of the success of the howitzers.

For some reason, only the Germans fully appreciated the fact that the Japanese shells had actually penetrated the Russian concrete, subsequent delays in capturing the fortifications being due to other factors. Accordingly, German artillerymen and industrialists produced a weapon capable of reducing the forts at Liège in a matter of hours. Timing was vital, because German strategy depended upon pushing their main striking force through Belgium as part of their opening – and victorious – gambit of the Great War in Europe. It is ironic that this plan had been devised because of the rival fortifications on both sides of the Franco-German boundary. They were of comparable strength, but whereas the French intended a spirited frontal attack on the German positions and a quick dash to Berlin, the Germans decided to outflank the French positions altogether. The bulk of their army would swing west, south and east to take the French in the rear, sweep them up and hammer them against the belt of German forts along the Rhine. To do that the German army had to go through Belgium – preferably peaceably, but if not, then forceably. And that meant taking out the Liège forts.

On 2 August 1914, Germany demanded passage through Belgium. This was refused and on 4 August the two countries were at war. Liège itself succumbed to surprise attack on 7 August 1914.

The other forts around Liège fulfilled their expectations; they stopped the German advance through the Meuse valley. Only at Fort Barchon was the 34th Division able to exploit dead ground to attempt a direct assault at close range. The defenders rushed out onto the parapets to drive them off, unaware of the fact that a battery of 3-inch (7.7-cm) and 4.1-inch (10.5-cm) howitzers

86 *The pre-First World War fort of Sedd-el-Bahr guarded the approach to the Dardanelles. Its magazine proved vulnerable to the latest 12-inch (30.5-cm) gunfire and blew up during British naval bombardment on 3 November 1914. It experienced further shelling on a number of occasions and was eventually stormed by infantry on 26 April 1915, the day after the British landing at Cape Helles.*

In both world wars older fortifications seemed valueless, but their safe dungeons and ruined ramparts and walls provided excellent cover for infantrymen and machine-gunners, and on occasions light field artillery. Even if the old castle became untenable, its massive bulk made it an obvious target, so such places often continued to attract the attention of gunners and bombers, who tended to ignore the actual defenders ensconced in camouflaged dugouts behind near-invisible barbed wire on the surrounding slopes.

from the 27th Division had worked its way round on the other side. With shells falling upon their unprotected backs, the garrison of Fort Barchon surrendered. However, the other forts were still holding out, dislocating the precise timetable of the Schlieffen Plan.

But *Dicke Bertha* (*Big Bertha*) was on her way, a 16.5-inch (42-cm) howitzer named in honour of the daughter of Krupp von Bohlen und Essen, the German industrialist. Weighing 42.5 tonnes, it was an unwieldy piece of battlefield artillery, but when dismantled into five great sections and towed by huge tractors, it was just about mobile. By the evening of 12 August 1914, *Dicke Bertha* was in position and had begun firing 1.15 tonnes of shell over a range of 9.4 kilometres with great accuracy. The eighth projectile established the range and by the next day another howitzer had been emplaced. Their shells plunged through earth and concrete, exploding inside the fortifications, stripping away whole sections of vertical retaining wall, blasting away the gun mountings from underneath. Cupolas and turrets were undermined, collapsed, and overturned, their exposed mechanisms smashed to pieces. And the garrison – soldiers of flesh and blood? They were pulverised, entombed, poisoned with fumes, driven mad, forced to surrender. On 16 August 1914 the last of the eleven fortresses capitulated and the German army was stepping out down the roads of Belgium on its way to victory. There were other fortresses at Namur, Maubeuge and Antwerp, but the *Kurz Marine Kanone Batterie No. 3* was now up to its full strength of four 42-cm sister howitzers.

In spite of what had happened at Liège, the Allied authorities still had great faith in their fortifications. But Namur was finished as a viable defence system on 26 August 1914, Maubeuge followed and Antwerp's defences were bombarded from 4 to 9 October 1914. Next day, the Germans were in the city.

The German advance was eventually stopped, and by fortifications, but these were temporary fieldworks consisting of trenches, dugouts and barbed wire. Allied counter-attacks foundered on identical obstacles and soon parallel, continuous lines of trenches stretched from Switzerland to the sea.

The front line was backed up by two or more support trenches, all joined by communications trenches. There were listening saps and mining tunnels, machine-gun posts and accommodation dugouts. Nothing was straight; everything zigzagged in traverses to prevent the entire trench being raked by fire from one end. Their sides were festooned with telephone wires and notices, the bottom of each trench was covered with duckboards.

Sometimes there were several belts of such trench systems, so arranged that the front-line troops could fall back, allow pre-ranged artillery to decimate the temporarily successful enemy – and then counter-attack, only to be lured themselves into another killing-ground. For the wartime propaganda machines had unleashed such a

fury of hatred against the enemy that there could be no question of peace through negotiated settlement; only the total annihilation of one side or the other could accomplish that.

As the war dragged on, this defence in depth became of greater significance, isolated shellholes and machine-gun bunkers with overlapping fields of fire often taking the place of continuous trenches. The Germans, in particular, became expert in siting and constructing permanent blockhouses, or what the British came to call pillboxes. These *Stutzpunkte* were of concrete which had been poured between wooden shuttering around an internal skeleton of iron rods, each 12–20 mm thick and erected according to a predetermined pattern. When set, these concrete walls could be 1.5 metres thick, overhead protection and camouflage being further enhanced by a layer of earth.

Stutzpunkte proved resistant to 8-inch (21-cm) shellfire, while the door was usually armoured and invulnerable, except for a direct hit – which was impossible because of a screening blast-wall or because the door was below ground level down a flight of steps (preferably with a right-angle turn in them). The only way a pillbox could be knocked out was for an infantryman to crawl forward and toss a hand-grenade in through the firing-slit. Right up against the wall of the pillbox, he was usually quite safe from the machine-gunners inside – but not from their distant neighbours, who though invisible in their hidden pillbox, could undoubtedly see *him*.

Most wartime photographs show lonely pillboxes as obvious targets for artillery, but that is because the cameraman had arrived after bombardment had blasted away all the trees and earth in the vicinity, leaving the *Stutzpunkt* virtually intact.

Trench warfare lasted for three years before mobility was restored to the battlefield. This was eventually due to three factors: the employment of tanks; the beginning of blitzkrieg tactics which tried to avoid or neutralise strongpoints instead of assaulting them; and the development of smaller offensives *in seriatim*, instead of massing the entire army in one 'Big Push'. This last tactic meant that the enemy was continually being compelled to retreat to prevent his being out-flanked. It also implied that the advancing force now had ample reserves of men and material and the ability to switch them from one sector to another. Obviously soldiers and supplies had to be accommodated at every stage of their journey from their basic training camp to the front line. An unprecedented demand was created for storage facilities of all kinds, the most famous – and the most durable – British contribution to this type of military architecture being the Nissen Bow Hut.

In 1916 Captain Nissen was commanding the 29th Company, Royal Engineers. He was a Canadian who was said to have been inspired by his observation of Eskimo igloos and beaver lodges. The Nissen hut was prefabricated and all its components (totalling 1.02 tonnes) fitted into a single horse-drawn General Service Wagon. The only tools required were a spanner and a hammer, and with one of these each, four men set to work as soon as they arrived at a suitable site.

First of all they laid out three parallel timbers 8.2 metres long and 17.8 × 10.2 centimetres thick.

There was no need to prepare foundations or previously level the site. The timbers kept the floor above the damp, while smaller pieces of wood or piles of bricks took account of any slope or hollows in the ground. Across the three bottom bearers were nailed sixteen floor joists, 10.2 × 5.1 centimetres thick and 49 metres long. To them were fixed the floor panels. Five bow-shaped frames 2.7 metres high went up next, arching from one side to the other and held rigidly by five purlins or thin longitudinal beams. Forty-eight curved sheets of corrugated iron were then bolted to this framework. Vertical panels blocked off each end. There was a door and two windows at one end, with a single window and a small round hole in the other end panel. All the joints were caulked and sealed, while insulation was provided by a layer of air trapped behind an inner skin of matchboarding or more corrugated iron. A Canadian drum stove was installed, its

87 *One of the Second World War Nissen huts erected at the American camp in Barwick Park (near Yeovil) still in existence.*

metal flue fed through the hole in the end panel – and four hours after they had started work, the four men moved on to the next job, while 24 other men moved into their new home.

There were innumerable authorised and unofficial modifications to adapt Nissen huts to a variety of functions. At least 25,000 were built between 1916 and 1918, thousands remaining in service years afterwards. Many were turned to civilian use, while Colonel Nissen himself produced plans for mass-produced private homes; the military architecture of the First World War influencing civilian engineering.

However, when most people, including military architects and engineers, thought of the Great War, they remembered the strongpoints and the trenches of the Western Front. On other fronts, too, fighting had been dominated by trench warfare; even if fluid situations did develop, they could be brought to a full stop by the simplest of earthworks. In that case, just imagine how effective a wide zone of carefully designed, well-sited, purpose-built and permanently constructed trenches and strongpoints would be. No

aggressor would be able to break through; caught out in the open, the assaulting army would be massacred. Established on the frontier, such a defence zone would make a country impregnable.

That was the reasoning behind the line of fortifications named after André Maginot, appointed French Minister of War in November 1929. He was its chief proponent, but the project had first been suggested by Marshal Pétain back in December 1925.

To those who said that the demolition of the Liège forts had proved the uselessness of permanent fortifications, it was explained that *La Ligne de Maginot* would be built without any of the defects embodied in that earlier Belgian construc-

88 *A Nissen Petren house in Yeovil, Somerset, built in 1925 at a cost of £513. The cavity walls are of concrete slabs. The unit consists of two semi-detached houses, each with two rooms downstairs and two upstairs, plus kitchen and bathroom. The second part of the name is derived from the two architects responsible for the civilian part of the design – Petter and Warren.*

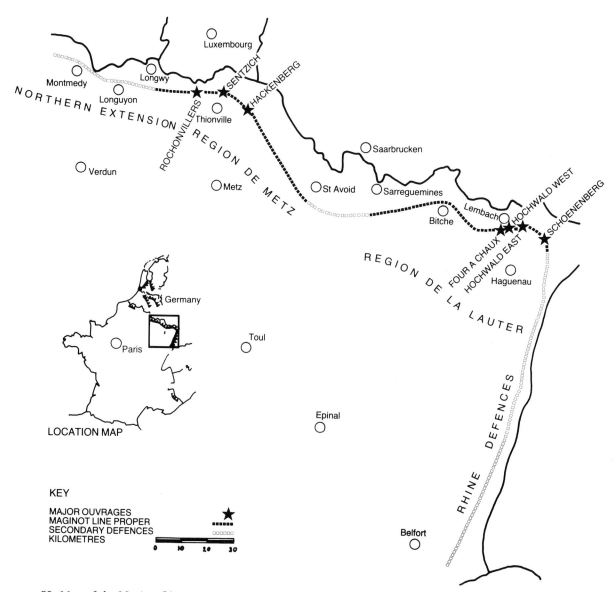

89 *Map of the Maginot Line.*

tion. First, those forts had been too far apart for mutual fire support. Second, there had been no mobile troops, no field army to deal with infiltrating infantry. The guns of the Liège forts were old and outranged by the German artillery, while the quality of their construction was poor, largely because the early users of concrete were ignorant of its properties. It had often been poured and allowed to set in layers, thus forming internal lines of weakness liable to fracture under stress. Nor had it been reinforced with steel bars, or any other form of internal bonding. The Liège forts had been badly ventilated and little attention had been given to water supply and sewage disposal.

Contrast their defeat with the valiant resistance of the newer French fortress of Verdun. That city's ring of forts had been built with steel cupolas instead of iron ones. They had been set in

90 *At the camouflaged stores entrance to* Ouvrage A19 (Hackenberg), *the narrow-gauge underground railway system of the Maginot Line comes out into open air and daylight. Pavé cobblestones provide firm access for road transport. In this photograph, it can be seen that the doorway is defended by embrasures for a 1.5-inch (37-mm) anti-tank gun (on the left) and for two machine-guns on the right, one firing across the portal.*

two layers of concrete, separated by sand to cushion the blast, the whole topped by a layer of earth, making an overhead protection 8.1 metres thick.

It was certainly true that the Germans had not been able to capture Verdun. It was also true that thanks to their better protection and deep shelters, the outlying forts had proved more capable of withstanding bombardment – including 42-cm shells – than had the Liège forts. But what had really saved Verdun had been the thousands of troops who had marched up *La Voie Sacrée* and had made the Germans pay dearly for every metre of ground they had conquered. Verdun had

been defended by French blood rather than by French masonry.

But no such sacrifice would ever be necessary again; *La Ligne de Maginot* would see to that, at a cost of 5,000 million francs. The Maginot Line was made up of a series of *ouvrages* or 'works'. At the heart of each, was a maze of tunnels and chambers, excavated out of the solid rock and lined with cement. Here, safely buried beyond the deepest penetration of the biggest shell or bomb, were the magazines and stores, power-stations, battle headquarters, hospitals, and barracks for up to 1,200 men, equipped with every facility for troop efficiency and welfare. Far above, fed by ammunition hoists, and controlled from separate command posts receiving reports from observation bunkers, were the steel cupolas, both fixed and disappearing types being mounted in reinforced concrete glacis. The biggest were four metres in diameter, mounting a 3-inch (75-mm) gun with a range of 12 kilometres. There were also 5.3-inch (135-mm) mortars, delivering a 21-kilogram bomb over a distance of 5.6 kilometres, plus a whole range of lesser weapons.

The largest *ouvrages* were in two blocks, infantry and artillery, being armed with lighter and heavier calibres respectively. Being up to 2.5 kilometres apart, the two blocks were linked by underground electric railway, which also ran to the entrances for personnel and material back behind the firing zone. These, too, were well protected with armoured doors, machine-gun slits and false entrances. Inside, at various positions along the tunnels, there were ambuscades and hidden mines to entomb unwary invaders, while the defenders had their own secret exits and sally-ports. Everywhere there were fireproof and gastight doors, exhaust vents and air intakes fitted with antigas filters.

In front of the *ouvrage* was a line of two-tier casemates, armed with anti-tank guns below, and lighter weapons above, each one a smaller version of the great underground forts. Their visible portions were surrounded by an anti-tank ditch, with vertical posts ('asparagus'), barbed wire, booby traps and mines forming further obstacles to mechanised and human advance.

About five kilometres in front of these casemates were the blockhouses, also of ferro-concrete. Ostensibly forward observation posts for the main line of *ouvrages* and casemates, they were equipped with anti-tank guns and automatic weapons. Their 30-man garrison was capable of putting up a sizeable fight on their own.

From here the German border was only two kilometres away. Every road junction from the blockhouses to the frontier was prepared for demolition; every bridge on the frontier itself covered by fire from a fortified house.

All that interlocking defence in depth was controlled from the one *ouvrage*, itself within 75-mm range of its neighbours. Every fortification was so strong that it could be bombarded by adjacent positions without damage, but with deleterious effect on any Germans clambering about outside.

And if, in spite of all this, any invaders did manage to run the gauntlet of the Maginot Line, then they would be mopped up by the French field army, while mobile anti-aircraft batteries and *L'Armee de l'Air* dealt with the *Luftwaffe*.

The Maginot Line was never intended to be a continuous solid fortification like Hadrian's Wall. Indeed, even the belt of defences which was completed was only as complex as this in two sectors: Rhin-Bas and Moselle (where there were the *ouvrages* of Schoenenbourg, Hochwald East, Hochwald West and Four-a-Chaux), and slightly farther west in Moselle and Meurthe-et-Moselle (the *ouvrages* of Hackenberg, Sentzich and Rochonvillers). Other sections of the Franco-German border were covered by lesser strongpoints, considered quite sufficient for those more mountainous regions. The Belgian frontier was not fortified at all for a variety of reasons: the flat land of Flanders was hardly the best soil for excavating deep underground fortresses; building what there was of the Maginot Line was absorbing too much money, material and labour (some work even had to be sub-contracted to German firms); it would be an unfriendly act to fortify the border of a neutral country like Belgium; besides, the German panzers could not operate in the narrow defiles of the wooded Ardennes mountains – and if they did, the French and British field armies would soon mop them up. As for coming through Belgium itself as in 1914, that was out of the question because of the Belgians' new underground fortress at Eben-Emael, dominating the bridges over the Albert Canal north of Liège.

For in 1939 every Continental country still had faith in continuing belts of fortifications as the best means of defending their frontiers. They were all fated to be disappointed.

First, the retracting cupola was too limited in size to be capable of mounting anything larger than a 3-inch (7.5-cm) gun. Anything bigger, and the cupola had to be lighter in weight (hence with thinner armour) or else it would be too heavy to operate. At the same time, the Germans were developing a 31.5-inch (80-cm) gun to deal with the strongest fortress – and nobody could foretell what size aerial bombs would reach.

But there are other ways of gaining access to strongholds, besides smashing your way in – as was demonstrated in 1938, when the Munich Agreement enabled Hitler to take possession of the Sudetenland fortresses (which the Czechs had modelled on the Maginot Line) without a shot being fired.

The Maginot Line itself was outflanked – by a German thrust through the Ardennes and Belgium in 1940.

And Eben-Emael? Nine gliders crashlanded on top of it. The German airborne troops they disgorged used hollow charges (like petards) to blow in the cupolas and embrasures, smothering others with flame-throwers. Nevertheless, some cupolas and casemates could not be knocked out. In spite of casualties and having to build barricades in the tunnels, the garrison (totalling 700) continued firing, not only at the airborne troops on the fort itself, but also at the German forces trying to cross the Albert Canal bridges. Units of the Belgian field army began organising counter-attacks and now it was the Germans' turn to dig in, take up defensive positions, and hold out for the promised reinforcements – who did not arrive till next morning, paddling across the Albert Canal in rubber boats. They assaulted the surviving casemates and about midday on 11 May 1940 Eben-Emael surrendered. The Belgians had suffered 82 dead and wounded; the glider-borne Germans, 21 casualties out of 55.

CHAPTER NINETEEN

The Second World War

You will enter the Continent of Europe.
(Instructions to General Dwight D. Eisenhower, on his
appointment as Supreme Commander, Allied Expeditionary
Force)

From 1940 to 1944 two mighty fortresses faced each other across the English Channel, the one a Continental citadel, the other the island bastion of a trans-Atlantic industrial stronghold. Both expected cross-Channel invasion, the British having to meet the crisis in a considerable hurry.

Their authorities decided upon a defence-in-depth system, similar to that employed on the Western Front in 1917 and 1918. Large numbers of pillboxes were erected, usually in groups with interlocking fields of fire. Sometimes they covered particular road junctions; sometimes they formed defensive belts across country or along the coast; and sometimes rings of them made up defensive 'islands' or 'hedgehogs'. Many pillboxes were built to look like garden sheds and other inoffensive structures. The great period of construction was in the summer of 1940, but building went on spasmodically for most of the war. In some cases, signed contracts had to be completed, while in other instances, Home Guard units built their own design of pillbox as local status symbols. Most subsequent construction was to protect newly built airfields against commando-style raids by German para-troops or marine units.

An important part of pillbox construction was the use of steel bars. Both ends of each bar were bent through 90 degrees for a distance of almost a metre. One set was laid with the ends projecting upwards, while those which were part of the roof projected downwards, being linked together by the others which formed the skeleton of the walls. The structure now resembled an enclosed cage, with small apertures for a door, ventilator and loopholes. The wooden shuttering was erected around this framework and the concrete poured in to a thickness of 45 centimetres, forming a completely solid, yet extremely resilient building. A small team of subcontractors could built a pair of pillboxes every six to eight weeks. Unskilled labour was sometimes quicker, but the completed work was not always as good as that of profes-sional engineers, whether civilian or military. It was not a question of appearance, but of strength – and of siting; some coastal pillboxes were soon subject to erosion.

A number of pillboxes seem to have been made of insubstantial brick, but that was in fact brick shuttering, employed where wood was in short supply. The brickwork was then left *in situ* around the set concrete, acting partly as camou-flage and partly as an additional bursting layer of protection. Wire mesh and other expedients had to be resorted to when the steel reinforcing bars were not available. Who knows whether some of the iron railings removed from house-fronts during salvage campaigns may not have ended up as ferro-reinforcement in some now-mouldering fortification?

Usually sited in association with pillboxes were anti-tank blocks called pimples or dragons' teeth.

91 *This two-storeyed pillbox near Ilton in Somerset was built in the same fashion as a single-storey one, its skeleton being formed of two steel cages, one on top of the other and integrally linked. From a distance, across the fields, only the top half is visible, covering the approaches to the other single-storey pillboxes in the area. The lower level provided fire along the now-disused Chard to Taunton railway line. Just above the ground-level door is the girder, which supported wooden steps to the upper entrance. Doors were usually located on the side away from the expected direction of attack. This pillbox and its companions were part of the Western Stop Line, intended to deal with a German advance eastwards after an invasion of the South-West Peninsula.*

They were cast in concrete, reinforced with pebbly rubble and wire mesh. They could be used as simple obstructions, blocking the road the Germans were likely to come along. They could funnel the invader into a 'killing ground', where he would fall victim to mine, machine-gun or anti-tank gun. Or they could provide simple cover for snipers and artillery – a modern form of merlon and crenel. If no regular troops were available, such defensive positions of pillbox and pimple would be manned by the local Home Guard. Even if unmanned due to shortage of personnel, weapons or ammunition, such obstacles could not be ignored or carelessly bypassed. The invader could not be certain that there were no hidden riflemen or gunners somewhere around; the blocks themselves might be booby-trapped; or the empty road curving past them might be mined. Infantry and engineers would have to check before the advance could get moving again. And every delay would gain time for the British to build up their strength in some other part of the island, and begin striking back at the German cross-Channel supply routes, even more vulnerable with the approach of winter.

Unlike the British the Germans had several

92 *During the Second World War much ingenuity was devoted to the development of anti-tank devices, both weaponry and static defences. The latter category included these cylindrical blocks or 'pimples' along the Basingstoke Canal near Dogmersfield in Hampshire.*

But all that was a generation ago. Now, these silent sentinels of a bygone age as remotely mysterious as the wooded ramparts of Danebury hillfort, thrown up more than 2,000 years before.

years to prepare their *Festung Europa* against assault from the sea. They put their faith in linear fortifications, concentrated around principal ports and likely landing-beaches, although their propaganda service implied that the whole coast-line of Europe, from North Cape to the Spanish frontier, was one continuous wall.

The work was undertaken by the *Organisation Todt*, an army auxiliary force of *Bautruppen* (or construction troops). At first it was composed of

German volunteers and conscripted building firms, but later on the bulk of the work was performed by virtual slave labour. Even so, the *Organisation Todt* continued to attract specialists from all over Europe, who volunteered either because they admired the Nazis, or because the pay was good, or because they were Allied agents reporting what they saw in otherwise prohibited areas.

An architectural feature of the Atlantic Wall was the massiveness of its structures. Concrete walls and roofs could be up to 3.5 metres thick, their external dimensions magnified by the use of concrete shuttering. Normally parallel wooden panels are erected, between which the concrete is poured, the panels being removed after the concrete has set. But that takes time, time in which British and American air raids could dislodge the shuttering at a critical stage. So, fairly thin pre-cast concrete blocks were stacked around the steel reinforcing rods, and the concrete poured in. The shuttering blocks were left *in situ* adding further solidity and cushioning effect to the main structure. Curved surfaces had to be sacrificed to the demand for hasty construction, being replaced by flat faces.

All these casemates, pillboxes and observation towers were fronted by a variety of beach devices for ripping apart landing craft, their flanks guarded by minefields, barbed wire and by infantry in fieldworks like trenches, foxholes and bunkers.

In fact, the Atlantic Wall was not typical of military engineering for army combat purposes, most of which was in the form of field fortification. Such improvisation made bombed cities, ruined castles and monasteries serve as formidable obstacles to all advancing armies.

Among the factors which enabled the Atlantic Wall to be breached was the accuracy of heavy naval gunfire and the employment of specialist tanks. The latter cleared paths through minefields, laid bridges across ditches, planted explosives against obstacles and pillboxes, and spewed flame at anything which looked suspicious. The petroleum gel employed by flamethrowers in the European Theatre of Operations was a thin mixture, producing a big bushy flame, its appearance often persuading the defenders to retreat. The Japanese in the Pacific were not so inclined to retreat or surrender. So, a thicker gel under greater pressure was employed. This enabled the smaller flame to be hosed in through the narrow slits of a bunker, ricocheting round every corner of the interior, igniting everything – and everybody – within.

Whether the Germans manning the Atlantic Wall defences in the Channel Islands would have put up such a suicidal defence is unlikely. However, they definitely expected the British to attempt an assault on them; that is what customarily happens when 'the sacred soil of the homeland' is occupied. As a result, the coast defence structures on the Channel Islands were the most formidable sections of the Atlantic Wall. They are also the most intact; the British declined the challenge, left the garrison alone and waited till the end of the war to reclaim their own without a fight.

Some German installations were given concrete raft foundations much greater in area than the structures they supported. This was because aerial bombs, missing the target, and exploding below the level of the normal foundations, could overturn the structures or at least dismount the gun or other equipment within. The 'concrete raft' idea either detonated near-misses above foundation level, or – if lower than that – distributed the shock of explosion throughout the structure.

For a new factor was influencing the design of military architecture – the threat from the air. The great industrial strongholds of Britain and Europe not only had to have horizontally-facing defence systems, they also had to have some sort of a roof. No longer were they simply bases for fleets and armies; they were also springboards for aerial bombardment and airborne assault – and in turn experiencing similar vertical attack.

The whole topic of aerial – and space – architecture (airports, launch-pads, runways and specialised manufacturing works) is a separate subject in itself. But in a study of this nature, there must be some reference to the military employment of such structures.

So, too, there must be mention of the provision of purpose-built shelter accommodation to protect both helpless civilians and vital workers producing the weapons of war – and by the twentieth century it had become impossible to differentiate between the two groups of people.

Purpose-built air raid shelters of the Second World War varied from small household ones to monster structures accommodating 20,000 people or more. Some were underground; others were monolithic structures towering ten storeys high and topped with anti-aircraft gun emplacements and radar aerials.

One way of preserving likely targets from air raid was to try to persuade the enemy to drop his bombs somewhere else. The type of decoy site built by the British was known as a 'Starfish'. It consisted of a dozen remote-controlled rocket launchers, and two large cisterns of oil and water, gravity-feed pipes leading to 26 braziers full of flammable materials. The operating crew (paid an extra six pennies a day danger money) con-

sisted of twelve RAF airmen under a sergeant. When an air raid developed, the team took up position in the remote-control room in fig. 96. They started the fires by electrically detonating the igniters under the braziers. They kept them blazing by occasionally flushing several gallons of fuel and water from the cisterns, which also simulated bombs exploding on the ground. Meanwhile the rockets were detonating high up amongst the bomber stream, giving the impression of anti-aircraft gunfire and tracers from night-fighters.

Besides such passive measures as shelters and decoy sites there were anti-aircraft gun emplacements and flak towers. Massive radar aerials gave advance warning of enemy aircraft, wireless masts transmitted signals between every level of

93 *This American type of control tower was erected in 1943 when the United States Army Air Force operated from Duxford Airfield. Now an outstation of the Imperial War Museum in London, Duxford is open to the public as a living airfield and store for large exhibits.*

command, alerting civil defence authorities and directing the counter-offensive in the sky. From purpose-built airfields climbed fighters and bombers, increasing in size and speed and complexity until they carried so many bombs and guns that they were called 'Flying Fortresses', and – from the Pacific island stronghold of Tinian – there rose a '*Super*fortress' carrying an atomic bomb.

94 *This brick-built air raid shelter in Alton (Hampshire) is typical of many produced in Britain for use by neighbouring families. Note the separate wall, screening the entrance from the direct blast of an exploding bomb.*

95 *In absorbing the shock of an exploding bomb it was likely that the blast wall itself might collapse, blocking the entrance. Indeed, this type of shelter was not proof against direct hits, especially when wartime conditions resulted in the use of inferior materials. British above-surface shelters were therefore provided with a small area of unmortared brickwork at the rear of the structure at ground level, so that the survivors could smash their way out if all other means of exit were blocked.*

96 *A decoy site ('Starfish') near the village of Odcombe in Somerset. It was intended to attract bombs destined for the Westland Aircraft Works at Yeovil, about five kilometres distant.*

Just in case the 'Starfish' did what it was supposed to do, and really did attract all the bombs intended for elsewhere, the personnel were provided with a deep shelter beneath the building seen here.

CHAPTER TWENTY

The nuclear age

A safe stronghold . . .?
(Martin Luther 'Ein Feste Burg ist unser Gott')

The atomic bomb was *not* the ultimate weapon.

It brought an end to the Second World War, but it did not bring an end to war itself.

Most nations, except the defeated ones – and they were soon allowed an armed gendarmerie for internal and coastal policing – still maintained armed forces. Some were small professional armies; others were massed armies of conscripts. However, there was so much spare military accommodation after the enormous construction programmes of the war that there was little need for new building. The exception was in occupied and liberated countries, where existing barracks had been destroyed. Such new construction as was undertaken was more comfortable than previous, having as many civilian facilities for labour-saving and recreation as possible.

The distinction between civil and military architecture became even more blurred with the widespread construction of married quarters and office blocks, indistinguishable from those erected by private firms and public authorities. The high standard of military accommodation became a symbol of military pride, while memories of past glories and sacrifices came to be enshrined in purpose-built monuments and museums. In both these movements, military architecture was reflecting – and continues to reflect – the social atmosphere of its age.

At the same time, traditional permanent fortifications disappeared from the map. There was no place in coastal defence for long-range guns firing at battleships 40 kilometres away; not with aircraft and missiles which could sink those same battleships as soon as they left their haven on the other side of the ocean.

On the other hand, there was a need for the close-range devices of siege warfare. In every country, buildings representative of the ruling authority have had to be protected against assault by disaffected members of their own populations, some resentful of official policy and wealth, others owing allegiance to some outside

97 *These postwar single-storeyed barrack blocks consisted of two parallel accommodation wings joined by a similar building. Inevitably they were known as 'H-Blocks', a term which has acquired a certain notoriety after surplus buildings began to be used as prison accommodation.*

98 *The Pentagon was built in 1941–3 to house all the US War Department offices in one building. It covers over 34 hectares of usable floor space.*

doctrine. External walls are fringed with barbed wire, windows made of armoured glass or completely blocked off by steel shutters. Unseen eyes inspect the interloper, electronic detectors frisk his person. There are turnstile-portcullises, only operable after the computer has accepted the correct plastic-card password. Everywhere there are guards, some discreetly – and in more suspicious places, openly – armed.

The rebellious subjects, too, have their own strongholds – caves and underground passages in the countryside; reinforced rooms and secret doorways in towns. These are really fieldworks, even in an urban environment, but their disguised entrances, peepholes, twists and turns, dead-end tunnels, ventilators, arms caches, escape routes and booby-traps, make them formidable complexes to overrun. This is especially so if social pressures prevent the military utilising the most violent means of knocking out the entrenched enemy; governments do not usually encourage the peacetime employment of heavy artillery to destroy a block of flats, just because a single sniper might be hiding in one of them.

The same posture of holding back from the extreme use of violent means to attain sociopolitical ends is also evident in international affairs. Countries have built up armouries of thermonuclear weapons, threatening their opponents with total destruction if the latter's missiles are detected approaching the home defence line. Whole continents have become massive strongholds, the means of production and the population to maintain that industry being jealously guarded by security services from defection to the other side. At the same time they are shielded by invisible walls of radar and lasers. These are linked by radio signal to complex computers whose faster-than-thought evaluation and microsecond reaction can initiate a state of readiness and launch retaliatory missiles against the aggressor without apparent human intervention.

This modern fortification is in two forms: active structures for launching missiles; and passive shelters for personnel and equipment. The former category includes underground silos, vertical tubes 25–50 metres deep (depending on the length of the rocket), and surrounded by the necessary apparatus for launch. All that is visible above ground is an upturned saucer of reinforced concrete eight metres thick. There is a small trapdoor in this carapace for personnel to gain access for occasional inspection of the silo and its missile, but normally the whole complex is left unmanned, the missile always fuelled and ready for launch. The flight launch control centre (also underground and built to resist the shock of subsoil explosions) may be anything up to $5\frac{1}{2}$ kilometres distant.

Upon receipt of the order to launch – and after the various fail-safe procedures have established that this is the real thing – the two officers activate the launch sequence of the ballistic missile under their command. A segment of the circular carapace is robotically pulled back, and within a minute, the missile is climbing away at 24,000 kilometres an hour on its irreversible journey up into space and down onto its target 12,000 kilometres distant.

The USA, the USSR, France and possibly China, all have this type of silo. It suffers from the disadvantage of having to be completely refurbished after every launch because the fiery exhaust gases of the rocket are temporarily confined within the silo. After that, some sort of monster transporter and crane have to be employed to load a missile into the silo. This lengthy procedure effectively precludes a second-strike launch from perhaps the only silo still undamaged by the enemy's nuclear bombardment. Another disadvantage of any nuclear age fortification is that even though they are widely distributed, satellite observation has pinpointed most silo locations, thus making them even more vulnerable.

One way of speeding up the process is to launch the missile from a canister, so that the silo walls and equipment are not harmed during firing. The canister can then be ejected and a replacement slid in. Obviously it is a rather more delicate and time-consuming operation than it sounds, and it still does not meet the problem of silo defence against enemy attack.

One proposal is that silos for the latest American MX missiles should be concentrated in Dense Packs or CSBs (Closely Spaced Basing), each containing a hundred missiles located about 500 metres from each other. Even though the silos would be superhardened and even though the complexes would be surrounded by anti-missile defence systems, it is recognised that these nuclear citadels would not be impregnable. What is anticipated, is that the detonation of an incoming Soviet missile would throw up so much debris as it hit its target that all other approaching rockets entering the area would be prematurely triggered when they struck that airborne cloud of soiled matter – what is known as nuclear fratricide.

An alternative suggestion is DUB (Deep Underground Basing), in which the whole of a launch and control complex is located a thousand metres underground in a mountainous area. The equipment stored down there would include a self-contained tunnelling machine so that, if targeted by a Soviet rocket, the launch crew can dig out a path to the sky for their own retaliatory missile.

Other experts suggest that mobility is the answer, launching the missiles from articulated trucks or railroad flatcars which never stop moving, from continually airborne aircraft, or

99 *The Thor raised to a vertical position for firing. Underground silos are now used for ballistic missile storage and launch.*

from submerged submarines – none of which can be classed as military architecture, even though their occasional needs have to be supplied by permanent bases and supply dumps of solid construction.

As these are often underground or otherwise shielded against blast, fire, radioactive fallout and unauthorised admission, they are similar in many ways to purpose-built shelters for personnel in the event of nuclear war. Virtually all countries have given some thought to the physical sheltering of their population during such an ordeal. The scale of protection varies from the advice issued by the British government on how to construct do-it-yourself shelters at home, to subterranean warrens in China which are rumoured to be spacious enough to house the entire population of Peking for three months.

Midway between the two extremes are the measures taken by countries like Switzerland and Sweden, which though non-aligned, are likely to get caught in a nuclear crossfire. The Sonnenberg Tunnel near Lucerne can accommodate 20,000 people at a time and contains a hospital, food stockpiles and emergency generators. In addition every Swiss newly built private house has to have its own integral fallout shelter.

Admittedly, all these civilian shelters – in any nation – are basically refuges for frightened people in time of trouble, like the brochs of ancient times, rather than stronghold bases of operations. However, neutral European countries have also given consideration to this sort of military architecture, building shelters big enough to take full-sized ships and aircraft.

From without, the mountainside looks just like any other tree-speckled cliff; and then the huge armoured doors open and the jets or fast attack craft surge out and away. This construction

100 *Aerial view of Thor Emplacement Number One where the first intermediate range ballistic missile launch took place. The dark object in the centre is a 'missile mount' with trailer (but without missile)* *backed into proper position. The two buildings on either side are where major ground support equipment is housed. To the rear is the shelter which rolls forward to cover the missile.*

provides a very effective means of re-establishing supremacy over a battlefield in the wake of a nuclear exchange.

These neutral nations point with justifiable pride to the steps they have taken to safeguard their populations during nuclear war. Indeed, although a procession of rockets trundling past, or an array of sky-pointing missiles against a background of radar aerials, looks impressive, these are the status symbols of weaponry. In military architecture, it is the underground shelter which has become the prestigious symbol, comparable with the proud strongholds of old. This is equally true – perhaps more true – in those countries which can only provide protection for the handful of soldier-scientists who tend the missiles, and for the national and regional administrators who have been charged with perpetuating some form of law and order in their immediate areas. After all, to know that you are so indispensable to the future of humankind that you are one of the chosen few whose survival is guaranteed, while the rest of the people perish, must indeed be the ultimate status symbol.

This is neither a surprising nor a novel quirk of human nature. As the history of military architecture has developed, we have seen how the rulers of the people have distanced themselves farther from their subjects in time of crisis. In ancient hillfort and city, the chief shared the privations of the siege, and – if defeated – was slaughtered with his people. Then citadels were built with concentric fortifications wherein the emperor could hold out for that extra length of time. Within the medieval citadel or castle there was a massive keep to which the baron could retire. By the sixteenth century the monarch's palace was as far as possible from his frontier and coastal defences. Throughout history there have been perfectly valid administrative and communications reasons why this should have been so. Modern nuclear command citadels, insulating the few inside, not only from their subjects, but also from the bulk of their defence and bureaucratic forces, are merely continuing that historic trend.

Another historic theme has been the place which castles have in folklore. In that tradition, legends have already grown up about these modern strongholds. Sometimes nuclear command bunkers are portrayed as impregnable hideouts, equipped with the means of producing their own air, living off their own recycled waste products. Such armoured filter-ventilators, observation slits and remote control cameras as are necessary for monitoring external conditions are proof against radioactive, chemical and bacteriological assault. Besides being provisioned for months and months, they have every facility for entertainment and sporting exercise. Other sections contain works of art, the Crown Jewels, bars of gold, preserving for posterity the priceless treasures of civilisation as we know it. All this is supposed to be in one of the *ouvrages* of the Maginot Line or perhaps in one of the old nineteenth-century forts or perhaps where a funny bit of iron sticks up out of a lonely field surrounded by a high chain-link fence. And, of course, on the appointed day, the great armoured airlock doors will open, disgorging hundreds of soldiers, civil defence workers, police and administrators to destroy the enemy, punish the disaffected, succour the afflicted, and reward the faithful – in a land bombed back to the Stone Age.

That is one side of the legend. At other times, nuclear command bunkers are regarded with cynical amusement. There are references to the claustrophobic neuroses and depression suffered by soldiers serving in the Maginot Line. Then there was the dampness and illness experienced by shelter-dwellers in the Second World War, who at least were in the open air during the hours of daylight. There are stories in newspapers about civil defence exercises which had to be cancelled after rain got in through ventilators smashed by vandals throwing stones at them.

Quite obviously the true efficacy of modern shelters and command bunkers must lie somewhere between these two views, and could only be realistically ascertained if a nuclear war did occur. In that event, those which survived until radioactivity reached acceptable levels would become like the castles of Norman barons; though professing allegiance to higher authority, in effect independent centres of law and order.

101 *The very nature of their construction (difficult access, high walls, solid gates and underground magazines) has made many old castles and forts suitable as safe repositories for all sorts of things – and people – which have to be kept under lock and key. Throughout history, they have been employed as prisons and treasure houses. Nowadays they can be utilised as stores for paintings and other precious artefacts which need a carefully controlled environment for their conservation. Others can contain security documents and other records, or communications equipment for public services. It is even rumoured that some – perhaps the* ouvrages *of the Maginot Line – may have been prepared as strongholds for the governance of post-nuclear Europe.*

But that is only if a nuclear war were to occur, for there has been a third theme running through the history of military architecture – a theme reflected in every age and every society – the unquantifiable influence exercised by taboo, custom and the rules of war.

It may well be that nuclear weapons do not make war unthinkable; they only make *nuclear war* unthinkable. The missile silos and command bunkers of the superpowers set out the global chessboard on which conventional wars can be fought. The combatants may be professional task forces or guerrilla units, massed conscript armies or even garrison troops in traditional fortifications, but they can conduct their operations according to certain rules and with certain limited objectives, which can be obtained by diplomatic or subversive means if these subsequently prove more expedient. The people directing the war know that if they break the rules and allow the conflict to escalate, they risk the ultimate punishment of irreversible global holocaust. In which case, victory or defeat in those wars of limited objective and of death by all forms except nuclear device, will rest, as always, upon the effort and will of ordinary men and women. Perhaps the only true stronghold lies within each individual's heart and mind.

But, as we have seen many times in this study of military architecture and its relationship to society, throughout history strongholds have been used to keep people in, as much as to keep people out. In exactly the same way, strong hearts and minds – may become *closed* hearts and minds.

102 *The Berlin Wall was erected in 1961. It divides East Berlin from West Berlin and although unique in its use of masonry blocks, is similar in layout and principle to the frontier barriers between all Western and Communist countries. There are belts of barbed wire, electrified fences and minefields covered by warning sensors, illuminated at night by floodlights, watched over and patrolled by soldiers and armed police. It may look like a defensive military barrier, but it is unlikely that it would present much of an obstacle to modern armoured forces. The key to its true purpose lies in the fact that it is erected just within Communist territory, most of its obstacles preventing access from that side of the frontier. The Berlin Wall is designed to keep people in, and prevent outsiders knowing what is happening within the Iron Curtain stronghold. There are gateways for carefully controlled intercourse between the cultures, while military experts and tourists may come and stare. But all that they can see of Communist intent is the blank face of the Berlin Wall. Perhaps one day future tourists will come and wonder at its ruins and speculate on the bygone age which found such construction necessary.*

Bibliography

Alcock, L., *By South Cadbury that is Camelot*, Thames & Hudson, 1972

Anderson, W., *Castles of Europe*, Ferndale, 1980

Anon, *A Handbook of the Boer War*, Gale & Polden (Aldershot), 1910

Ashe, G., *The Quest for Arthur's Britain*, Pall Mall Press, 1968

Bain, R., *The Clans and Tartans of Scotland*, Collins, 1966

Baramki, D.C., *The Road to Petra*, Anton Nazzal (Amman, Jordan), 1973

Barton, Sir W., *India's North-West Frontier*, John Murray, 1939

Batsford, H. and Fry C., *The Cathedrals of England*, B.T. Batsford, 1954

Baynes, N.H., *The Byzantine Empire*, Thornton Butterworth, 1925

Bellew, Sir G., *The Kings and Queens of Britain*, Pitkin.

Bottomley, F., *The Castle Explorer's Guide*, Kaye & Ward, 1979

Breeze, D., 'Bearsden', *Current Archaeology*, Vol. VII, No. 11, 1982

Brice, M.H., *The Royal Navy during the Sino-Japanese Incident*, Ian Allan, 1973

Brice, M.H., *The 15-Inch Guns*, Imperial War Museum, 1968

Brown, R.A., *English Medieval Castles*, Batsford, 1954

Brown, R.A., *Orford Castle*, HMSO, 1964

Brown, R.A., *Rochester Castle*, HMSO, 1980

Bryant, A., *The Age of Chivalry*, Reprint Society, 1965

Butler, R.M., *The Bars and Walls of York*, Yorkshire Architectural & York Archaeological Society, 1974

Caesaris, G.I., *De Bello Gallico Commentarii*, Macmillan, 1905

Campbell, D., *War Plan UK*, Burnett, 1982

Chalet, K., 'Listed Nissen is Social History', *Western Gazette*, 18 November 1983

Chant, C., *How Weapons Work*, Marshall Cavendish, 1976

Clarke, D.T.D., *Colchester Castle*, Colchester Borough Council, 1980

Clarke, D.T.D. and Davies, G.M.R., *Roman Colchester*, Colchester Borough Council, 1979

Colledge, J.J., *Ships of the Royal Navy*, David & Charles (Newton Abbot), 1969

Collingwood, R.G. and Myers, J.N.L., *Roman Britain and the English Settlements*, Oxford University Press, 1936

Coombs, R.E.B., *Before Endeavours Fade*, Battle of Britain Prints International, 1976

Corney, A., *Southsea Castle*, Portsmouth City Museums, 1968

Corswant, W., *A Dictionary of Life in Bible Times*, Hodder & Stoughton, 1960

Council for British Archaeology Group 12, *Newsletter*, April 1983

Craster, O.E., *Hurst Castle*, HMSO, 1969

Cruden, S., *St Andrews Castle*, HMSO (Edinburgh), 1958

Cullingford, C.N., *A History of Dorset*, Phillimore, 1980

Cunliffe, B., *Danebury*, The Open University Press (Milton Keynes), 1976

Davies, H., *A Walk along the Wall*, Quartet, 1976

Davies, R.W., *Hadrian's Wall*, Sunderland

College of Education, 1972

Dendy Marshall, C.F., *History of the Southern Railway*, Ian Allan, 1968

Dottin, G., *The Celts*, Editions Minerva (Geneva, Switzerland), 1977

Duggan, A., *Devil's Brood*, Arrow, 1960

Edwards, I.E.S., Gadd, C.J. and Hammond, N.G.L., *The Cambridge Ancient History*, Cambridge University Press, 1971

Elliott, Major-General J.G., *The Frontier 1839–1947*, Cassell, 1968

Farwell, B., *Queen Victoria's Little Wars*, Allen Lane, 1973

Fedden, R. and Joekes, R., *The National Trust Guide*, Cape, 1973

Fisher, H.A.L., *A History of Europe*, Edward Arnold, 1949

Fox, A., *Prehistoric Maori Fortifications in the North Island of New Zealand*, New Zealand, 1970

Fry, P.S., *Castles*, David & Charles (Newton Abbot), 1980

Galer, D., *Tower 73*, Borough of Eastbourne, 1979

Gardiner, N., 'Giant Fake Fires to Fool Nazi Bombers', *Hampshire Magazine*, July 1983

Gibbon, E., *Decline and Fall of the Roman Empire*, Bison, 1979

Gillingham, J., *Richard I*, Weidenfeld & Nicolson, 1973

Glover, T.R., *The Ancient World*, Pelican, 1961

Guise, S., *The Great Redoubt*, Eastbourne Borough Council, 1979

Guy, J., *Kent Castles*, Meresborough Books (Rainham, Kent), 1980

Hale, J., 'The Development of the Bastion, 1440–1534', in *Europe in the Late Middle Ages*, ed J. Hale, J.R.L. Highfield and B. Smalley, Faber & Faber, 1965

Handford, S.A., *The Conquest of Gaul*, Penguin, 1978

Harbottle, T. and Bruce, G., *Dictionary of Battles*, Rupert Hart-Davies, 1971

Harding, D., *Prehistoric Europe*, Elsevier-Phaidon (Oxford), 1978

Harrison, D., *Along Hadrian's Wall*, Pan, 1973

Haslam, R., *Powys*, Penguin, 1979

Hedley, O., *Her Majesty's Tower of London*, Pitkin, 1976

Helm, P.J., *Exploring Prehistoric England*, Robert Hale, 1971

Hogg, I.V., *Coast Defences of England and Wales 1856–1956*, David & Charles (Newton Abbot), 1974

Hogg, I.V., *The History of Fortification*, Orbis, 1981

Holt, J.C., *Magna Carta*, Cambridge University Press, 1965

James, R.R., *Gallipoli*, Batsford, 1965

Jane's Weapons Systems, 1976 *et seq*

Johnson, P., *The Civilisation of Ancient Egypt*, Weidenfeld & Nicolson, 1978

Johnson, S., *Roman Fortifications on the Saxon Shore*, HMSO, 1977

Kaplan, F.M. and Keijzer, A.J., *The China Guidebook*, Eurasia (New York), 1982–3

Kightly, C., *Strongholds of the Realm*, Thames & Hudson, 1979

Koch, H.W., *Medieval Warfare*, Bison, 1978

Laski, M., 'The Albigensian Crusade', *Man, Myth & Magic*, No. 15 (BPC 1970)

Leasor, J., *Mutiny at the Red Fort*, Corgi, 1959

Li, D.J., *The Ageless Chinese*, Dent, 1968

Life Magazine, 'The Epic of Man', Time-Life International, Nederland, 1962

Lloyd, A., *King John*, David & Charles (Newton Abbot), 1973

MacGregor, P., *Odiham Castle*, Alan Sutton, 1983

Mackie, E., *The Megalith Builders*, Phaidon (Oxford), 1977

Macksey, K., *Land Warfare*, Guinness Superlatives (Enfield), 1976

Mallory, K. and Ottar, A., *Architecture of Aggression*, Architectural Press, 1973

Mason, Colonel F.O., *Interview*, Imperial War Museum, Department of Sound Records No. 000049/08

Melegari, V., *The Great Military Sieges*, New English Library, 1972

Miller, F.T., *The Photographic History of the Civil War*, Thomas Yoseloff (New York), 1957

Ministry of Public Building and Works, *Hadleigh Castle*, HMSO, 1963

MPBW, *Portland Castle*, HMSO, 1965

MPBW, *The Tower of London*, HMSO, 1967

Montgomery, Field Marshal, Viscount, *A History of Warfare*, Collins, 1968

Morley, B.M., *Henry VIII & the Development of Coastal Defence*, HMSO, 1976

Muir, R., *Riddles in the British Landscape*, Thames & Hudson, 1981

North, A., 'The Nissen Hut Story', *Army & Navy Modelworld*, Vol. 1, No. 2 (June 1983)

O'Neil, B.H.St, *Deal Castle*, HMSO, 1966

Parkes, O., *British Battleships*, Seeley Service, 1966

Perks, J.C., *Chepstow Castle*, HMSO, 1978

Pfeiffer, C.F., *The Biblical World*, Pickering & Inglis, 1966

Powell, T.G.E., *The Celts*, Thames & Hudson 1980

Prebble, J., *The Lion in the North*, Penguin, 1973

Pryor, F., 'Down the Drain', *Current Archaeology*, Vol. VIII, No. 4, 1983

Ramsey, W., 'Fort Eben-Emael', *After the Battle*, No. 5 (1974)

Reed, A.W., *An Illustrated Encyclopaedia of Maori Life*, A.H. & A.W. Reed (Wellington, New Zealand)

Richmond, I.A., *Roman Britain*, Penguin, 1955

Rigold, S.E., *Temple Manor*, HMSO, 1962

Rigold, S.E., *Portchester Castle*, HMSO, 1965

Saunders, A.D., *Tilbury Fort*, HMSO, 1960

Scottish National Portrait Gallery, *The Royal House of Stewart*, Edinburgh, 1960

Seignobos, C., *The World of Babylon*, Leon Amiel (Geneva), 1975

Shrubb, Lieutenant-Commander R.E.A. and Sainsbury, Captain A.B., *The Royal Navy Day by Day*, Centaur (Fontwell), 1979

Simpson, C., *This is Japan*, Angus & Robertson, 1975

Simpson, W.D., *Bodiam Castle*, National Trust, 1971

Singer, C., Holmyard, E.J. and Hall, A.R., *et al*, *A History of Technology*, Oxford University Press, 1958

Storry, R., *A History of Modern Japan*, Penguin, 1960

Sutcliffe, S., *Martello Towers*, David & Charles (Newton Abbot), 1972

Thompson, M.W., *Farnham Castle*, HMSO, 1961

Toy, S., *The Castles of Great Britain*, Heinemann, 1970

Toynbee, A., *A Study of History*, Oxford University Press, 1972

Trevelyan, G.M., *History of England*, Longman, Green, 1952

Vale, M., *War and Chivalry*, Duckworth, 1981

Vatcher, F. de M. and Vatcher, L., *The Avebury Monuments*, HMSO, 1976

Warner, P., *A Guide to Castles in Britain*, New English Library, 1981

Warner, R., *Athens at War*, Bodley Head, 1970

Warren, W.L., *King John*, Eyre Methuen, 1978

Weekley, I., 'Yamajiro', *Military Modelling*, July 1983

Wheeler, H., *The Wonderful Story of London*, Odhams, 1956

Wheeler, Sir M., *Still Digging*, Pan, 1958

Wilkinson, F., *The Castles of England*, George Philip, 1973

Wills, H., 'Pillboxes', *Current Archaeology*, No. 69, November 1979

Wise, T., *Forts & Castles*, Almark, 1972

Wise, T., 'French Foreign Legion Forts', *Airfix Magazine Annual*, No. 6

Wright, N., *Beautiful Castles of Britain*, Marshall Cavendish

Young, P. and Emberton, W., *Sieges of the Great Civil War*, Bell & Hyman, 1978

103 *The Castle of Hohenzollern in Baden-Württemberg whence came the dynasty of the Emperors of Germany.*

Index